Their Master's Voice

Their Master's Voice

The Major Prophets Speak Today

CHRIS WOODALL

WIPF & STOCK · Eugene, Oregon

THEIR MASTER'S VOICE
The Major Prophets Speak Today

Copyright © 2020 Chris Woodall. All rights reserved. Except for brief quotations in critical publications or reviews, no part of this book may be reproduced in any manner without prior written permission from the publisher. Write: Permissions, Wipf and Stock Publishers, 199 W. 8th Ave., Suite 3, Eugene, OR 97401.

Wipf & Stock
An Imprint of Wipf and Stock Publishers
199 W. 8th Ave., Suite 3
Eugene, OR 97401

www.wipfandstock.com

PAPERBACK ISBN: 978-1-7252-7520-1
HARDCOVER ISBN: 978-1-7252-7521-8
EBOOK ISBN: 978-1-7252-7522-5

Manufactured in the U.S.A. 10/15/20

Contents

Permissions		vii
Acknowledgments		ix
Introduction		xi
1	Isaiah	1
2	Jeremiah	40
3	Lamentations	80
4	Ezekiel	117
5	Daniel	156
Conclusion		196
Bibliography		199

Permissions

All Scripture quotations, unless otherwise indicated, are taken from the Holy Bible, New International Version, NIV, copyright © 1973, 1978, 1984 by Biblica, Inc. Used by permission of Zondervan. All rights reserved worldwide.

Scripture quotations marked ASV are taken from the American Standard Version, copyright expired.

Scripture quotations marked Darby are taken from The Holy Scriptures: A New Translation from the Original Languages by John Nelson Darby, copyright expired.

Scripture quotations marked EHV(NT) are taken from the Evangelical Heritage Version of the New Testament, copyright © 2019. Used by permission of the Wartburg Project, Inc. All rights reserved.

Scripture quotations marked ESV are taken from the English Standard Version, copyright © 2001. Used by permission of Crossway, Carol Stream, IL 60188. All rights reserved.

Scripture quotations marked GNT are taken from the Good News Translation—Second Edition, copyright © 1992. Used by permission of the American Bible Society, Philadelphia, PA 19106-2155. All rights reserved.

Scripture quotations marked HCSB are taken from the Holman Christian Standard Bible,® copyright © 1999, 2000, 2002, 2003, 2009 by Holman Bible Publishers. Used by permission. Holman Christian Standard Bible,® Holman CSB,® and HCSB® are federally registered trademarks of Holman Bible Publishers.

Scripture quotations marked KJV are taken from the King James (Authorized) Version, crown copyright.

Scripture quotations marked LXX are taken from The Septuagint (Greek Old Testament), copyright expired.

Scripture quotations marked MSG are taken from The Message, copyright © 1993, 2002, 2018 by Eugene H. Peterson. Used by permission of NavPress. All rights reserved. Represented by Tyndale House Publishers, a Division of Tyndale House Ministries.

Scripture quotations marked NASB are taken from the New American Standard Bible, copyright © 1960, 1962, 1963, 1968, 1971, 1972 by the Lockman Foundation, La Habra, CA 90631. Used by permission.

Scripture quotations marked NLT are taken from the New Living Translation, copyright © 1996, 2004, 2007. Used by permission of Tyndale House Publishers Inc., Carol Stream, IL 60188. All rights reserved.

Scripture quotations marked NRSV are taken from the New Revised Standard Version Bible, copyright © 1989 by the National Council of Churches of Christ in the USA. Used by permission. All rights reserved worldwide.

Scripture quotations marked RSV are taken from the Revised Standard Version of the Bible, copyright © 1946, 1952, 1971, 1973 by the National Council of Churches of Christ in the USA. Used by permission. All rights reserved worldwide.

Scripture quotations marked Wycliffe are taken from A Modern Spelling Version of the Fourteenth-Century Middle English Translation of the Bible by John Wycliffe, copyright © 2001 by Terence P. Noble. Used by permission.

Scripture quotations marked YLT are taken from Young's Literal Translation, copyright expired.

Acknowledgments

The second greatest expression of gratitude I must acknowledge is to those whose names appear in the text that follows; the greatest is to their Maker, regardless of whether they would acknowledge him so.

Any errors in interpreting the wealth of information to have come my way by means of research are entirely my own.

Introduction

For those of you who are familiar with my earlier work on the Minor Prophets, this will seem like a logical next step. Sometimes, however, God doesn't necessarily choose that which is obvious to us. I required more than a mere gut instinct or a casual nod to rationality. It came in a most unexpected way; and yet, when dealing with divine initiatives, the unexpected is somehow also bizarrely anticipated.

While reading through some of the earlier books of the Old Testament as part of my personal devotions, I became aware of an idea for a study (and a proposed title) that required the present work before it could be tackled. To say "I became aware of an idea" is the least offensive way I can put it. Some might prefer "I decided," "I thought up," "It seemed reasonable to me," or any other means to describe a proposition that effectively relegates the role of the Holy Spirit to that of a casual bystander. To my closest friends and those of a similar persuasion, I would say that God directed my thoughts thus. However, that belongs to another day. We cannot jump from step A to step C without first negotiating step B.

I propose to adopt a similar schematic approach here to what I employed for *Minor Prophets in a Major Key*: a section for each Major Prophet, including a historical and personal background, an overview of the whole work, and then trusting God's leading once again, a look at a key verse or two from each prophet's contribution, which I believe he would have us consider in the context of a twenty-first century Christian milieu.

This is almost where the similarity between the two works begins and ends. Because I always have in mind a target word count of eighty- to ninety-thousand words, dividing such a number between twelve Minor Prophets gave us manageable bite-sized pieces for each; doing the same for five works by the Major Prophets might place us in the territory of potential indigestion. I shall endeavor to avoid placing the reader in such danger.

Another latent hazard with the Major Prophets is the exact opposite of what I found with their Minor counterparts. With them, I took great pains to emphasize the apparent lack of respect we often pay them as chosen representatives to declare God's message to all generations. Despite the sheer wealth of material at our disposal, many of the passages from Isaiah, Jeremiah, Lamentations, Ezekiel, and Daniel are so well known to us that we risk the plight of dispatching them to that part of our brains that deals exclusively in matters that are deemed both to have been read and their meanings fully exhausted. Would that no part of Scripture should ever find itself consigned there.

Earlier, I mentioned that the similarity of my treatment of the Minor and Major Prophets almost finds its resting place with the literary style I adopt for them both. Almost, but not quite. The prevailing human condition throughout the ages ensures that while circumstances, cultural developments, and technological advancements do change with time, the underlying sinful disposition of humankind remains constant in every epoch. Mercifully, God's messages to both victim and perpetrator alike are similarly unchanging, as we shall see.

Of the five books that make up the Major Prophets in the Old Testament, three are among the largest in the Bible: Isaiah, Jeremiah, and Ezekiel. As if to underscore their Major status, each is significantly longer than the Minor Prophets combined. Although the specific details of each prophet's contribution differ, a more general overarching theme may be discerned in them all: to remind their respective target audiences of their covenantal obligations. Aligned to this is the covenant dictum: "I will be your God and you will be my people" (see Exod 6:7; Jer 30:22). Implied by and to be inferred from this are the promises both that blessing will follow obedience and betrayal will yield the gravest of consequences.

Are the lessons provided by these Old Testament saints applicable to us as Christians in the twenty-first century? Before I draw your attention to the New Testament by way of demonstrating that it is so, allow me to pose a couple of slightly different questions: "Is God our God?" and "Are we his people?" Whether you responded with a "Yes" or a "No," the answer to all three should be precisely the same. If God is not your God, then you cannot count yourself among his people, and will presumably fail to see the significance today of what Scripture reveals of Israel's Old Testament history.

However, for those whose response to any of this is somewhat less negative, it might be an idea to contemplate the company you keep, for "what fellowship can light have with darkness? . . . What does a believer have in common with an unbeliever? . . . As God has said: 'I will live with them and walk among them, and I will be their God, and they will be my people'" (2

Cor 6:14–16). And again: "But you are a chosen people, a royal priesthood, a holy nation, a people belonging to God, that you may declare the praises of him who called you out of darkness into his wonderful light. Once you were not a people, but now you are the people of God" (1 Pet 2:9–10).

Although the context for Paul's words and those of Peter is separation from that with which we were previously most comfortable, the principle behind their counsel of detachment is that what was said of Israel in the Old Testament is now equally valid for those who find themselves in Christ. This potentially opens up before us a whole host of avenues down which we might consider venturing. But we must resist at all costs the temptation to genetically modify the seed of God's word in order to achieve a predetermined response. Nor should we be ignorant of the fact that neither apostle was motivated by an inert desire simply to remind their readership of their status before God, as wonderfully liberating as that was for them and surely is for us, too. Rather, they were spurred to action for the same reason as the prophets of old: poor discipline and indifference on the part of their immediate recipients. Do their words still speak today? Only if Christian believers are still prone to such folly as chasing disposable pleasures instead of choosing meaningful pursuits.

1

Isaiah

HISTORICAL BACKGROUND

Although the precise dating of any of these books remains beyond us, we are able to assert that Isaiah and Jeremiah belong to the pre-exilic period, while Ezekiel and Daniel were written after the exile had taken place. Lamentations effectively forms the link between the two. Much of the historical background for Isaiah is shared by Micah and Hosea, and is provided for us by other biblical accounts (see 2 Kgs 15–20; 2 Chr 26–32).

As far as we are able to discern, Isaiah began preaching sometime during the mid-eighth century BC. Shortly afterwards, Judah's king, Uzziah (also known as Azariah), died in 740. Coincidentally or otherwise, Uzziah's demise also marked the termination of a period of sustained peace for the southern kingdom. Thereafter, Assyria's policy of militant expansion meant that none of her neighbors would enjoy further respite from the threat of overthrow for the foreseeable future. As one ruler succeeded another, and then another, the increase in ambition was matched only by the intensification of their aggression as a justifiable means to that end.

So real was the peril, and so far had Judah's leaders distanced themselves from their covenant God, that in 735 BC, King Ahaz seriously considered the possibility of forming an anti-Assyrian tripartite coalition with her sister nation to the north and Aram (that is, Syria). Undeterred by either the reality of the pending calamity or the reputation of his audience, Isaiah challenged Ahaz to make a choice regarding the object of his trust: divine might or military prowess. Ahaz was not renowned for championing God's cause, nor did he particularly have the stomach for a fight unless the odds were heavily stacked in his favor. It comes as no surprise, therefore, that he found a third way more to his liking: he asked Assyria's king, Tiglath-Pileser III, for help, thereby making Judah a vassal state in all but name. It was not merely a rebuffing of God's messenger, nor even the more serious matter of refuting the first and greatest commandment, but what each represented: the rejection of God himself. Ahaz was without sincerity and wholehearted only in his pursuit of sinfulness.

Two years later, Israel to the north began to surrender large territories, including Galilee; by the end of 721, its capital, Samaria, had fallen to Shalmaneser V, signaling the beginning of the end of Israel's nationhood. Within twelve months, the destruction was completed by Sargon II. Towns, the names of which will be familiar to any Old Testament scholar, such as Shechem and Tirzah, were simply wiped out. Paul Johnson has recorded this melancholic epitaph:

> Thus the first great mass tragedy in Jewish history took place. It was, too, a tragedy unrelieved by ultimate rebirth. The holocaust-dispersion of the northern people of Israel was final. In taking their last, forced journey into Assyria, the ten tribes of the north moved out of history and into myth.[1]

Isaiah foretold that a not-entirely dissimilar fate awaited Judah, though not at the hands of Assyria, but through an as-yet impotent but steadily emerging yokemaster: Babylon (see below).

In 701 BC, Sennacherib of Assyria threatened Jerusalem, whose king by now was the eminently more faithful firebrand, Hezekiah. Hezekiah sought neither to grovel nor to ally himself with the ungodly, but rather prayed fervently to his God. This was no last-ditch attempt to curry favor from the Almighty, but was fully symptomatic of one described by Irving Jensen as "a true God-fearing man whom God used to purge the corruptions of Ahaz and restore true worship to the kingdom."[2] A remarkable victory ensued, with 185,000 Assyrians being slaughtered by the Angel of the Lord (see 2 Kgs 19:35). In the New Testament, James tells his readership that "the prayer of a righteous man is powerful and effective" (Jas 5:16). Older English translations inform us that such prayers "availeth much" (KJV). Whichever you prefer, both may be said to apply equally to Hezekiah's experience.

---

1. Johnson, *History of the Jews*, 70.
2. Jensen, *Survey of the Old Testament*, 203.

Extraordinary though the victory was, however, it was not entirely unexpected. There is a small, but significant, missing link in the sequence I have just described; let us momentarily identify it simply as x. Sennacherib threatens, Hezekiah prays, x, God intervenes. The identity of x is unveiled for us in fifteen verses, subheaded in the NIV as "Isaiah Prophesies Sennacherib's Fall." It begins:

> Then Isaiah son of Amoz sent a message to Hezekiah: "This is what the Lord, the God of Israel, says: 'I have heard your prayer concerning Sennacherib king of Assyria. This is what the Lord has spoken against him . . . '" (2 Kgs 19:20–21)

The footnote in my Bible tells me that Isaiah's message to the king was unsolicited. That may well be so, but it was hardly unprecipitated. Moreover, it is a clear and unequivocal example that, in this brief hiatus of otherwise darkest gloom, God remained faithful to those who remained faithful to him. There is also an abiding lesson here for us all: we must allow God to answer our prayers in the light of his infinite wisdom, not in accordance with our own whim or intellect.

In many ways, Isaiah and Hezekiah were kindred spirits. Both were fervently passionate concerning their obligations and each was particularly sensitive to the burden they bore on behalf of and toward others. Neither was perfect, their zeal often driving them into situations that required hasty retreat. But their differences lay in their respective roles and how they functioned within them. This is perhaps no more clearly evident than in the occasion of their final conference together (Isa 39:3–8). Having welcomed political envoys from Babylon and given them a tour of the palace treasury (Isa 39:1–2), Hezekiah was confronted and challenged by Isaiah, who prophesied that Judah would become subject to Babylonian captivity (Isa 39:5–7), no doubt enunciating every syllable with the suggestion that he alone was privy to the freight of despair conveyed by each. Hezekiah's response betrayed his lack of concern beyond the immediate: "'The word you have spoken is good,' Hezekiah replied. For he thought, 'There will be peace and security in my lifetime'" (Isa 39:8).

When applying the phrase *Historical Background* to any of the prophets, we must do more than simply state the context of their circumstances and how events conspired to produce such a framework. This is especially so of Isaiah, because he saw it quite differently. To him, history entailed more than the unfolding of interrelated outcomes in the past; rather, it consisted in those outcomes being at the behest of an actively involved Supreme Being. It is fitting, therefore, that long after Isaiah's words had themselves passed into history, they became the subject of New Testament quotation far more than those of the other prophets put together.

PERSONAL BACKGROUND

It is worth noting at this point that of the four major prophets known to us, the pre-exilic Isaiah and Jeremiah contained the covenant tetragrammaton *yhwh* in their names (-iah), while the post-exilic Ezekiel and Daniel had the more generic *El* as their suffix. Moreover, the ministries of each were perfectly complementary to those of their periodic counterparts. Where Jeremiah and Ezekiel were more ecclesiastically aware, Isaiah and Daniel were more politically astute.

In common with his eighth-century BC contemporary Hosea, Isaiah's name [*Yesha'yahu*] is also a derivative of Joshua, meaning "Yahweh is salvation." His hometown was Jerusalem and he was possibly of noble ancestry. There are clues to this in the way he conducted his affairs, but it is also hinted at by the oft-repeated phrase that he was the "son of Amoz," as if his heritage was called upon as some guarantee of authenticity. Indeed, there is the suggestion within Judaistic tradition that he may have been of royal descent, conceivably even first cousin to King Uzziah. That Isaiah not only ministered during the reigns of four of Judah's kings (i.e., Uzziah, Jotham, Ahaz, and Hezekiah; see Isa 1:1), but also served at their court seems to add weight to such an argument, as does his undeniable expertise in matters that could come easily only to one afforded a decent education—or have been blessed by God. Whatever the truth of his upbringing, it must be acknowledged that his express sympathies lay not with the aristocracy, but with the vulnerable, the widowed, the orphaned, the ejected, dejected, and evicted, and with the disenfranchised casualties of the affluent and oppressive.

The opening verse of Isaiah's account of himself suggests that he was a particular type of prophet: a seer of visions. Much of what follows is sufficiently detailed to be descriptive of such revelation, but Alec Motyer remains unconvinced. He accepts that the Hebrew *hazon* and *haza* "can refer to 'visionary experience' . . . but both more usually express the heightened 'perception' of truth which the Lord granted by special revelation to the prophets."[3] This may well be true, but it hardly disproves its etymology. We should also anticipate some consistency of proximal usage. Isaiah himself employs this same *hazon* to speak—albeit metaphorically—of visions of the night, that is, divinely appointed dreams (Isa 29:7). He then goes on to give graphic descriptions of what may be seen by those subject to such

---

3. Motyer, *Isaiah*, 49.

an experience. To be fair to Dr. Motyer, he does conclude his paragraph on the matter with a statement that surely can find little disagreement: "The Isaianic literature, then, is 'the perception of truth which came to Isaiah by divine revelation.'"

What is most unusual about Isaiah is that, though unidentified by name, his wife is also described as a prophetess (Isa 8:3). They had two sons, the names of whom are prophetically relevant to the messages their father conveyed:

Shear-Jashub	—	a remnant will return; and
Maher-Shalal-Hash-Baz	—	quick to plunder, swift to spoil.

The circumstances of Isaiah's death are not revealed to us by the pages of Scripture. However, according to Talmudic tradition he is said to have been sawn in half during the reign of Hezekiah's son and idol-worshipping successor, Manasseh. If so, then the writer to the Hebrews possibly had him in mind when composing the so-called *Heroes of the Faith* chapter (see Heb 11:37a; 2 Kgs 21:16). It must be conceded, however, that the link is tenuous, grounded in nothing more substantial than supposition and surmise. Arrows of true wisdom must not be winged by feathers of conjecture.

A significant number of erstwhile scholars claim multiple authors for the book that bears Isaiah's name. Their alleged reason for doing so almost invariably involves the apparent stylistic differences between the first thirty-nine chapters and the remainder (that is, chapters 40–66). There are, however, some obvious consistencies between the two sections, most notably the uniformity of vocabulary. There is perhaps no more glaring example than the use of the phrase "the Holy One of Israel." Isaiah uses this twelve times in the unchallenged section, and it finds itself employed fourteen times in the so-called Deutero-Isaiah (Deutero- and Trito-Isaiah, if you further ascribe chapters 56–66 to a third author); it appears only six times in the remainder of the Hebrew Scriptures. Moreover, New Testament writers—and those of whom they write, including Jesus—quote liberally from all parts without qualm or further comment.

The assumed difference in style between the two contentious sections in Isaiah can be explained by the specific historical setting of each, the circumstances thus evoked, and the maturing process of the prophet. Given these factors alone, we might have cause to be more suspicious if they produced little or no change at all. A clue may also be provided by a closer inspection of what detractors would claim to be the closing chapters of true Isaiah (Isa 36–39). In the context of arguments favoring the unity of Isaiah, these chapters proffer a perfect historical interlude. Also, if I may borrow a musical term, the cadence with which Isaiah would otherwise end at chapter thirty-nine is imperfect and unresolved without what follows to the end of chapter sixty-six. In short, I can only find myself in agreement with those who suggest that the notion of plural authors for Isaiah creates at least as many difficulties as it seeks to address,[4] and this is never an encouraging sign.

Some commentators have noted a marked shift of emphasis in Israel's cultic obligations from Isaiah onwards. Where Yahweh had thitherto been perceived (and presented) as the God amongst gods, they argue, there is a distinct move in Isaiah's words "towards a pure monotheism."[5] The supporting evidence is almost convincing. However, equally valid might be the premise that what was previously only implied becomes more overtly extrapolated from Isaiah on. The turning point seems to come about two-thirds of the way through Isaiah's contribution: "This is what the Lord says—Israel's King and Redeemer, the Lord Almighty: 'I am the first and I am the last; apart from me there is no God'" (Isa 44:6). In other words, the essence of which find their echo on Patmos around eight hundred years later,

> Behold, I am coming soon! My reward is with me, and I will give to everyone according to what he has done. I am the Alpha and the Omega, the First and the Last, the Beginning and the End. (Rev 22:13)

OVERVIEW

Chapters 1–35: Prophecies of Condemnation

Prophecies against Judah (chapters 1–12)

As we might expect, chapter 1 of Isaiah sets the tone for all that follows. It might even be that this chapter circulated independently of the rest until their later composition and collation without raising any serious query as to authorship. In many ways, God's words through this prophet were no different to what had been said before. This is because the conduct of his people remained largely unchanged, any deviation being only in the degree to which they were prepared to exercise their disobedience. In this context, the key verse comes early on and epitomizes much of the Old Testament canon: "Stop doing wrong; learn to do right!" (Isa 1:16b).

---

4. See Motyer, *Isaiah*; Archer, *Old Testament Survey*.
5. See Johnson, *History of the Jews*, 76.

It is in this section where we first learn of Babylon(-ia) as the chosen instrument by which God would execute his judgment upon the southern kingdom through captivity (Isa 11:11). Although it is true that many worthy commentators prefer to interpret this regathering in an exclusively eschatological milieu rather than a more immediate one,[6] the very nature of prophetic fulfilment suggests that the one does not automatically preclude the other.

Prophecies against the surrounding nations (chapters 13–23)

The condemnation facing these nations was not simply because of their proximity to God's covenant people, but because they had all at one time or another abused that privilege by leading God's people away from their cultic obligations:

Babylon	Isa 13:1—14:23;
Assyria	14:24–27;
Philistia	vv. 28–32;
Moab	15:1—16:14;
Damascus/Syria	17:1–14;
Cush (i.e., ancient Ethiopia)	18:1–7; 20:3–6;
Egypt	19:1—20:6;
Babylon (again)	22:1–10;
Dumah (i.e., Edom)	vv. 11–12;
Arabia	vv. 13–17; and
Tyre	23:1–18.

Isaiah's foresight saga (chapters 24–27)

Often referred to as "Isaiah's Apocalypse," these chapters not only speak of a coming universal judgment (Isa 24:1–3), but also outline the reason for it: to purge sin that God might reign in righteousness (Isa 22–23). If read in isolation, then the reader might be overwhelmed by the sheer intensity of the composite symbolism employed to describe the final verdict. The purification is but a means to an end; the overriding theme is not one of prolonged endurance, but of exuberant praise.

---

6. E.g., Motyer, *Isaiah*, 120.

The four chapters here may be sub-divided under five distinct headings:

i. A city in ruins (Isa 24:1–20);
ii. A King who judges the mighty (Isa 21–23);
iii. Gratitude for provision; preserved by grace (Isa 25:1–12);
iv. A city of refuge for the righteous (Isa 26:1–21); and
v. An Israel without struggle (Isa 27:1–13).

Prophecies of judgment and blessing (chapters 28–35)

This first section concludes with another series of woes directed toward Ephraim (Israel), Ariel (Judah), Assyria (as God's vehicle of judgment), and all nations who reject Yahweh as the true God, the "Holy One of Israel." The basis of this final judgment seems to be in whom they have placed their trust in times of crisis: God, man, or idols. All is not doom and despair, however, as promises of blessing for the faithful punctuate the pending gloom. Note especially the Messianic context of such favor (Isa 32:1–5; 35:1–10), the contrast of which is not lost on John Phillips:

> One moment Isaiah's book is black with the thunder and the darkness of the storm. The next, the rainbow shines through, and he sweeps his readers on to the Golden Age that still lies ahead for the world.[7]

Isaiah's poetic use of Ariel for Jerusalem is interesting (see Isa 29:1–8). Linguistic students are correct to identify its use as sounding similar to the Hebrew for "altar hearth" (see also Ezek 43:15), but the suffix *-el* conveys also that it is an altar hearth of divine appointment. Historically, it relates to the site of burnt offerings. This was symbolic of the Lord's enduring presence, the purpose of which was to provide the means of atonement for unintentional sins, but also where God's people expressed their complete surrender to him through covenant (see Lev 6:8–13). It was, in effect, the means of their salvation; or it could be the seal of their peril.

Chapters 36–39: A Historical Interlude

Other than in a purely devotional setting, these chapters are better read in conjunction with 2 Kgs 18–20 and 2 Chr 29–31. They thus enrich the

---

7. Phillips, *Exploring the Scriptures*, 131.

student's understanding of the collapse of the northern kingdom of Israel by Assyria, how and why Judah to the south was temporarily spared, and the introduction of Babylon on to the world stage.

King Hezekiah is the focal point of these chapters, his sin being the turning point. As my pastor is very fond of reminding me, a turning point very often proves also to be a significant teaching point. Or, to put it another way, with each change of emphasis comes also an opportunity for illumination. We shall return to these verses later. Suffice for now to concur with Alec Motyer's appraisal that Hezekiah's decision "[t]o choose security in an alliance with Merodach-Baladan (Isa 39:1–4) was to throw the divine promise of security and deliverance (Isa 38:6) back in God's face and to abandon the way of faith."[8]

Chapters 40–66: Prophecies of Comfort

Israel's redemption (chapters 40–48)

By this stage, the term "Israel" may be used only of the remnant tribes forming the southern kingdom of Judah. Their comfort is to be found not only in the promise of redemption, but also in the facts underpinning that promise. Foremost amongst these is God's character, which ensures the reliability of his word (Isa 40:8), guarantees his potency to bring about what he has said (Isa 12–17), and renders him beyond comparison (Isa 18–26).

It would be unwise to dismiss these chapters (and the rest that follow) as belonging to Isaiah's authorship solely on the basis of the hitherto absent exultant tone. It is not entirely missing from the previous thirty-nine chapters, though it must be conceded that such rejoicing is both sporadic and minimal by comparison. The reason for this is fairly obvious. Until these chapters, there was very little to arouse such elation. Even in the opening words of this section, however, we can almost hear the Handelian major chords ringing out: "Comfort ye my people . . . " (Isa 40:1).

Israel's Redeemer (chapters 49–59)

The Messianic context alluded to earlier now begins to gather momentum as Isaiah's emphasis shifts from the temporal setting of Judah's near-future deliverance from Babylon to that of a more distant global Redeemer (see Isa 55:1). Indeed, it has been suggested that Isaiah speaks of Christ with

---

8. Motyer, *Isaiah*, 19–20.

virtually the same comprehension and comprehensiveness as any other writer, including those of the New Testament.⁹ It seems quite astonishing, therefore, that the intertestamental years saw the development of expectation amongst God's people for a Messiah who would come as a warrior-like enforcer. This is especially so in view of Isaiah's portrayal of the Christ in his fifty-third chapter:

- there would be nothing physically extraordinary about him (v. 2);
- he would generally be rejected by humankind (v. 3);
- his death was to be a product of divine judgment upon the sin of humanity (vv. 4–7a);
- he would humbly accept his lot in life (v. 7b);
- his grave would be that of a common criminal (v. 9);
- the death he was to die would be by divine appointment (v. 10a);
- only through such a death could satisfaction be guaranteed in the Godhead (v. 11); and
- it was to be for sinners that he would come (v. 12).

Israel's restoration (chapters 60–66)

The circumstances facing Isaiah's original hearers would have conditioned their understanding of his words—so much so that it is difficult to imagine anyone from that time interpreting them in any way other than as a postexilic return to the geographical location of their forbears. It is only those of us at this side of the BC/AD divide who are able to rejoice in something approaching the full measure of their intended meaning, both Messianic and eschatological.

Arguably the most familiar segment of this final section is chapter 61, especially the opening verse and first line of verse 2. The significance of Jesus' reading of these words in Nazareth's synagogue is surpassed only by the implied application of them to himself (see Luke 4:14–20). It is equally noteworthy that Jesus sat down, having ended his reading on a high note: "the year of the Lord's favor" (Isa 61:2a; Luke 4:19). Again, I think Motyer puts it best when he says, "What Isaiah saw as one messianic work, the Lord Jesus divided into two: the salvific purpose of his first coming . . . and the judgmental component of his second coming."¹⁰

---

9. See Jensen, *Survey of the Old Testament*, 332.
10. Motyer, *Isaiah*, 426.

THE ODYSSEY

Readers of my earlier work on the Minor Prophets may notice one or two stylistic differences as we consider the lessons to which I want to draw your attention from the book of Isaiah. First of all, the text in question here (see below) is so lengthy that it does not appear in full at the outset, but I would ask you to read it in your translation of choice before going much further.

Secondly, there will be four main headings, which is something of a radical departure for me, if only for the fact that I am not used to dealing with even numbers. There will, I'm sure, be some surprises along the way, challenges perhaps to the odd predetermined mindset, and admissions that may sit uncomfortably with those for whom biblical study is but a tool for further pigeon-holing God.

I should also advise that whatever routine preparations the reader may make in their approach to material of this kind, you might want to add a glass of water and a ready supply of headache relief. Be assured that normal service should be resumed from Jeremiah onwards.

Now, please read Isaiah 10:5–34.

Just a Crooked Stick

As early as this is in Isaiah's deliberations, it is not the first time he introduces us to the idea of Assyria being used to exercise God's judgment upon his covenant people (see also Isa 8:1–10). It might even be argued that Isaiah himself played a precipitative role by virtue of his "How long?" plea in chapter 6. Nothing of what the prophet saw in Judah, whether through his natural eyes or by divine vision, seemed to make much sense to him. What, we might ask, would he have made of the Almighty's choice of Assyria as his weapon of wrath?

So, Assyria: upholder of virtue or paragon of arrogance? Although these are concepts not necessarily as mutually exclusive as we might first think, in Assyria's case they most certainly were. The historical record could hardly be more unequivocal. The burying alive of rebel leaders in a pyramid of recently decapitated heads is but one example of Assyria's brutality. To cite any more would be as gratuitous as it would be grotesque. However, it is not just the extent of their cruelty that is hideous, but also the shameless boasting of it by their politicians and the graphic representations produced by their noted artists. How could God possibly choose to use them to exert his judgment upon his own people? Is it not as abhorrent as it is absurd?

Perhaps what we should rather be asking is what lessons we may learn from the fact that he did. That he did must surely be beyond any reasonable doubt. Notice the divine responsibility attested to early on in our reading:

> Woe to the Assyrian, the rod of my anger, in whose hand is the club of my wrath! I will send him against a godless nation, I will dispatch him against a people who anger me, to seize loot and to snatch plunder, and to trample them down like mud in the streets. (Isa 10:5–6)

There is no case here for a distinction between God's perfect will and his permissive will. What we may say with confidence is that God's people cannot justifiably expect to avert the ramifications of inconstancy in human affairs any more than those they cite as examples of such behavior. What we are able to affirm with equal boldness is that God is not averse to employing malevolent individuals or nations to exercise judgment upon the evil of others, even if to our finite understanding the measure of wickedness in those being judged seems less than that of those being used as instruments of their judgment. Moreover, that which is seen of the evil is seldom the worst of it. And if it is at least four hours since your previous dose, now might be a good time to top up on that headache relief before you re-read the last two sentences.

How glibly we often claim God to be King of kings without realizing that this is precisely what it entails: his kingdom rule extending to include divine sovereignty over earthly events, the decisions precipitating those events, and the consequences emanating from them! Alec Motyer makes the following observation:

> . . . this passage asserts a philosophy of history, how the historical facts arise from hidden supernatural causes, and how the human actors who are the hinges on which history outwardly turns are themselves personal and responsible agents within a sovereignly ordered and exactly tuned moral system.[11]

Just a minute: Who's in control again? God is! And who's responsible for our actions? We are! Maybe that doesn't sit satisfactorily with our theology, but neither our theology nor our comfort with it are of prime concern to God. Historically, as with almost every similar truth, where two apparently contradictory statements appear in Scripture, each one has attracted adherents to the exclusion of the other, simply because they appear to be beyond reconciliation. But they are beyond reconciliation only to the human mind or to finite understanding. And therein lies the real root of the problem. So

---

11. Motyer, *Isaiah*, 108.

loftily have we elevated human intellect that we dare not concede of anything beyond its grasp. We will return to this principle in due course. For now, be assured that there is an answer, but be warned also that it may well be one that you will not wish to discover.

Russian roulette

When we pause to consider, history is awash with examples of those who have been instrumental in purging the earth of evildoers, even when those responsible have themselves earned something of a reputation for wickedness. And we don't necessarily need to view the pages of history from a Christian perspective to detect such episodes. The rise of successive imperial powers has usually followed this format, with one evil empire finally meeting more than its match, and thus being overthrown.

In more recent times, who could possibly have imagined that the resistance of Joseph Stalin's Red Army to the German threat would effectively secure an end to the possibility of Hitler's plan for Nazi globalization? There were other factors too, of course, but none were as unexpected as the Russian resurgence. In 1941, the Soviet system had seemed all but destroyed. So disdainful of it had members of the German high command been that propaganda minister, Joseph Goebbels, predicted it would collapse like a pack of cards at the first sign of trouble. His words did not appear empty. Within six months of engaging battle, five-million Soviet soldiers were either dead or captured. Brave they may well have been, but they were also ill-equipped, irresponsibly led, and had inferior training mechanisms in place for the task before them.

By November of the following year, however, the transformation was as remarkable as it was unmistakable. Not only did they learn from their own errors, but they also discovered some of the secrets of the earlier German success and simply mimicked them. Soviet military strategies were now a match for the best of the German panzer divisions. Intelligence and communications techniques were improved beyond recognition, and training regimes were redesigned to reward resourcefulness. In some measure, Stalin had a hand in all of this, but arguably his most decisive contribution was the appointment of a deputy, Marsal Zhukov, who was given the freedom to command the Soviet General Staff on the battlefield.

All hail comrade Stalin? Not really! Just like Assyria two millennia earlier, the Soviet Union was but the rod of God's anger, the club of his wrath in the hand of the Almighty, a crooked stick with which to draw a straight line.

Indeed, some of the straightest lines drawn have been made with the most warped of sticks. Let us consider a couple more.

Another Joe

Out of Jacob's sons came the tribes that together formed the people of Israel, the covenant nation of God. Is there any way in which they could be described as crooked sticks? Well, their jealousy-fueled intentions toward their brother Joseph hardly fell into the category of straight dealing (Gen 37:12–36). Joseph survived and eventually prospered, but that is not what his siblings had planned for him. On the surface, it might seem that only a combination of fortunate circumstances (Gen 37:25), personal greed (Gen 37:26–27), and guilty remorse (Gen 37:21–22, 29) contributed to the report to their father of Joseph's death being a lie (Gen 37:31–36). They had certainly wanted it to be true (Gen 37:17–20).

But this was even better, wasn't it? Sure, they were guilty, but not of murder. After all, as far as they were aware, Joseph was still alive. And even if he wasn't, his life had not been taken by their hands. He was out of the way, which was all they had really wanted. Absorbed and obsessed in equal measure, they were each a couple of shekels to the good and, if they played their cards right, there was now a vacancy in the Jacob's-favorite-son department. Though their father seemed presently inconsolable, they had succeeded in fooling him. But they had not managed to hoodwink their heavenly Father.

Indeed, their actions had—albeit unwittingly—presented the perfect environment for God's sovereign purpose to begin to unfold. Along the way, Joseph was to learn that his brothers' betrayal was only the first in a sequence of unpalatable events that were to find meaning only from a loftier perspective. Even at gutter level, Joseph's prospects appeared to be raised considerably once in Egypt compared to those feared from the dank, dark, dingy cistern in Dothan. But his hopes were not lifted for long. Potiphar's wife and a negligent cupbearer saw to that. If Joseph was to learn anything from these episodes of treachery and neglect, then it was surely that God's purpose is as much about timing as it is about anything else.

In due course, Joseph's elevation far exceeded the level of his disgrace—so much so that he might have been forgiven for imagining the pinnacle of it was to have been given Pharaoh's daughter as his wife and all its accompanying privileges (Gen 41:41–45). A man of faith? Certainly! But here is what the writer to the Hebrews considered to be his single most faithful act: "By faith Joseph, when his end was near, spoke about the exodus of the Israelites from Egypt and gave instructions about his bones" (Heb 11:22). What? Is that it? Ray Stedman captures the significance perfectly when he writes of Joseph:

> [Joseph,] whose life was filled with dramatic examples of the power of faith, did not let his impending death alter his certainty that God would fulfil his promises concerning Israel. He gave instructions that when Israel would leave Egypt (over two centuries later), they should carry his bones with them and bury them in the land of promise. This Moses did . . . and Joseph's tomb is still visible at Shechem . . . [Such] men were not dreamers or merely wishful thinkers; they "saw" invisible realities, and adapted their own lives and [those] of their descendants accordingly.[12]

Head and shoulders loses out

The incident between David and Goliath is widely known, even amongst those of no religious persuasion. Cited as an example to encourage the weak against the strong, it has become a metaphor for all manner of situations in which we may find ourselves: the feeble overpowering the potent, youthful exuberance versus battle-scarred experience, and naïve impetuosity up against the wiles of tactical might all have the potential to attract a reassuring "this is your Goliath moment." It is an episode worthy of consideration for inclusion here. But there is a better one.

So why mention it at all? Simply because David's victory over Goliath provides the background for a far more significant and lasting battle, which is perhaps frequently overlooked in favor of its more illustrious cousin. I give you King Saul, but we first need to dip into a little of the circumstances leading to his monarchical appointment.

Prior to Saul, Israel had no human king; God was their sovereign. Of course, God was still in charge long after Saul's nomination, but Israel demanded a physical presence to lead them. Samuel the prophet was no longer a young man and his sons did not share their father's integrity or sense of moral rectitude (see 1 Sam 8:1–3). Moreover, when their hostile neighbors asked who directed them in battle, it was increasingly becoming an embarrassment to keep pointing at the sky and saying things like: "He rides on a cloud." So, they asked for a king and God appointed Samuel to anoint Saul.

In fact, Saul was Samuel's choice, based on nothing more qualifying than his extraordinary appearance (1 Sam 9:1–2), though given the reason

---

12. Stedman, *Hebrews*, 127.

for Israel's insistence, that is hardly surprising. The actual wording here is noteworthy: "[Kish] had a son named Saul, an impressive young man without equal among the Israelites—a head taller than any of the others" (1 Sam 9:2, NIV). Other versions give a more accurate translation of the original: "He stood head and shoulders above everyone else" (NLT, NRSV). The significance of this is that the head is often spoken of in Scripture as representative of human wisdom, while the shoulders imply human strength. Not only do these two qualities form the essence of the king of Assyria's pride in his dealings with Israel centuries later (Isa 10:13), but compare them also with God's own affirmation of David's kingship in rejecting Saul: "your kingdom will not endure; the Lord has sought out a man after his own heart and appointed him leader of his people, because you have not kept the Lord's command" (1 Sam 13:14). Should the heart ever be allowed to govern the head? Apparently so!

Thereafter unfolded one of the most intriguing relationships in the whole of the Bible. Although aware of the divine hand upon his life from an early stage, David sought to remain faithful to Saul in the most trying of circumstances. For Saul's part, his actions were dictated by the overriding mood swing of the day, which usually ranged from goodwill to dread. In the end, Saul's hotheadedness got the better of him and David was eventually crowned his successor. David's reign was far from perfect, but it did coincide historically with the golden years of Israel's monarchy. What it might otherwise have been had David not experienced the early years of Saul's hostility can only ever be a subject for conjecture. What we do know is that God used those events to shape David's development. In that sense, the crookedness of Saul's jealousy, resentment, bitterness, and impulsiveness was an instrument in the hand of God to draw what would become an all too brief straight line in Israel's history.

A byword for disloyalty

The word "betrayal" is a difficult one to assign against one who seems to be beyond the reaches of treachery. After all, we often think of betrayal in terms of letting others in on a secret, known only to ourselves, either in isolation or as part of a privileged few. The secret known could be a hidden weakness, a vulnerability, a sinful act, or an illicit thought. None of these are consistent with Jesus' profile, so how could Judas be guilty of betraying Jesus? We must not allow our usual dealings with imperfect beings to condition our understanding of how the word might relate to one so perfect.

Etymologically, the word "betrayal" and its derivatives come from the Latin verb *tradere*, meaning "to hand over," usually into the hands or power of an enemy. There need be no legitimate basis for such a hand over other than a suspension or abandonment of trust by the betrayer or those party to the betrayal. In these simple terms, it might reasonably be argued that Peter was as guilty as Judas.

Despite the claims of a recently discovered pseudo-Gospel or the imagination of Hollywood directors determined to boost public interest, Judas was not following secret orders from Jesus himself, nor is there any unequivocal evidence to suggest that he had a hidden agenda from the outset. As far as we may tell—and, for the Christian, that must mean on the basis of what Scripture actually teaches—Judas' profession in the Gospel accounts was genuine. He was numbered amongst the twelve and we have no reason to doubt that he was actively involved in all the pursuits attributed to that group as a whole, including empowerment and authority over demons and disease (Luke 9:1-2).

Moreover, for three years Judas had first-hand experience of the greatest role model it is possible to have. He didn't just see the miracles from a distance, but he actively participated in the unfolding of many of them, such as the feeding of the five thousand (Matt 14:13-21). He was as panic-stricken as the others in the boat until Jesus calmed the storm (Mark 4:35-41). When Jesus raised Lazarus from the dead, we have no rational grounds to suspect that Judas was absent (John 11:1-44). Not only did Judas see with his own eyes, he also heard all the wonderful teaching with his own ears and, along with the other disciples, had the advantage of having some of the difficult parables more fully explained (Matt 13:36-43; Mark 4:10-12; Luke 8:11-15).

Just for the record, I happen to believe in the principle once saved, always saved. This is not to say that I am oblivious to or choose to ignore the potential obstacles or arguments against such a doctrine. It is simply that I currently believe the weight of evidence to tip the balance in that direction. On this basis, should I also conclude either that Judas was ultimately saved or that he never was? I lean toward the latter for this and no other reason: Judas had access to the best possible example, the most compelling evidence imaginable, and the finest teaching known to humanity. All must surely have contributed to the perfect environment in which to foster faith. And yet his heart appears to have been wholly unaltered.

Of course, Judas was a pawn in the hands of Satan (John 13:2, 27), but he was not without personal culpability. The dark path he walked was of his own choosing. Given a client so riddled with bitterness, so beset with avarice that the key to the purse became merely a means to keep one's own pockets lined, so inordinately jealous as to plot your Master's downfall, despite the overwhelming evidence to support his innocence of the charges that must be brought for a conviction to be secured, would possibly cause any twenty-first century defense lawyer to look to his upbringing. "He didn't stand a chance." "It wasn't really his fault." "Verily, verily: his parents are to blame." Doomed and damned he may have been, but it was for no other reason than that he consciously chose for it to be so, even if that choice consisted in nothing more sinister than refusing to avail himself of the ample opportunities for it to be otherwise.

Even the one who appeared to be pulling Judas' strings was not as in control as he imagined. As the cross began to cast its shadow in reality, how Satan must have greeted its emergence with glee! All his schemes to thwart God's master plan seemed to be coming together. Even as the Son of Man hung there, it is unlikely that the devil would have had any inkling that this *was* the plan, or that his part in the drawing of it had been but another crooked stick. It really doesn't matter who dances to the devil's tune when it is the hand of God in which rests the baton that directs the orchestra of history.

Judging the Instrument of Justice

There is not much to be read into the introductory "Woe" of verse 5 of our main text, as this could just as easily be translated "Ho," as in a call to heed the message about to be delivered. However, no such ambiguity surrounds verse 12 and the seven-verse stanza that follows:

> When the Lord has finished all his work against Mount Zion and Jerusalem, he will say, "I will punish the king of Assyria for the willful pride of his heart and the haughty look in his eyes" ... Does the axe raise itself above him who swings it, or the saw boast against him who uses it? As if a rod were to wield him who lifts it up or a club brandish him who is not wood! Therefore, the Lord, the Lord Almighty will send a wasting disease upon his sturdy warriors; under his pomp a fire will be kindled like a blazing flame ... the splendor of his forests and fertile fields it will completely destroy as when a sick man wastes away." (Isa 10:12–18)

I have intentionally stopped short of verse 19, the reason for which will become apparent in due course. What we are able to discern from these verses without too much difficulty is that, having employed Assyria as the instrument of his justice against his covenant people for their unrighteousness, God is thereafter free to exercise further judgment against the tool of his choosing. This is not to suggest that he was thitherto incapable of doing so, except insofar as he was bound by the unfolding of his own purpose.

The harbinger of fallenness

God had made perfectly clear through his prophet that Israel did not succumb to the Assyrian threat due to their lack of political prowess or to any deficiency of military expertise, but because of their spiritual falsehood. They were not so much careless as contemptuous, having placed their trust in such worthless non-entities as idols and images (Isa 10:10–11). Assyria's blameworthiness, however, was to be found in failing to acknowledge God's hand in their conquest. Just read the verses I have omitted from the above text at the first ellipsis:

> For [the king of Assyria] says: "By the strength of my hand I have done this, and by my wisdom, because I have understanding. I removed the boundaries of nations, I plundered their treasures; like a mighty one, I subdued their kings. As one reaches into a nest, so my hand reached for the wealth of the nations; as men gather abandoned eggs, so I gathered all the countries; not one flapped a wing, or opened its mouth to chirp." (Isa 10:13–14)

I realize, of course, that this is an example of prophetic précis designed to convey the attitude of a third party, but we must surely expect it to be an accurate one. Just count the personal pronouns of self-glorification: nine appear in the span of two verses. It reads like the transcript of an egotistical contestant on *Blind Date*, trying with unwarranted vigor to impress. Indeed, had the Assyrians at this time been familiar with the Latin tongue, their king's attitude might possibly have been summarized: *Veni, vidi, vici*.

The king of Assyria was judged punitively because of "the willful pride of his heart" (Isa 10:12). Indeed, those who contend that this is the basis of all divine judgment will receive no argument from me. Although the apostle Paul's counsel to the young Timothy is such that "the lust of money is the root of all evil" (1 Tim 6:10, KJV), both the definite article preceding "root" and "evil" as an overarching principle rather than manifold expressions are not as fully supported by the original as we might imagine. While the first part is correctly translated "the lust of money" and not money *per se*, what follows is more plausibly "a root of all kinds of evil," though inclusion of the definite article in this case does little to affect the overall meaning.

This being allowed, the key motif must then be seen to be pride. Even this is perhaps not so much pride for its own sake, but that such pride might give occasion for boastfulness or an arrogant display (Greek, *alazoneia*) of those things in which we take pride (see 1 John 2:16). We might thereby conclude that pride is truly *the* root of all evil. This includes original sin and all those party to it. But we must take a step further back than even this to identify the link between pride and boasting: it is self-achievement. Just read those verses relating to the king of Assyria again with this in mind. Now consider the following from the Genesis account of Adam's fall:

> "You will not surely die," the serpent said to the woman. "For God knows that when you eat of [the forbidden fruit] your eyes will be opened, and you will be like God, knowing good and evil." (Gen 3:4–5)

I am not entirely sure that Eve's ears were still attuned by the time the devil got to that bit about "knowing good and evil," except perhaps that we might infer it from the fact that she considered "the fruit of the tree [to be] . . . desirable for gaining wisdom" (Gen 3:6). What we do know is that her actions introduced a sequence of events that have since been imitated beyond measure. Pride, self-achievement, boasting, self-reliance, further boasting, self-government, arrogance in the extreme. How often we are able to trace this pattern being replicated in individuals and nations! So much so that it might even be identified in societal behavior, leading initially to the rise but ultimately to the fall of empirical structures, including that of the neo-Assyrian here before us. Indeed, John Bright describes the reason for Assyria's downfall as "its godless hubris [exhausting] the divine patience."[13] How prophetic of the proverbialist to instruct that, not only does pride precede disgrace (Prov 11:2), but very often also destruction (Prov 16:18)!

Ignorance borne of arrogance

We must take a moment here to stress that, as heinous and as susceptible to judgment as Assyria's pride certainly was, it was equally not misplaced. There is nothing in the record, either here or elsewhere, to suggest that the king of Assyria was overestimating his power. The "strength" and "wisdom" of which Isaiah speaks are each bound by the same quality of effective ability. That is not in question. There is absolutely no doubt that, in terms of military prowess, the Assyrian ruler was capable of achieving just about anything he set his mind to. It is his refusal to acknowledge his indebtedness to Yahweh as but an appointee of divine choice that earns him such stinging rebuke.

---

13. Bright, *History of Israel*, 293.

In many ways, we could hardly expect better behavior of the Assyrians. Apart from the reputation they had worked so hard to attain, they were not God's covenant people, and so perhaps it is a little unfair to anticipate the kind of allegiance that such status would attract. It is not as if Assyria was entirely godless; far from it. They had a god for almost every scenario imaginable: a goddess of love (Ishtar), the sun god (Adramelech), the goddess of grain (As Shalla), the god of medicine (Anasas), the god of farming (Nisroch), and the god of wisdom (Nabu) are but a sampling. Their "god of gods" was the capital's patron, Assur. Although each god was believed to be endowed with specific functional power, they also had one thing in common: the tasks required of them were all subject to the nationalistic whims of the resident king. This is a problem with gods created in man's image: they can only ever be perceived as amplified humanity.

It has been suggested that nationalism is intrinsically neither good or bad, but what makes it one or the other is its principal motivating factor: survival or expansion. It is an interesting theory, were it not for the countless historical examples where the one has invariably provided the basis for the other. Governments flirting with the idea of hierarchical citizenship based on ethnicity is not a latter-day phenomenon, while the tactics employed to impose it and the consequences of having done so vary only in their degree of monstrosity. The end product is racism. Having gained a firm foothold on home territory, to then seek to extend the parameters of that rule into other lands is to step across the border into imperialism. International laws and conventional agreements will not assuage the ambition of those whose appetite has not been sated by their own prosperity and security; it becomes their perceived moral obligation to inflict their newfound way on neighboring countries, all under the misguided notion that "It's for their own good," or "They'll thank us one day." And so, acts of barbarism, deranged paranoia, institutional theft, and warped tyranny are excused as ultimately noble deeds. They are, in fact, the workings of delirium.

It is neither my duty nor my desire to inflict painful reminders upon anyone, but we do not need a degree in social history to recall instances where nations must accept a guilty verdict. What might seem baffling to us is that one-time victims often make the most avid victors. Perhaps it shouldn't come as such a great surprise, as it is really a form of bullying but to the nth degree. Those of us who can remember our worst school days will know that those who were previously bullied often made the cruelest bullies themselves, even if our own experience of it was merely that of an embarrassed onlooker.

Guiltless by dissociation

It is hardly a novel idea to suggest that some of the worst atrocities committed have been in the name of religion. Most of those reading a work like this will probably have some allegiance to Christianity. It may even be exclusively so. I would also guess that for the majority reading that opening sentence, minds were immediately drawn to things like the carnage of 9/11 in New York, the Boston marathon bombings, or the various orchestrated suicide attacks at numerous sites in London in July 2005. All of these tragedies are fairly recent and all were carried out ostensibly by Islamist militants against the perceived Christian enemy.

A broader sweep of the historical record will show that those claiming to be followers of Christ have often been the perpetrators rather than the casualties of such mayhem. Although no authoritative figures exist, it is estimated that between 1095 and 1453 AD, well in excess of one million lives were lost as a direct consequence of the so-called Christian crusades. This was at a time when the global population was only marginally over 5 percent of its current 7.7 billion. The official defense is that they were an attempt to introduce the heathen to Christ as an evangelistic tour *par excellence*; there is at least as much evidence to support the theory that such fervor was born of a desire to increase the then-Pope's territories for taxation purposes. Fast forward a couple of hundred years and papal power was showing no signs of dilution. Around 300,000 individuals were subject to the ignominy of the Inquisition, with one in five of those being put on trial facing execution.

In more recent times, the systematic starvation, alleged constructive infection by issuing blankets riddled with disease, and the administratively engineered relocation on foot during the harshest of wintry conditions for native Americans is perhaps a little too close to home for comfort. Well, what about the racially motivated barbarism of groups like the Ku Klux Klan? Though officially denounced by almost every Christian denomination, their claim looks for support to a Christian moral code.

But not everyone who claims to be a follower of Christ is a follower of Christ. Neither is being a Christian like helping yourself to the pick 'n' mix at the local sweet store and then announcing that you are a connoisseur of confection to all and sundry. To follow Christ is primarily to adhere—or, at least, to seek to adhere—to the principles of his example. How dare we cite him as our exemplar in such ungodly conduct? I am as embarrassed as I am ashamed to be identified with any of it.

Although I fail to buy into the modern trend for historical accountability, which asserts that I must apologize and, where possible, make reparation for the sins of my ancestors, I do think we should remove the blinkers. Pretending these things didn't happen or excusing them on the basis that those responsible were merely products of the generation in which they found themselves will not suffice. The history of the Christian church is not so much a comedy of errors as a corridor of mirrors. But neither should we entirely dismiss the possibility of circumstantial mitigation. An anachronistic imposition of twenty-first-century values on other ages can only ever present a distorted view of events. Faced with the same choices, would we have acted so very differently? Anarchy or order, liberty or oppression?

Targeted duplicity

This is not to say that we are necessarily wrong to judge; only to ensure that we do so from the surest foundation imaginable. When Jesus counselled his gathered audience not to judge, lest they themselves be subject to judgment (Matt 7:1–2), he was not altogether ruling out the declaration of an opinion on someone's conduct or of using that opinion as the basis for punitive measures. Only by taking these verses in isolation could we arrive at such a conclusion. And so, the text out of context becomes a pretext for a subtext.

If we read on, however, it becomes increasingly clear that the real issue is one of hypocrisy. I have understood this for years; or, at least, I thought I did. But until recently, I saw it only in general terms: "How do I have the right to criticize my brother when there are things in my own life that may be obscuring my capacity to view it correctly?" But it is more specific than that. "Log," "speck of sawdust," "beam," "mote," "plank," and "splinter" are all differing measures of the same product. It is not just that we are prone to see mischief in others when we are free from being blameless, nor even that the measure of sin we can see in others is magnified by our own guilt. More often than not, the area of misdemeanor is precisely the same.

When I was a small child, my grandparents would often take me shopping with them to one of the many local towns. Rarely did we make such a visit without being approached by someone selling pin-on flags or shaking a collection bucket in our direction. My abiding memory is of my hand being more tightly squeezed, our pace suddenly quickening, and the accompanying invariable retort from grandad: "Charity begins at home!" Of course, it really does in the sense that we must look after the needs of those for whom we are most responsible before we are in a position to broaden our charitable horizons. What my grandad actually meant might well have been adapted from Dickens' *A Christmas Carol*: Charity begins *and* ends at home. In its real sense, charity does indeed begin at home; and so, too, must judgment.

There is a theory that we often see specific faults in others in areas where we ourselves are free from trouble. It is a plausible one and probably supported by the personal experience of many. And so, the timid see even minor acts of unkindness as gross cruelty. But the ruthless see it even before it has been manifest. Arrogance in others is no more easily discerned than by those of a proud disposition. And sexual impropriety cannot be hidden from the gaze of an adulterer.

As Christians, we are not prohibited from judging, but let us first bring our own misdeeds under the microscope and deal with them. We may then find that what previously appeared to be blatant acts of haughtiness, betrayal, or lewdness on the part of others were exaggerated by our own distorted view of them—so much so that we may even discover them to be non-existent: "To the pure, all things are pure" (Titus 1:15). Please do not misunderstand what I am saying here. Removing the beam from our own eye does not make us blind to reality. It is just that this newfound reality is often very different to how we had thitherto perceived it.

Mutual discipline is far from discouraged by the writers of the New Testament, providing it is preceded by self-discipline (see 1 Cor 6:1–6; Gal 6:1–6). By all means, take every opportunity to speak the truth, but we must ensure that we do so in love; it is the only prescribed way to grow towards maturity in Christ (Eph 4:15–16). Perhaps it would be beneficial for all parties if we hesitated in passing judgment for a moment to consider our motives for doing so. Are we aiming to find a solution or merely to be proved right? Do we wish to tear our brother down so that our own status might thereby be elevated in the minds of others? Is it our overriding desire to see our sister restored or humiliated? A human being with no perception of true spirituality demands justice; only those who recognize God's righteousness and their own standing before it cry out for mercy (see Mark 10:46–52). Which of these is more likely to bring glory to God?

How reassuring that we come back to that question? Bringing glory to God—or, rather, failing to do so—was at the heart of his dealing with both Israel and Assyria. It is perhaps not without significance that arguably the most comprehensive picture we have of God's glory is also provided by Isaiah (42:18—43:21):

- God as Creator (Isa 43:1a, 7);
- God as Redeemer (v. 1b);
- God as Preserver (v. 2);
- God as Savior (v. 3a);
- God who takes intimate delight in his creation (v. 4);

- God whose purposes will not be thwarted (vv. 5–6); and
- God's sovereign right to glory (vv. 8–13).

While the precise nature of the relationship between God's sovereignty and man's responsibility is not obvious to us, the biblical presentation is such that we can know of its existence. What this means in practical terms is that even the despots of the world are subject to divine design. Failure to acknowledge their indebtedness serves only to compound their tyranny further. Isaiah makes no attempt to explain the paradox any more than Peter did during his sermon on the day of Pentecost:

> Men of Israel, listen to this: Jesus of Nazareth was a man accredited by God to you by miracles, wonders, and signs, which God did among you through him, as you yourselves know. This man was handed over to you by God's set purpose and foreknowledge; and you, with the help of wicked men, put him to death by nailing him to the cross. (Acts 2:22–23)

An Insoluble Enigma

As I write, it is nineteen years ago this week since I prayerfully considered my options, having recently gained a Master's degree in Theology. Advice from cronies and critics alike was in ample supply. They ranged from "Carry on regardless" to "Call it a day," with plenty of variation between the two. Prominent amongst the former was the possibility of continuing my studies toward a PhD. My reluctance owed nothing to false modesty, but rather to what I considered at the time to be a realistic appraisal of my capabilities. As I sought God's counsel, I became aware of what I thought to be a two-word title: *The Odyssey*. In circles that I have frequented in the past, this would have been described as hearing from God. I remain unafraid and unashamed to use that phrase, but not without further qualification. There was no audible voice, no finger writing in the sky, and no Bible verse jumping out at me from the page. I simply became aware of a thought, the construction of which I was not conscious of having made any contribution towards: *The Odyssey*.

Over the next few days, other words were added. By the end of the week, I seemed to have a full working title for my doctoral studies: *The Odyssey: A Doctrinal Analysis of Divine Justice in the Light of Human Suffering*. Those of you who are more theologically astute than I was in 2001 will, of course, already see where this is heading. I mentioned it to the Dean of the University, who patiently and graciously introduced me to the word

"Theodicy." For the next four years, I wrote over eighty-thousand words on the nature of God as we are able to understand it, natural and moral evil and our response to them, and sought where others had largely failed to resolve once for all the problem of evil. I, too, not only joined their company, but in so doing also became self-appointed CEO of the Institute of Adding Not Much Really.

Unlike the likes of Plantinga and Hick, however, I did reach a startling deduction. In fairness, they probably arrived at the same conclusion, but for reasons known only to themselves chose not to disclose it. It is of such importance that you might want to take a moment before you read on. Find a notepad, pencil, highlighter pen, check the date, and take a deep breath, because this may just change your outlook on the Divine Being. My conclusion to the problem of evil at the end of 2004, which remains unaltered in 2020, was simply this: I do not know!

Acknowledging our limitations

I don't know why the apparently innocent suffer. I don't know why we haven't found a cure for cancer yet. I don't know why some are so prone to cruelty that the only way we can find to describe them is as those who are purely evil. But I also discovered something else. Without the drama of my earlier revelation, it is this: however much we cry "Why?" or "How could God . . . ?" there is no evidence in any of it that negatively impinges upon either his existence or his inherent goodness. Or, to put it another way, there is nothing in the existence of evil to suggest that the righteousness of God is thereby annulled.

And that is the issue before us in this passage. God's capacity for all that we have looked at so far in this section relating to him exercising judgment, and the tools he chooses to employ for that purpose, do not make him complicit in evil. This is not just difficult to comprehend; it is impossible. But that is not the same as to say that it is irreconcilable. When two truths appear to be inconsistent, but are not, this is known as an antinomy (not to be confused with antimony). Indeed, the word "antinomy" may be defined as "a contradiction between two beliefs or conclusions that are in themselves reasonable; a paradox."[14]

So, how is it possible to say that these two truths—the simultaneous existence of evil and God's righteousness—are not irreconcilable? Well, first of all we must look beyond the parameters of ourselves. Arguably the single largest stumbling-block to grasping difficult theological truths is not lack of

---

14. *Concise Oxford English Dictionary*, s.v. "antinomy."

personal intellect, but a reluctance to lay aside the idea of human intellectual infallibility. The truths before us will not be reconciled in, with, or by finite minds; they find resolution only in the mind of God.

When the same prophet is used some forty-five chapters later to convey the idea that "[God's] thoughts are not [our] thoughts, neither are [his] ways [our] ways" (Isa 55:8), the difference is not by measure or degree. We are not here invited to compare the eighth-century-BC equivalent of two former high-school graduates, one with a handful of qualifications and the other with straight-As in every subject taken. A clue regarding the true picture is to be found in the following verse: "As the heavens are higher than the earth, so are [God's] ways higher than [our] ways and [his] thoughts than [our] thoughts" (Isa 55:9). The difference between the two is as much about vantage point as it is to do with quality.

Our limitations cause us to question the existence of God, or at least to fail to find any positive purpose in the path he seems to have chosen for us, when we or a close friend or family member are beset with health concerns. An overdue bill that we have no fathomable means to pay can be a challenge to our faith. Plans we make with all noble intentions that fail to come to fruition make us think that God is no longer interested in us. We arrive home from the afternoon seminar on trusting in the Almighty, the pithy title of which was *Letting Go and Letting God*, just in time to catch the early evening news bulletin on TV: dozens of innocents killed and hundreds of others seriously maimed in a terrorist attack on the other side of the planet; scores of children, weak and dying from malnutrition on the African continent; a church full of Christians bombed for no other reason than they refused to cease worshipping Jesus in their Middle Eastern enclave. God's ways are not our ways because his view of the same incidents is unrestricted by the calendar date on which they unfold.

Before we look at a New Testament context for this concept, let us pause briefly to consider what it might be like if this was not the case. If God's ways, thoughts, deeds, and experiences were no different from our own, then would he be worthy of worship? Theologians speak of the communicable and non-communicable attributes of God: those perfections within his Being that he has either conferred upon humankind in some measure or completely withheld from the pinnacle of his creation. Let us for a brief mad moment imagine a "god" of our creation with whom we have invested something of human nature: a "god" whose ways and thoughts bear a strong resemblance to our own.

Such a "god" would surely be self-serving, though at the same time dependent upon others to meet the needs of that self-service. In a spirit of political correctness, he would not be "he," but gender neutral. He would still be interested in the plight of the downtrodden, the underprivileged, and the disenfranchised, but especially so if to advertise the fact would raise his public profile and ensure a favorable reception for his latest hit single. He would never have announced satisfaction with his creation, because who knows what Microsoft or Apple might be able to offer by Christmas? It is unlikely that he would be three persons because, well, two's company and all that. He would not have made us male and female, because don't we have the right to decide for ourselves when we are in full command of our faculties? No doubt he would have ensured that only those things which may be contained within the comprehension of his creation are valid, while those things that stand outside it thereby become untrue.

Thank God that God is God and that his ways and thoughts are not only not ours, but that some of them remain beyond finding out. Give praise to him, too, that though Christianity is not unreasonable, there are truths annexed to Christianity that reason is entirely impotent to penetrate. It is here that reason must defer to resolution.

One way is accessible

In the midst of such potential frustration, let us all the more eagerly hold on to those things of which we are encouraged to be certain. We may not always be able to discern God's ways, but he has made the way to him accessible to us. Allow the writer to the Hebrews to instruct us:

> Therefore, brothers, since we have confidence to enter the Most Holy Place by the blood of Jesus, by a new and living way opened for us through the curtain, that is, his body . . . Let us hold unswervingly to the hope we profess, for he who promised is faithful. (Heb 10:19–23)

As if further clarification was required, Jesus identifies himself as this "new and living way":

> Jesus answered [Thomas]. "I am the way and the truth and the life. Nobody comes to the Father except through me." (John 14:6)

Whenever I have heard this text being announced as the basis for the preacher's message (and there have been many such occasions), what followed invariably involved a perfectly delivered three-point sermon, with each facet of Jesus' reply being given equal time and ranking. But the trisection, valid as it may be for the purpose of analysis, detracts also from the unity of what Jesus was saying. He is the way in no small measure by virtue of the fact that he is also the truth and the life; he is the truth because he is the way and the life; the life he has to offer is available to us because he is the way and the truth.

The capacity of this, too, is beyond our comprehension. Jesus is the way and the truth and the life not only to the fullest extent imaginable and to the exclusion of all that might otherwise seek to countermand that reality, but infinitely so. There is no box within which the truth to be found in Christ may be contained, not because none of sufficient size can yet be found, but because the discovery of such a container would reveal it also to be of infinite size and, therefore, not truly a box. The only "object" that seems to fit the bill would be God himself as the Divine Being. And it is to this Being that we have access through Jesus, this "new and living way," the truth (again, definite article) having set us free to live once again in fellowship with our Maker.

One of the criticisms for my earlier writings has resulted from my willingness to challenge some of the findings of William Hendriksen. The truth is that I so rarely stumble across anything in Hendriksen's work with which I find myself in disagreement that it is an occasion worthy of note. Here's what he has to say on the matter before us, with which I fully concur:

> Truth and life are nouns, not adjectives. Christ is the truth and the life, just as well as he is the way. Nevertheless, the context indicates that the idea of the way predominates. The meaning appears to be: "I am the way because I am the truth and the life." When Jesus reveals God's redemptive truth which sets men free from the enslaving power of sin, and then he imparts the seed of life, which produces fellowship with the Father, then and thereby he, as the way . . . has brought them to the Father.[15]

Taking a closer look

Having established the unity of Jesus' statement, we may now unpack its components separately for closer inspection. Although the writer to the Hebrews leaves room for reasonable doubt, Jesus' use of the definite article and the consistent testimony of Scripture elsewhere is unequivocal: He is *the* way. As if to close the door on uncertainty once for all, he adds: "Nobody comes to the Father except through me" (John 14:6b). Cults and religions that acknowledge Jesus as just one amongst many, even first among equals,

---

15. Hendriksen, *John*, 268.

are guilty of nothing less than blasphemy. And yet, even this was insufficiently clear to some of his disciples. Having already had the answer spelled out for them, Philip, by effectively repeating the same question, showed that he had about as much a clue as might Joey Tribbiani.

The thing about truth is that it is unaffected by and independent of belief in it to remain true. Just as the capacity to sincerely believe in something (or someone) adds nothing to its veracity, so unbelief diminishes it not one jot. Much of late-twentieth-century faith teaching failed at just this point. So much so, in fact, that at times such teaching has more resembled a combination of wild supposition and wholesale superstition. The Bible teaches that "faith comes by hearing and hearing by the word of God" (Rom 10:17), but how many otherwise godly Christians have been caught out by the snake oil philosophy of just needing to conjure up enough belief by saying "Get thee behind me" to doubt? Unfortunately, it has a ring of legitimacy about it, just enough to get us hooked. But if God hasn't spoken, we haven't heard. To imagine otherwise is to reduce faith to baseless optimism.

The point here, however, is that truth is not affected by how many people do or do not believe in it. In other words, it is not subject to democratic process. We rightly rejoice when we hear of unbelievers coming to Christ, especially in large numbers or remote regions. Although some might argue that Christ's return at the end of the age is made more imminent by such news, his status is neither enhanced nor moderated by it.

By way of example, consider the principles of nature. They are God-assigned laws, some knowledge of which he has entrusted to us through science. Imagine for a moment that a nation or continent decided to hold a special event to celebrate its human autonomy, but there was just one obstacle to the success of that event: gravity. What to do? "I know," enthuses the minister for the environment, "let us have a referendum of all those over the age of eighteen to decide whether or not we should temporarily suspend gravity, just for the duration of the formalities." Well, they could hold their ballot. They could even vote in favor of the proposal. But it wouldn't make the slightest difference to gravity.

Jesus is the way. There used to be an old Pentecostal trend to affirm such statements with: "The Bible says it, I believe it, that seals it!" Well, it is sealed simply by the Bible saying it. If everyone on earth believed it, Jesus would be the way. But equally, even if nobody on the planet believed it, he would still be the way. Precisely the same could be said about him being the truth, as it could of him being the life. Though they try, the best theologians find its explanation beyond them. In simple terms, we are only really able to explain that which is embraced by our understanding. To claim to understand such matters renders us subject only to pity or ridicule.

Faith is the key, but not the command

Faith is not entirely unreasonable. Even the writers of Scripture, under the guidance of God's Spirit, sought ways to define faith, provide examples of faith, often through personal testimony, contrast faith with its opposites, and compare it to like and complementary virtues, all that our understanding of it might be enhanced and our experience of it enriched. Ultimately, however, the infinite nature of faith's object renders its observation to be beyond finite boundaries.

According to the apostle Paul, faith is one of three enduring qualities, the others being hope and love (1 Cor 13:13). For this reason, I have often heard it said that together they form a triumvirate of Christian identification. It is not, perhaps, an idle notion. At first glance, however, it is somewhat at odds with what Jesus presented as the hallmark of a Christian.

When I came to Christ in the mid-1970s, a great deal was made of the need to make those within my social circle aware of this newfound way of life. Some of the terminology used was confusing to one without any church-related background, while others sounded positively cultish. I remember, for example, in the very early days being completely freaked out by an elderly spinster at a local church convention, who casually asked if I'd been "washed in the blood." "Walking with the Lord" conveyed less sinister images, but only marginally so. Even the biblical concept of living by faith was presented in a way that suggested survival with no visible means of support; a bit like a spiritual marionette.

All of these were designed to show an unsuspecting—and hitherto unprepared—world that the present version of us was forever changed from what had gone before. Just in case it was not obvious from my behavior, I favored the winning and oft-lamented combination of car sticker and lapel badge. Then I discovered the following verse, which seemed to make more sense than the advice I had thus far received from other well-meaning souls:

> A new command I give you: Love one another. As I have loved you, so you must love one another. By this all men will know that you are my disciples, if you love one another. (John 13:34–35)

The final clause is conditional: "if." But what precisely is it that depends upon the condition having been met: the subjects' discipleship or third parties being made aware of that discipleship? True enough, loving one another is issued as a command, reaffirmed by the emphatic "you must," but commands are susceptible to violation. It is possible to be a Christian and show none of the distinctive marks of that status. Otherwise, salvation would be by works and not by faith. But unbelievers will not be attracted to Christ by us theorizing over doctrine or pointing to an event two-thousand years ago, however much gusto or stagecraft we introduce to our presentation. We will simply be "a resounding gong or a clanging symbol" (1 Cor 13:1). Faith, hope, and love will abide, "[b]ut the greatest of these is love" (1 Cor 13:13b).

Always a Remnant

Good news! It may have taken us quite a while to arrive, but here it is at last. In the midst of the fire of God's judgment, there is yet a remnant of those who will once more express covenant faithfulness:

> In that day the remnant of Israel, the survivors of the house of Jacob, will no longer rely on him who struck them down but will truly rely on the Lord, the Holy One of Israel. A remnant will return, a remnant of Jacob will return to the Mighty God. (Isa 10:20–21)

The most striking thing to note is that this is no reward for maintaining allegiance. This is clear from the suggestion that the remnant who survive will come once more to rely on the Lord, having previously abandoned him to put their trust in the oppressor. Commentators are divided concerning the identity of this oppressor. The immediate context leans toward Assyria, but it might equally apply to the northern kingdom's alliance with Aram (Isa 7:2), with whom its earlier dealings could hardly be described as amicable (see 2 Kgs 6:8–25). The principle at stake, however, remains utterly unaffected: "A remnant will return" (Isa 10:21a).

A chance to begin again

There is an interesting—perhaps even significant—allusion to the theme toward the end of the previous stanza. Simile and metaphor combine to present a graphically detailed account of what Assyria can expect to experience at the hands of the Almighty. So progressive is the judgment to be meted out that the reader practically expects it to lead to a final perfect cadence of total destruction, with Assyria being entirely wiped from the face of the earth. Our quench almost feels unsated by: "And the remaining trees of his forests will be so few that a child could write them down" (Isa 10:19).

It may well be presented in a negative tone, but be that as it may, it is not entirely devoid of hope, even for that nation of ungodliness. When the prophecy was fulfilled, it was both rapid and radical (Isa 37:21–38). So many lay dead in the Assyrian camp that a census of the living would have required little skill; but at least there were some left to number. An opportunity perhaps undeserved, but ultimately squandered.

No mere leftovers

Concerning the remnant of Israel, however, a few minor observations should be made from the immediate text before we can press on to consider the consequences of its fulfilment. First of all, the word "only" is not a verbatim translation of the original, though it may be implied by the contextual contrast (Isa 10:22). Even allowing for this, I'm not entirely convinced by its necessity, as the very nature of a remnant suggests a remaining smaller part of an originally (or previously) larger whole. Thus "only" may be inferred even in its absence, making its use somewhat superfluous.

Secondly, the basis of the reconciliation between the two parties is not to be mutual compromise, but acquiescence on the part of Israel. This should be so obvious as to require no further explanation, but my experience of such matters deems it necessary to make the point. The remnant's return is correctly described as being directed "to the Mighty God." The terminology throughout, however, is specifically covenantal: "the Lord, the Holy One of Israel." I have written exclusively on this subject elsewhere.[16] Suffice to say here that Scripture knows essentially of two types of covenant: those between peers and those between a superior and an inferior party. In the former, the details may be negotiated at length before agreement is reached. In the case of the latter, the role of the inferior party is solely to accept or reject the terms and conditions being offered by the superior party. They are not even at liberty to ignore them, for in so doing they are effectively rejecting them. And so it is here that Isaiah speaks of a time when a remnant of God's covenant people will return to him and thereby also the covenant he has already established with them.

My wife and one or two of her friends occasionally make their own clothes. I once came home from a walking trip to find her on the phone to one of them, waxing lyrical about Celine, imagining her to be an old school friend with whom they may recently have become reacquainted, only to discover some embarrassing moments later that Celine is, in fact, the name of a dressmaker's dummy. Sewing machines, specialist scissors, highly tested tensile cottons, and multi-functional presser foot accessories all conspire to confuse and confound the naïve innocents amongst us. As a sometime beneficiary, it is not difficult to overlook the odd overlocker, but some things do require explanation.

16. Woodall, *Covenant*.

Apparently, the best places to buy fabric are at Saturday markets. On this occasion only, your understanding will be helped immeasurably by thinking of the word "best" as a synonym for "cheapest." Each weekend, former mill towns in the north of England are beset by those on the lookout for just the right shade of puce with which to fashion a fleece sweater for their as-yet-unsuspecting and ultimately ungrateful nearest and dearest. Material widths off the roll are usually sold in meter lengths, though older custodians of the cloth may still sell it by the yard. The less there is left, the cheaper it becomes. This is called the remnant. There may only be enough left at this stage to make a pair of fingerless gloves. So far, that fits perfectly well into our earlier definition of a remnant: a smaller remaining quantity of an original (or previous) larger whole. In the rag trade, however, the remnants are often also those pieces that, in the process of earlier purchases, have been rejected because of some flaw or imperfection. These will often be bought to make items of clothing that are hidden from public view, such as my undershirts.

Chosen by grace

Although both definitions are given equal support by most current English dictionaries, this latter idea is entirely absent from the Bible's understanding of the word "remnant." The most neutral definition we may ascribe to the Hebrew *shear* and its derivatives (e.g., *sheerith* and *sheruth*) is "a surviving residue." The context usually determines whether this is to be viewed with hope or pessimism, though Paul's treatment of the theme, particularly his identification of it with the grace of God, should not be ignored. Here's how he related it to the believers at Rome:

> Isaiah cries out concerning Israel: "Though the number of the Israelites be like the sand by the sea, only the remnant will be saved. For the Lord will carry out his sentence with speed and finality." (Rom 9:27)

The context is made clear by the heading in the NIV: *God's Sovereign Choice*. What is also highlighted in the rest of the chapter that may not be quite so evident elsewhere is that such choosing is not without justification. God is not given to whimsical decision making, but he is entirely rational in his thought processes, even if his reason lies beyond human comprehension. It seems that Israel's downfall was not the product of willful disobedience *per se*, but that their non-compliance consisted in attempting to attain righteousness by unprescribed means: works instead of faith (Rom 9:30–33).

A couple of chapters further on, the apostle spells out with yet more clarity precisely what is meant by this "remnant" of which the prophets spoke, a people elected by God through grace:

> So too at the present time there is a remnant chosen by grace. And if by grace, then it is no longer by works; if it were, grace would no longer be grace. What then? What Israel sought so earnestly it did not obtain, but the elect did. (Rom 11:5-7a)

Less than three verses and yet so pregnant with meaning. The latter part seems to militate against the principle behind Jesus' earlier teaching that finding always follows seeking (Matt 7:7). According to Paul, Israel not only sought, but did so earnestly (which is consistent with the original). Their endeavor, however, was restricted by their self-imposed parameters of a works-related philosophy. They were hardened against God's chosen means and so found the end product to be beyond their reach.

Although the larger context seems to pit works of the law against the grace of God, the principle holds true for all works of any kind. The doctrine of election has confounded and frustrated theologians for centuries. Why should God choose so and so in favor of such and such? The very asking of the question suggests misunderstanding. First of all, we might better ask why he should choose any. Secondly—though not in measure of importance—the determinant factor of election is not anthropocentric but Theocentric, or more specifically: Christocentric.

It must also be noted that the cause is constant. When Paul says, "it is no longer by works," we should not thereby infer that it ever was, but has now become or evolved into something that previously was not the case. Rather, Paul is referring to the authoritative affirmation that salvation has been demonstrated to be by grace, so that his readership now no longer has any excuse for believing that it might be by works.

Self-effort can never satisfy

It is not easy to throw off the shackles of a salvation-by-works mentality. For many of us, particularly in the West, our upbringing conditions us to believe that everything of value must be earned. Any suggestion that it might not be, and we become expertly entrammeled with guilt and obligation. As far as social structure is concerned, such a system is not necessarily unprofitable. Allowing that principle to govern every area of life, however, is not always beneficial. From a very early age, I was brought up by my maternal grandparents. For the most part—and I mean well in excess of 90 percent—I have only fond memories. Even the missing few percentiles contributed toward fashioning me in ways that I have learned to view positively, though I must acknowledge that others may not quite see it that way.

I am a perfectionist; without professional qualification, some might suggest to the extent that I register on the autism spectrum. Given that the classic symptoms include profound difficulty with social communication and interaction, restricted interests, and repetitive behavioral patterns, it is admittedly troublesome to find much of a defense. As with many similar conditions, there is some debate as to which contributes most: nature or nurture. What I can say is that I am able to point to specific incidents in my childhood where particular seeds of pedantry were sown. The last thing I want is for this to develop into a pity party, but often my very best was never quite good enough.

I was one of only a handful on my first day at primary school who had already been taught to read at home. Consequently, I always did very well in the weekly spelling tests. However, scores of nineteen out of twenty were never greeted with a heartwarming, "Well done!" It was more likely to be, "How did you manage to screw up the one you got wrong?" Fast forward five years to me playing football for the school team against our local rivals from the neighboring village. We won five-two and I scored three of our team's goals, but also managed to miss a straightforward chance. Guess which part of my performance received the microscope treatment.

And so, the dissatisfaction of others soon became my own frustrations. Hobbies became obsessions, but not for long. I quickly moved on to something else as soon as I discovered the limitations of my ability had been exhausted. If I couldn't excel, I would rapidly make my exit. In later years, I have learned to manage this much better. But my early years as a Christian were especially problematic. This was the mid-1970s and the level of advice you could expect as someone new to the faith consisted of little more than: "Go away, pray, read your Bible, and don't smoke!"

So, I did. I had no idea about reading plans, and have never used one even when I became aware of their existence. The motto in those days seemed to be something like: "A chapter a day keeps the devil away." This was fine for most of the time. But my first job on leaving school, which pretty much coincided with becoming a Christian, was spent as an apprentice mechanic at my local colliery. Not only did I spend much of those first three years underground, but it also involved shift work and involuntary overtime. I found it impossible to stick to my self-imposed routine of a chapter a day, but the guilt meant I also had to find an alternative. So, on my days off, I'd play catch up. Never quite free to enjoy my portion of daily bread on Thursday until I had gorged on Monday-to-Wednesday's leftovers.

Faith and love revisited

Even as I write this, I know that some will think it ridiculous, if not scandalous; others will possibly be able to identify with it, even if only in measure; still others will have some vague memory of similar things that they thought had been consigned to utter forgetfulness, and quickly try to convince themselves that they once knew someone like that. You see, being saved by faith and then trying to live a life worthy of that fact by works is more commonplace than we often care to admit. This is why the Christian experience is described in terms of *living* by faith, that is, a present continuous drawing upon faith in order to meet the demands of each day as a believer.

There is a relationship between the two, which must be acknowledged. But we are saved *to do* good works; we are not saved *by* them. This is not new to us. But we must be clear in our understanding that the good works, which we are saved by faith to do, neither add to nor subtract from our standing as Christians. Even the continuation or absence of faith exercises cannot do that (this is not the same as continuing in the faith or failing to do so). Living by faith as a progressive life pattern enables us to grow and develop as Christians; choosing not to do so fosters only devolution and an arrest in our maturity. It is as futile as it is foolish, but it is no more than that. Francis Schaeffer puts it like this:

> Christianity is not just a mental assent that certain doctrines are true. This is only the beginning. This would be rather like a starving man sitting in front of great heaps of food and saying, "I believe the food exists; I believe it is real," and yet never eating it.[17]

It would be tempting to leave matters as they are, having promoted only the positive idea of faith being the basis for every avenue of the Christian experience, thereby leaving the reader to conclude that the inverse is equally true. However, Paul does not omit to emphasize the negative also: "everything that does not come from faith is sin" (Rom 14:23). Many commentators skip over this as but the flip side to what Paul had said earlier in the chapter, and might have been inferred anyway. But its importance lies in helping us to avoid any inappropriate deductions. To choose not to live by faith in any detail, however apparently minor, is not neutral but positively sinful. Partial belief is unbelief.

The context is again one of eating and drinking, but that is only the example chosen by the apostle to illustrate a life principle. Those whose faith is weak are not faithless, but faithful in lesser measure than those whose faith is strong. As such, they are expected to live in accordance with the measure

---

17. Schaeffer, *Death in the City*, 147.

of faith they have. To do otherwise at the behest of or to impress those who are stronger in faith would be to do so with impure motives: it would be an act motivated by sin. If anything, the strong should adjust their practical application of faith when to give it free rein might cause the weaker believer to stumble. This is more than mere toleration or the turning of a blind eye; it is choosing not to please ourselves for the sake of the convictions of others. In practical terms, it may well call for restraint and understanding on the part of both the weak and the strong. At its root, however, is a desire to express what we looked at in the previous section: Jesus' command to love one another (John 13:34).

And so, we find ourselves several steps removed from God's promise through Isaiah of a remnant. Or do we? Remember, I described that remnant as "those who will once more express covenant faithfulness." Even for the Old Testament saints, this consisted in obligations toward their fellow human beings as well as to Yahweh (see Exod 20:1–17). We have also seen that Jesus initiated the new covenant by issuing also a new commandment, not just to love one another, but to follow his example in so doing.

When we speak of loving one another even as Christ loved us, I wonder what specific images are developed in our minds. Do we see Jesus feeding the thousands or being hailed as a great teacher? Does his compassion for the diseased and disenfranchised captivate us more than all else? Perhaps the fact that he always seemed able to disarm the religious authorities with just the right combination of words and inflection contributes most toward him earning our respect. Is the Son of Man really only a kind of spiritual superhero to us? Or do we see him as one who was prepared to forsake all personal ambition, to resist every temptation to pursue self-glorification outside of the Father's purpose, and to suffer indignity, ignominy, and death rather than abandon us to the wiles of the devil? And would we be prepared to follow *that* example, if necessary? I'm guessing a remnant would.

Summary

Few readers will have been surprised to find me discussing such issues here as divine sovereignty, human responsibility, and covenant faithfulness. But who would have thought that a study beginning with God's dealings with a heathen nation could possibly lead us on a journey that also considers Christian discipline, reasonable faith, and Jesus' command that his disciples should love one another? I must confess to being almost as astonished as anyone else.

It is to that fourth-century bishop, Augustine of Hippo, that the following couplet regarding the Testaments is customarily attributed: "The New is in the Old concealed; the Old is in the New revealed."[18] This is especially true of typology. Of course, typological interpretation of Scripture is fraught with danger. The same might be said of many valid hermeneutical tools, and with equal legitimacy. This should not cause us to completely disregard their value, however; rather, we should handle them with care. As we continue to work through my gleanings on the books of Jeremiah, Lamentations, Ezekiel, and Daniel, please keep asking questions of the text, don't hesitate to challenge my assumptions, carry on praying for God's direction, and maintain contact with those whom he has placed over you for your spiritual development.

---

18. Augustine, "Questions on the Heptateuch," 2.73.

2

Jeremiah

HISTORICAL BACKGROUND

We are treated to the relative luxury of being able to give fairly precise dates for Jeremiah's contribution to Scripture, from his call to be a prophet in 627 BC (Jer 1:2) to the year when Evil-Merodach became king of Babylon in 561 (Jer 52:31; see also 2 Kgs 25:27). Judah had known some politically blustery times, but none as tempestuous as those covered by Jeremiah's input. He had justifiable cause to attract the nickname "the weeping prophet," being actively involved during the reigns of five kings of Judah: Josiah, Jehoahaz (Shallum), Jehoiakim (Eliakim), Jehoiachin (Jeconiah), and Zedekiah (Mattaniah).

Josiah (640–609 BC)

During what might be described as "the Dark Ages" for God's covenant people, few non-prophets emerge with reputation intact, fewer still from the ranks of the politically motivated. Here is how the chronicler sums up Josiah's contribution, however:

> Josiah was eight years old when he became king, and he reigned in Jerusalem for thirty-one years. He did what was right in the

eyes of the Lord and walked in the ways of his father David, not turning aside to the right or to the left. (2 Chr 34:1–2)

Josiah's loyalty was beyond question, though his judgment failed him when he lost his life at Megiddo in an attempt to halt the Egyptians on their way to help Assyria in battle with the Babylonians (2 Kgs 23:29). It is not clear from this account, but the chronicler gives details of a verbal warning from Pharaoh Neco to Josiah, claiming divine authority for his mission. At face value, this might seem contrived, though the chronicler's verdict suggests not:

> Josiah, however, would not turn away from him, but disguised himself to engage him in battle. He would not listen to what Neco had said to him at God's command but went to fight him on the plain of Megiddo. (2 Chr 35:22)

The nature of Josiah's death shared many features with that of Ahab of the northern kingdom of Israel (see 2 Chr 18:29–34). One area where they differ is that Ahab was not sufficiently mourned by any of God's prophets to merit the composition of laments in his honor (35:25).

Jehoahaz (609 BC)

There seems to be no consensus concerning why the fourth son of Josiah took precedence over his brothers with regards to the throne on his father's death. The firstborn, Johanan, is mentioned only once in the whole of Scripture (1 Chr 3:15), so he may have predeceased his father. The other two did eventually accede to the throne, but none of the three behaved so virtuously as to replicate Josiah's biblical epitaph (see above). It may well have been that the nobility made their preferences known on account of an appealing rebellious streak in Jehoahaz, which seemed lacking in his siblings. Although there is no conclusive evidence to support such a claim, he was certainly prepared to resist the Egyptian threat, though to no lasting avail.

The reign of Jehoahaz was as fleeting as that of his nephew later proved to be, before he was deported in stages by Pharaoh Neco. Jehoahaz died in exile in Egypt, in fulfilment of Jeremiah's prophecy concerning him (see Jer 22:11–12). It is perhaps significant that Jeremiah uses his personal name rather than his throne name, given their rather distinctive meanings: Jehoahaz means "Yahweh has grasped," while Shallum is closely linked to the idea of retribution.

Jehoiakim (609–598 BC)

Having deported the hapless Jehoahaz, the Egyptians installed his brother, Jehoiakim, to rule in his stead, but under their jurisdiction. This arrangement lasted until 605 BC, when the Babylonians won a decisive battle at Carchemish, whereupon Jehoiakim ruled for a while as vassal for the victors. Three years later, and again counter to Jeremiah's counsel, Jehoiakim rebelled against Nebuchadnezzar (2 Kgs 24:1). Jehoiakim's confidence proved to be ill-placed, his downfall guaranteed. Nebuchadnezzar dispatched local garrison troops to attack Judah, but notice how Scripture presents this information:

> The Lord sent Babylonian, Aramean, Moabite, and Ammonite raiders against [Jehoiakim]. He sent them to destroy Judah in accordance with the word of the Lord proclaimed by his servants the prophets. (2 Kgs 24:2)

Jehoiakim died *en route* to captivity aged only thirty-six. Although there is no biblical record of his burial, Jeremiah foretold that his body would be discarded outside the city walls, without ceremony and devoid of dignity (Jer 22:18–19). Hardly a paragon of perspicacity and social sensitivity, it would be a fitting end: likened to an ass in death, as he had proved himself to be in life. According to the first-century AD historian, Josephus, this is precisely what happened, and at Nebuchadnezzar's instigation.

Jehoiachin (598–597 BC)

Appointed at the age of eighteen by Judah's Babylonian overlords, Jehoiachin's transitory reign was sufficiently marked by evil to attract Jeremiah's prediction of not only its termination, but also the end of his short dynastic line (Jer 22:24–30). Jeremiah's words were fulfilled to the letter (see 2 Kgs 24:10–16). There may even have been a note of regret on the part of Nebuchadnezzar in appointing Jehoiachin. There certainly seems to have been some incident or sequence of events to have changed Nebuchadnezzar's mind in such a brief period of time. Perhaps the evil Jehoiachin did was not only "in the eyes of the Lord" (Jer 22:9).

Jehoiachin was imprisoned in exile, but afforded certain privileges on account of his royal pedigree. After Nebuchadnezzar's death in 562, his successor, Evil-Merodach, allowed Jehoiachin to be released from prison, effectively into his personal custody (2 Kgs 25:27–30). Given this king's penchant for wanton lawlessness, perhaps he saw in Jehoiachin a kindred spirit from whom he could learn, thereby adding to his own growing reputation. If this was his intention, Evil-Merodach had little occasion to avail himself of the opportunity, as he was killed the following year by troops belonging to his brother-in-law, Nergal-sharezer.

Zedekiah (597–587 BC)

Zedekiah was no more than a puppet king, installed by Nebuchadnezzar of Babylon to replace his nephew (2 Kgs 24:17). There is more than a hint of irony, perhaps by design, that this final monarch of the southern kingdom had his name changed from Mattaniah (i.e., "hope of/from the Lord"); if ever anyone failed to live up to what might have been expected of him given his name, then it was Zedekiah (i.e., "Yahweh is my righteousness"). He was both erratic and impotent, succumbing to any who had the audience and audacity to exert sufficient pressure on him to direct his paths according to their preference.

Zedekiah stubbornly refused to alter course when, having followed his advisors' counsel to seek an alliance with Egypt against Babylon, the latter laid siege to Jerusalem. Jeremiah advised surrender, but Zedekiah declined (Jer 21:3–10; 38:17–18). After a brief respite, Judah's hungered capital collapsed, Zedekiah was captured in flight toward the Jordan Valley, and the very last thing he saw was his sons being executed before his eyes were put out and he was deported with the final phase of exiles to Babylon (2 Kgs 25:4–7). Zedekiah was around thirty-two years of age at this stage; however many days he lived beyond this were spent imprisoned in exile (Jer 52:11).

PERSONAL BACKGROUND

There is a worrying trend amongst many latter-day preachers to temper their "messages" in such a way as to curry popular support. Some seem to perceive their congregations as consumers of entertainment rather than the covenantally elect of God. Jeremiah would not have sat comfortably in such company. Indeed, had his ministry been suspended until now, he would no doubt have been labelled a non-conformist. Imagine these words being spoken today at the local monthly gathering of the *Apostles and Prophets "R" Us Convention*:

> "Hear this, you foolish and senseless people, who have eyes but do not see, who have ears but do not hear: Should you not fear me?" declares the Lord. "Should you not tremble in my presence? . . . But these people have stubborn and rebellious hearts;

they have turned aside and gone away... The prophets prophesy lies, the priests rule by their own authority, and my people love it this way." (Jer 5:21–31)

But he did fit the mold of the biblical prophet very well, especially those of the Old Testament. Like many of his contemporaries, Jeremiah had no time for the religious establishment—most notably those who peddled their neatly packaged, socially acceptable version of truth for personal gain. Even Josiah's policies of temple reform were not exempt from Jeremiah's scathing rebukes, though the object of his ire was more likely the opportunity that such prescriptive guidelines gave for feigning obedience rather than a true heart response (see Jer 3:5).

Much of the disapproval with which Jeremiah was met probably stemmed from the fact that many of his directives seemed heavily laden with defeatist terminology. The reader will search for his lighter side in vain. From his perspective, however, we must note two not entirely unrelated factors:

i. He could only prophesy as God's mouthpiece; to do otherwise would have been presumptuous; and

ii. Whatever else may be said of Babylon, this "foe from the north" (Jer 1:13–16; 4:5–8) was merely an instrument in the hand of an offended God.

And so, Jeremiah was not so much a product of the age into which he was born as a divinely appointed counter-product to that age. Much of what we otherwise know of him is revealed to us in the opening verses of his first chapter. It should come as no surprise for us to learn of Jeremiah's priestly background when we know that he came from Anathoth, as this was one of four Levitical towns nominated in the tribal allocation of Benjamin (see Josh 21:17–18). Anathoth was a town of pagan origins just three miles northeast of Jerusalem, its name associated with the plural form of the Canaanite goddess of war (i.e., Anat). The name survives today as Anata, which is very close to but not precisely on the ancient site of Anathoth.

Jeremiah was the son of Hilkiah, whose priestly heritage could be traced back to the time of Solomon. His name was not uncommon, especially so amongst families with priestly connections. But neither is the fact that his parents chose to name their son Jeremiah without significance, as it can mean either "Yahweh appoints" or "Yahweh throws down"—the latter in the sense of being laid as a foundation; thus, by derivation, to be firmly established.

More is revealed of the personal nature of the prophet in Jeremiah than may be said of any other prophet's writings. Part of the reason for this is that he comes across as one who tends to wear his heart on his sleeve, a quality (or weakness) with which I can readily identify. My mother used to say of me that I was a victim of the tear duct and the sweat gland to the point of incontinence. But I think the main contributing factor for us having such intimate knowledge of Jeremiah's character is his use of a personal secretary (Jer 32:12–16; 43:1–6).

Baruch's legacy is perhaps that his name is so well-known to many of us, despite the fact that it appears only four times in the whole of the Bible, all in the book of Jeremiah. Of course, part of the reason for this may be in relation to the deuterocanonical work, *The Book of Baruch*. This is held to be part of Scripture within both Roman Catholicism and Eastern Orthodoxy, though it is omitted elsewhere, as are any claims to authentic authorship. The apocryphal *Apocalypse of Baruch* is similarly well-known due to its inclusion in the Septuagint version of the Hebrew Scriptures, though its composition is equally doubtful. What we are able to discern from the unchallenged texts in Jeremiah is that Baruch has earned his reputation as a faithful servant. His status is implied rather than stated, especially given that the role of scribe in Judah in the late-seventh to early-sixth centuries BC was a prominent position, often reserved for those with experience of high royal officialdom.

The extent of Baruch's faithfulness toward Jeremiah was such that he served him in his ministry for almost two decades through arguably the most turbulent period of Judah's history. It is highly likely that other less troublesome options would have presented themselves to him; he was under no obligation to remain loyal to one who insisted on placing himself directly in the line of such hostile opposition. No obligation, that is, but his own convictions. How does this help us in our evaluation of the character of Jeremiah? Simply by enabling us to see something of the caliber of the man whose temperament attracted such enduring devotion.

At first glance, Jeremiah's natural sensibilities seem to make him ill-suited to the commission to which he was engaged. Given the severity of the words he was to convey, the status of those who were to receive them, and the level of potential humiliation should it not go according to plan, a priest renowned for his timidity would not have been my choice. But then again, I don't particularly specialize in making upside-down decisions. This is how John Graybill sums him up:

> That [Jeremiah] tenaciously clung to his assigned task through
> the succeeding years of rejection and persecution is a tribute

both to the mettle of the man and to the grace of God, without which his personality surely would have gone to pieces.[1]

Nothing is known for certain of Jeremiah's demise. Tradition suggests that he was stoned to death in Egypt, but there is no other evidence for this. Paul Johnson simply concludes:

> After the fall of [Jerusalem] . . . a group of the citizens dragged [Jeremiah] with them and settled across the Egyptian border, where he continued, in great old age, to denounce the sins which had brought on the Lord's vengeance, and to put his faith in a "remnant," a "small number" who would see his words justified by history. There his voice faded into silence, the first Jew.[2]

OVERVIEW

Chapter 1: God's Call to Jeremiah

What we might otherwise think of as God's calling upon the life of Jeremiah (Jer 1:10) was actually a more detailed unveiling of his plan for him. Jeremiah had been the object of divine choice since before he had even been born (Jer 1:5). In my NIV translation, the same English verb is used of both actions: "appoint." However, the original Hebrew is subtly, yet perhaps significantly, different. The first word is *dastika*, which means "to reserve," "to put by," or "to mark out for future reference." The second word, *qadtika*, is complementary and relates to something or someone being put to use having been reserved at an earlier time. Both may apply to inanimate objects as well as persons, such as the storage of grain or crops to be used in the event of a future famine.

The significance of this, I believe, is crucial to our understanding not only of Jeremiah's calling, but also of God's dealings more generally. He is a proactive God rather than a reactive God. Obviously, omniscience and foreknowledge play key roles in that. But he doesn't respond to world events on the hoof, as if they caught him off guard. Yahweh's choice of Jeremiah was not a haphazard last-ditch response to a sudden crisis; it was merely the latest step in the process of Jeremiah's journey from conception to consecration.

---

1. In Pfeiffer and Harrison, *Wycliffe Bible Commentary*, 656.
2. Johnson, *History of the Jews*, 79.

Chapters 2–45: A Mouthpiece to Judah

Judah Condemned (chapters 2–29)

All the tools of the prophet's trade are employed in this section: analogy, parabolic illustration, personal representation, warnings from history, and symbolism:

- A bride's love gone cold (Jer 2:2–20);
- A vine metaphor (2:21);
- Israel divorced because of adultery (3:1–8);
- False prophets unmasked and repudiated (5:12–13; 7:28; 14:14–16; 23:9–40);
- A linen belt oracle (13:1–11);
- A lonely prophet, but never alone (16:1–9);
- The potter's house reveals its secrets (18:1—19:13);
- The sign of Passhur (20:1–6);
- Unfaithful shepherds denounced and replaced (23:1–8);
- The two baskets of figs (24:1–10);
- The seventy years in exile (25:1–11);
- The sign of the yoke (27:1—28:17); and
- A letter of encouragement to the exiles (29:1–28).

The promise of restoration (chapters 30–33)

Leaving aside its denominational use, the word "restoration" is usually linked to the re-establishment of a former condition or previous ownership. Acceptable synonyms might include restitution, recovery, or repair. Its biblical use (Hebrew *shub*; Greek *apokostasis*) embraces all of these, but also seems to include a built-in multiplication factor or an exponential improvement upon the original. Paradise, for example, is not Eden merely restored but transcended.

In the chapters before us, this is not quite so obvious initially until we arrive at arguably the key section to the whole book. God promises to restore both Israel *and* Judah to the land he had given them (Jer 30:3), to rebuild the city ruins of Jerusalem (Jer 30:18), and to give them back their nationhood (Jer 31:1), each a cause for rejoicing in its own right. But then he introduces a new twist on an old theme:

"The time is coming," declares the Lord, "when I will make a new covenant with the house of Israel and with the house of Judah. It will not be like the covenant I made with their forefathers ... This is the covenant that I will make with the house of Israel after that time," declares the Lord. "I will put my law in their minds and write it on their hearts. I will be their God and they will be my people." (Jer 31:31-33)

Judgment unfolds (chapters 34–45)

The beginning of these chapters subverts chronological sequence by returning the reader to the reign of Jehoiakim. Certain travel restrictions were placed upon Jeremiah (Jer 36:4), which meant that his messages could not be delivered first-hand. This is why he dictated his prophecies for Baruch to write down and take to be read before their intended audience, the king (Jer 36:4-7). Jehoiakim's response was as irreverent as it was arrogant: he simply cut up the scroll from which Jeremiah's words were being read and burned the fragments (Jer 36:23-24). Such contempt was to be the final straw.

The narrative then moves on to find Zedekiah reigning as Babylon's vassal king in Judah. Because Jeremiah's counsel fell far short of triumphalism, he was perceived as a traitor to his country (see Jer 37:1-13) and imprisoned at the behest of the captain of the guard (Jer 37:14-15). Jeremiah continued to prophesy defeat for the king at the hands of the Babylonians (Jer 37:19) and was soon cast into a nearby cistern for his troubles, where he would surely have died but for the intervention of a Cushite palace official (Jer 38:1-13). Still Jeremiah would not alter the direction of his message and his words finally proved true (Jer 39:1-9). The rest of the section is concerned with Jeremiah's release by Nebuzaradan (Jer 40:1-4), the conspiracy and assassination of the appointed governor of the occupied territory (Jer 41:1-2), and the people's refusal—yet again—to heed Jeremiah's advice (Jer 42:1—43:6). The consequences this time were far worse than they could possibly have imagined.

Chapters 46–51: A Voice to the Nations

Egypt	Jer 46;
Philistia	chapter 47;
Moab	chapter 48;
Ammon	49:1–6;
Edom	49:7–22;
Damascus	49:23–27;
Kedar and Hazor	49:28–33;
Elam	49:34–39; and
Babylon	chapters 50–51.

A comparison of this list with those surrounding nations against whom Isaiah prophesied (see p. 7) reveals a number of notable additions (Ammon, Kedar, Hazor, and Elam) and omissions (Assyria, Cush, Arabia, and Tyre). Those common to both are Egypt, Philistia, Moab, and Babylon. Much could be written about all of them (and has been), but for the purposes of this example, allow me to say just a few words about Babylon.

As has been noted, Babylon was chosen by God as the instrument by which he would execute his judgment upon the southern kingdom of Judah for their wanton disobedience. There was nothing on the part of Babylon that might be considered meritorious in this decision. It did not excel where Judah lacked, nor were its people better exemplars of moral rectitude. It was simply a matter of sovereign choice. That choice did not extend to Babylon replacing Judah as ambassadors of God's covenant, nor did it exempt them from judgment on their own account. One of the names missing from Jeremiah's catalogue of woes was that of Assyria; the leaders of Babylon should have taken note.

Chapter 52: The Epilogue

As the previous section concludes with: "The words of Jeremiah end here" (Jer 51:64), this final chapter forms a historical coda; it may have been a later scribal addition, perhaps by Baruch. Although the wording varies slightly from the account in Second Kings (24:8—25:30), the differences are negligible. Disagreements over dates (see 2 Kgs 25:8; Jer 52:12) could be accounted by scribal error or, if more than one source was used, different calendar settings might have been employed. Alternatively, the earlier date could have alluded to Nebuzaradan's arrival at Jerusalem, while the later date might be applied to the beginning of its destruction. The material facts are not altered and can be verified from other sources. For example, archaeological evidence confirms the depopulation of Judea at around this time.[3]

What is particularly noticeable—both here and elsewhere—is the insistence to date the captivity in relation to Jehoiachin's reign (Jer 52:31; see also Ezek 1:2). Despite the evil he had wrought amongst God's people, those same exiled people continued to measure their circumstances in accordance with the ongoing Davidic covenant and God's faithfulness to it. Nervous expectation or casual habit? Perhaps a bit of both.

SPRINGS AND CISTERNS

> Hear the word of the Lord, O house of Jacob, all you clans of the house of Israel. This is what the Lord says . . . "My people have committed two sins: They have forsaken me, the spring of living water, and have dug their own cisterns, broken cisterns that cannot hold water." (Jer 2:4–5a, 14)

To the best of my albeit vague recollection, I have only heard this text used as the basis for a sermon once in over forty years as a Christian. Though I am unable to remember much about that occasion, I suspect it was probably misused, as the context was purely evangelistic. The preacher highlighted the folly of self-dependence on the part of the unsaved in the light of the fact that God offers an infinitely greater resource. "Not much wrong with that," you might think, and you'd be right. But the "not much" is quite significant: Jeremiah is not being employed as God's channel to address the heathen, the alien, Israel's enemies, or any of their kings, but his own covenant people.

It doesn't seem that long ago that the word "sin" was in danger of vanishing altogether from the Christian vocabulary. The influence of political correctness and a desire to keep our pulpit rhetoric non-believer friendly conspire to make some choose less-hostile alternatives. It never quite disappeared, but it has perhaps suffered some dilution of meaning. For the sake of clarity, I proffer a slightly different rendering for verse thirteen:

> For my people have committed two evils; they have forsaken me, the fountain of living waters, and hewed them out cisterns, broken cisterns, that can hold no water. (Jer 2:13, KJV)[4]

---

3. See Albright, *Archaeology of Palestine*, 140–42.
4. Compare with NASB, RSV, Wycliffe, and YLT.

Two Sides of the Same Coin

In this opening section, I wish to draw the reader's attention briefly to the obvious and the omitted, before going on to consider the overt in some detail. First of all, the language employed by Jeremiah is typically prophetic metaphor. That is, he conveys a mental image by use of everyday objects, situations, or circumstances, the qualities of which will help to enrich our understanding of God's true meaning.

Secondly, though two sins/evils are cited, and the one might be said to compound the other, they consist in essentially the one act. This is especially true because there is no third way: not drinking is not an option. Water is not a luxury, but a necessity for sustaining life, and so failing to avail ourselves of God's supply means we must search elsewhere. To look at it from the opposite direction, the very act of choosing self-sufficiency is a rejection of divine provision. At this point, I must reiterate what I alluded to earlier: at this stage, at least, the addressees are still considered to be God's people.

A cistern's arrest

Perhaps the chasm between the two options is not immediately apparent to many of us in the twenty-first century. In the UK, for example, the word "cistern" is often attributed to the small household tank for storing domestic water, usually as part of a flushing toilet system. While not to be recommended as an unfiltered drinking source, neither is it particularly what the seventeenth-century translators of the King James Version of the Bible had in mind; it is certainly not what was intended by the original Hebrew.

Before we all dash off to consult our lexicon of choice, let us consider the word's use elsewhere in Scripture. A comprehensive comparison of biblical characters that featured Joseph and Jeremiah would be an interesting one, not least for the fact that they shared the ignominious experience of having been cast into a cistern by those intent on doing them harm:

> So Joseph went after his brothers and found them near Dothan. But they saw him in the distance, and before he reached them, they plotted to kill him . . . So when Joseph came to his brothers, they stripped him of his robe—the richly ornamented robe he was wearing—and they took him and threw him into the cistern. Now the cistern was empty; there was no water in it. (Gen 37:17b–24)

> Then the officials said to the king, "[Jeremiah] should be put to death. He is discouraging the soldiers who are left in the city, as

> well as all the people, by the things he is saying to them. This man is not seeking the good of these people but their ruin." "He is in your hands," King Zedekiah answered . . . So they took Jeremiah and put him into the cistern of Malkijah, the king's son, which was in the courtyard of the guard. They lowered Jeremiah into the cistern; it had no water in it, only mud, and Jeremiah sank down into the mud. (Jer 38:4–6)

Derived from the Hebrew verb *ba'ar* (to dig), these subterranean bell-shaped storage facilities are still to be found in parts of Palestine, both in private homes and those for public use. In Old Testament times, however, cisterns were mainly dug outside the city walls in an attempt to retain some rainfall during the dry season (from May to September). Even those annexed to royal households could boast only the most primitive of plaster coating to the floor and lower walls, though the upper part was often exposed earth and rubble. It was presumably the brokenness of this partial lining that impinged negatively upon its capacity to retain water. You might not flinch at the prospect of bathing in such contamination as a last resort, or even to drink of it if you were trapped and close to your last breath, but to do so otherwise by choice is unimaginable.

By contrast, the natural filtration process makes spring water purer and, therefore, more beneficial for both human and animal consumption. The consequences of this might range from merely a more refreshing experience to tangible nutritional advantages. Moreover, the hydrospheric system of cracks, fissures, and channels can mean an almost constant supply of top-quality groundwater. Even before we begin to look at any more detail, we can surely agree that Irving Jensen's exclamation is but an echo of what is currently foremost in our minds:

> How astonishing and horrifying that [Israel] should forsake a continuous fountain of living waters for broken cisterns that could hold no water![5]

The wrong means to a distorted end

The horror and astonishment only intensify as we delve deeper. Staying with the metaphor for a moment longer, the choice is essentially one between what God has to offer, which is satisfying, abundant, life-sustaining, and limitless, or going our own polluted, impure, bacteria-ridden, vomit-inducing way. In modern parlance, it's a no-brainer, isn't it? Well, you'd think so.

---

5. Jensen, *Jeremiah and Lamentations*, 24.

But once we identify the cisterns with man-made attempts to find spiritual fulfilment, even within a Christian milieu, then perhaps our amazement takes something of a battering.

When compared to God's grace, a works-related "righteousness" is not only found to be a broken cistern, but also a deficient system, doomed to end in abject failure and utter frustration. But what about the relationship God has in store for his people versus the idolatry our hearts often crave? And before we dismiss the notion of a Christian entertaining such a weakness, think of an idol less in terms of a wooden statue and more as anything or anybody that might seek to displace God as our source of delight, focus, satisfaction, hope, ambition, or investment.

Even otherwise godly things in the wrong context, or those given inappropriate recognition, can supplant God in our affections. They are often more dangerous because they are more subtle and we, therefore, excuse them because of their perceived kingdom value. And so, because others see us, for example, as vital members of the church music group, perhaps with a principal role in leading the congregation toward the utmost in praising their Redeemer on Sunday morning, we feel perfectly justified in cutting ourselves more than a little slack in our personal devotions. After all, we're surely still in credit on the divine balance sheet.

Not personally troubled by this? Perhaps the career you have forged for yourself has become a broken cistern. It may even be that the work you do is a direct result of God having at some time been involved in the process: you prayed for guidance, asked for his calming influence at the interview, and frequently included him in the decisions you had to make. It all began with you looking to the living stream as your source of refreshment, but the pressures of the day-to-day routine, often having to work long hours and weekends, temptations associated with out-of-town conferences, and weekly target schedules that are designed to stretch you to the limit, perhaps these have taken their toll on your capacity to draw from God's designated source.

Maybe much of what I have just described applies to you, but you have justified your circumstances by the fact that you are a church pastor. It's not so much that you blame it on the "my ministry" syndrome; but you do use it as an excuse. Your daily devotions are now more of a potential sermon scan, a visit to the frail always has one eye on the lookout for that much-sought-after humorous anecdote, and prayer times are dominated by pleas rather than praise. And your preparation notes for leading tomorrow night's midweek home group, which used to consist of the overflow of your private times with your Father, are now hastily scribbled around the evening meal table, often as the first of those entrusted to your care are beginning to arrive.

Church leaders are not exempt from adopting a broken-cistern existence. If anything, they are perhaps more vulnerable than most and eminently more susceptible. The transition from one to the other is subtle, it is sly, and it is fiendishly successful in achieving its objective. No prizes, then, for guessing who I'm going to name as the sole instigator. Here's a clue: Who stands to gain the most by causing Christians to become sidetracked? His name is Satan.

Hope that is prepared to pay the price

The first Christian biography I read was *Through Gates of Splendor*, the account of Jim Elliot's life, ministry, and death by his widow, Elisabeth. On the first Tuesday of January 1956, Jim and four colleagues arrived by plane on a small strip of land, surrounded by the jungles of Ecuador. It was a dangerous landing, but one they had been praying about and planning for some considerable time. They were motivated by a burning desire to reach the Auca Indians with the gospel of Christ.

The Aucas' notoriety was not undeserved; there was a reason they were numbered as an unreached tribe. Earlier missionaries had managed to make initial contact, offering supplies as tokens of their peaceful intentions, but always inciting only a hostile reception. Fully aware of the dangers, for three months Elliot's crew had been regularly flying over the area, dropping gifts and shouting greetings. On landing, they built a hut and waited for the Aucas to come and find them.

They didn't have long to wait. Three days after their arrival, the team was approached by a delegation of three: one man and two women. They exchanged greetings. The missionaries had reason to believe they were making good progress and offered to take their male visitor up in the plane. This, remember, was the Friday. On the following Sunday, they were due to make routine radio contact with their base at 4:30 in the afternoon. No such message was forthcoming. When radio silence showed no signs of being broken, and an aerial reconnaissance reported no sighting, a search expedition was dispatched. Four bodies were recovered, all speared to death. The fifth was never found. It seems they had been ambushed.

Jim Elliot's diary was found by the rescue party. As they had waited for the Auca Indians to arrive, he made this final entry:

> I walked out to the hill just now. It is exalting, delicious, to stand embraced by the shadows of a friendly tree with the wind

tugging at your coattail and the heavens hailing your heart, to gaze and glory and give oneself again to God—what more could a man ask? Oh, the fullness, pleasure, sheer excitement of knowing God on earth! I care not if I never raise my voice again for him, if only I may love him, please him. Perhaps in mercy he shall give me a host of children that I may lead them through the vast star fields to explore his delicacies whose finger ends set them to burning. But if not, if only I may see him, touch his garments, and smile into his eyes—ah then, not stars nor children shall matter, only himself.

O Jesus, Master and Center and End of all, how long before that glory is yours which has so long awaited you? Now there is no thought of you among men; then there shall be thought for nothing else. Now other men are praised; then none shall care for any other's merits. Hasten, hasten, Glory of Heaven, take your crown, subdue your kingdom, enthrall your creatures.[6]

Nothing but the truth

Heartrending and heartwarming at the same time. Quite a story! But why tell it here? Because if we are to be people of truth, then it has to be the whole truth; if I am in some small measure responsible for presenting before you what I consider to be the counsel of God, then as much as it is within my gift to do so, it must be the whole counsel of God. As true worshippers, we are not at liberty to cherrypick the attributes of God that are aesthetically suited to our own personality or the cultural *zeitgeist*. And here's the rub: drinking from God's unpolluted stream is always the best option; that is an indisputable truth that I would defend with everything within me. But it is not always the safe option. Whether we are faced with brute force or *faux bonhomie*, it is seldom risk-free; it is never without cost, and yet it is always ultimately satisfying.

As Son of God, it might be possible for some to imagine that this is one area where Jesus was not "tempted in every way, just as we are" and, therefore, not fully able "to sympathize with our weaknesses" (Heb 4:15). Let me qualify my use of the word "possible": it is "possible" only if those who take this option are prepared also to challenge the veracity of the episode in which Jesus was confronted by the devil in the wilderness at his weakest moment apart from the cross (Matt 4:1–11).

---

6. Elliot, *Through Gates*, 156.

Sermon fodder this is not; but neither is it as analogous as some preachers have perhaps contended. "He was hungry" (Matt 4:2) means precisely that; it isn't code for something that only those in the know would understand. However, at the risk of being perceived as if I am simply adding to the list of unnatural interpretations, I don't think it requires such a leap of faith or a stretch of the imagination to identify the choices with which Jesus was faced: he either continued to receive sustenance from the pure waters of his Father's delight or he settled for what the devil's broken cisterns might provide.

Jesus was, indeed, "tempted in every way, just as we are." My temptation in writing that last sentence was to substitute "in every way" with an ellipsis, but I am not convinced that would have been correct. I don't think he was "tempted . . . just as we are," because the measure of the intensity of his temptation was far greater. His sinlessness, specifically expressed in his resistance to temptation because of that perfection, means he was forced to endure more until finally the devil gave up. Our sinfulness does not give rise to such inexhaustible defiance.

Why Would You Make the Wrong Choice?

This is the obvious question, isn't it? So much so, in fact, that if asked in conversation it could easily pass rhetorically with no more than a cavalier shrug of the shoulders in reply. But it is a serious question that warrants a sober answer. Why, when offered the opportunity to indulge themselves with the finest of fare, freely and without limit, would anyone with a modicum of common sense opt for something that is not only second best, but comes trailing behind by some considerable distance? It is both devoid of cohesion and defies comprehension.

A clash of instincts

I believe there are a number of conceivable reasons, and most of us are guilty of at least some of them. Judging by the weight of New Testament apostolic emphasis, arguably the most common factor is the constant battle between the sinful nature and our newfound spiritual allegiance. Paul had to address this on more than one occasion, but it is perhaps in his counsel to the churches in Galatia that we find the clearest instruction:

> So I say, live by the Spirit, and you will not gratify the desires of
> the sinful nature. For the sinful nature desires what is contrary

to the Spirit, and the Spirit what is contrary to the sinful nature. They are in conflict with each other, so that you do not do what you want. (Gal 5:16–17)

Well, that's fine advice, but when a desire pushes itself to the surface, how do we know to which nature it belongs? Without any claims to either being exhaustive, the apostle helpfully draws up two lists contrasting some of the features of each combatant nature:

> The acts of the sinful nature are obvious: sexual immorality, impurity and debauchery; idolatry and witchcraft; hatred, discord, jealousy, fits of rage, selfish ambition, dissensions, factions and envy; drunkenness, orgies and the like . . . But the fruit of the Spirit is love, joy, peace, patience, kindness, goodness, faithfulness, gentleness and self-control. (Gal 5:19–23)

When we look at the traits associated with the sinful nature, we must agree with Paul: they are obvious. And yet, with as much *pathos* as we can muster, we still excuse ourselves when we yield to them, often on the presumption that there are grey areas and: "We weren't quite sure where the boundaries were." Given the context, it may also be that Paul is saying that, though the desires themselves may be hidden, the deeds emanating from those desires and the consequences of them are not so easy to conceal. "If in doubt, don't," would seem to be the safest advice. But does our entrapment by such acts affect our status as Christians? Yes and no! It certainly inhibits our Christian experience, because our indulgence in them hampers our growth toward Christlike maturity. Paul warned his readership (the companies of believers in Galatia and elsewhere) of the struggle in which they were engaged.

But notice his admonition toward the end of the section on "the acts of the sinful nature": "those who live like this will not inherit the kingdom of God" (Gal 5:21b). The original Greek *prasso* means "to be in the habit of doing,"[7] thus implying the present continuous tense. A more accurate rendering, therefore, might be: "those who continue to live like this," which I have found to be explicit only in the Evangelical Heritage Version of the New Testament.

Many of those traits listed as characteristic of the sinful nature are readily identifiable in society two thousand years on. We kid only ourselves in typically Galatian fashion by pretending that Christians are entirely beyond their pull. We are similarly deceived if we think this is anything other than choosing to drink from broken cisterns rather than God's spring of

---

7. See Vine, *Expository Dictionary*, 322.

living water. But aren't these simply examples of our doing so rather than answering the question: "Why?"

Perhaps a better clue might be derived by looking at some of the qualities annexed to living by God's Spirit. Our perception of love is often conditioned by a subjective rationale. We look for joy in all the wrong places, we expect to find it in the company of those who are prepared to promise it only for a season, and we pursue exploits that are designed to bring fulfilment only in the moment. Kindness and goodness are all too frequently measured by how someone or something makes us feel there and then, rather than by their potential for long-term benefits. Faithfulness is not only perceived to be temporal, but we actually welcome the fact that it is; that way, we have a built-in get-out clause, just in case things don't work out. Gentleness very rarely finds itself elevated beyond the realm of the sensual, and "self-control"? "Yeah, right!"

Act in haste, repent at leisure

Did I miss one? Ah, yes: patience. Herein, I believe, lies the key to answering our question: we choose broken cisterns because we are too impatient to wait for God's perfect timing. When I became a Christian in the mid-1970s, the buzz slogan doing the rounds was: "If it feels good, do it." Tragically, it even infiltrated certain corners of the Christian room, though thankfully not those I was encouraged to frequent. In more recent times, we have a major sports company to thank for enticing us to "Just do it!" with the implication that there is not a moment to lose.

We live in an age of the instant and the immediate. Well-meaning advertisers tell us that if we don't get what we can while we can, we might never do so. So, hop aboard the gravy train now before it gathers momentum, because it won't be slowing down for the tardy or the vacuously insipid. I even remember this being promoted from the pulpit of a well-known charismatic church in the north of England some years ago. Under the heading, *Quitters, Campers, and Climbers*, the more robust "super-Christians" were effectively encouraged to embrace a Christianized "survival of the fittest" mentality, in some bizarre Darwinian bastardization of the gospel. "Don't wait for them to catch up; press on toward the goal," went the cry of ambition. By all means press on, and if you're going to do so, there's no better target than the goal God has set before you, but the New Testament emphasis seems to be that we treat those who may be weaker amongst us with patience and understanding. I'm sure we'd expect it of those who are stronger than us.

Scripture gives plentiful examples of patience being regarded as a virtue, often by recording incidents where impatience ends in folly. Arguably the most well-known is the one involving Esau and Jacob (Gen 25:27–34). Although twins, as the slightly older of the two, it was Esau who held the birthright. Their respective characters could hardly be more different, Esau being "a skillful hunter," used to spending time outdoors, while Jacob was more meditative (Gen 25:27). We are told that Isaac favored Esau, but Rebekah loved Jacob (Gen 25:28), each parent possibly taking a particular shine to the reflection of their own image they saw in their sons.

On one occasion, Jacob was practising his culinary skills, while his brother was out in the open country, doing whatever it is boys of that age find to do in the open country. We are not told what it was, and so may only speculate what it might have been that caused him to be so incredibly hungry when he arrived home. So desperate was Esau that he offered no argument when Jacob told him that the price for a portion of his homemade broth was the family birthright (Gen 25:29–32). Thus were sown the seeds of division, which grew thenceforth until it became full grown. Of course, we can read that story knowing that it was God's means of effecting his purpose for what would become his covenant people through Jacob. From Esau's perspective at that time, however, his own actions thereby irrevocably closed the door on what might otherwise have been his. And all because of impatience. The lesson is as salutary as it is sober.

But I have also known some Christians who have settled for an inferior experience genuinely believing they are living the real deal. Having never been exposed to the kind of teaching that might challenge their understanding, they have had no viable alternative but to swallow the lies, partial truths, and downright distortions they have been drip fed. Even when this has not been the case, the flaunted arrogance of some of those who claim to be living life on the highest plane can often be grossly disconcerting. It can sometimes seem like more a case of God's best for the pretentious and the obnoxious than anything with which Oswald Chambers might have been familiar.

An example worth following

Twenty-odd years ago, Christian teens across the globe began sporting bracelets, T-shirts, car stickers, pencil cases, and street banners bearing the meme WWJD—What Would Jesus Do? It wasn't long before marketing companies saw an opportunity and added to their catalogues an array of items like the WWJD teenage lingerie and nightwear range, the WWJD picnic set collection, and WWJD toddler fashion accessories. Even those opposed to the gospel message jumped on the bandwagon by virtue of political parody and satire, while those with a complaint against any perceived ungodly stance by the church would demonstrate outside its buildings posing the same question.

I don't doubt that the original concept was well-intentioned, even useful up to a point. But it can also be unacceptably misleading, if only by virtue of the fact that the answer is too often determined by subjective opinion. It's not so much what we know Jesus would do, but what we think he might do. There is also the added difficulty that many of the things we know Jesus would do remain beyond us, such as taking command of adverse weather conditions with just a word (Mark 4:35–41) or meeting the immediate dietary needs of a crowd of thousands from a small boy's picnic lunch (John 6:5–13).

I think we could hazard an educated guess at what Jesus would do if faced with the same choice as Jeremiah's audience: he would not settle for a broken-cistern existence. Do I really need to provide supporting evidence? Well here it is:

> When it was almost time for the Jewish Passover, Jesus went up to Jerusalem. In the temple courts he found men selling cattle, sheep and doves, and others sitting at tables exchanging money. So he made a whip out of cords, and drove all from the temple area, both sheep and cattle; he scattered the coins of the money-changers and overturned their tables. To those who sold doves he said, "Get these out of here! How dare you turn my Father's house into a market!" (John 2:13–16)

The synoptic accounts all substitute John's "market" for "den of robbers" (see Matt 21:13; Mark 11:17; Luke 19:46), each reflecting its Old Testament root (Jer 7:11). It is John alone, however, who we have to thank for the disciples' association of Jesus' actions with what the Psalmist had to say: "His disciples remembered that it is written, 'Zeal for your house will consume me'" (John 2:17; Ps 69:9).

What image does this text conjure in your mind? Zeal is not difficult to understand here, except perhaps in its intensity: to be so zealous for God's house that it engrosses us. But is that an appropriate understanding of the verb "consume"? It might not look out of place in John's summary of the incident, but the context of its original setting in the Psalms might provide a better clue:

> May those who hope in you not be disgraced because of me, O Lord, the Lord Almighty; may those who seek you not be put

to shame because of me, O God of Israel. For I endure scorn for your sake, and shame covers my face. I am a stranger to my brothers, an alien to my own mother's sons, for zeal for your house consumes me, and the insults of those who insult you fall on me. (Ps 69:6–9)

The Greek word translated "consume" in John's account is *kataphagetai*; the Hebrew in the Psalmist's original is *achalateni*, both of which convey the idea of being devoured to the point of destruction. On this occasion, Hendriksen seems so concerned with the change in tense from the original (present continuous) to the Gospel writer's use of it (future) that he omits to define either.[8] This is how Brendan Byrne views it:

> At one level, this simply refers to a zeal for the purity of temple worship that could lead any prophetic figure to act as Jesus does here. At a deeper level (perhaps not evident to the disciples at this point), the text is a comment upon what is driving the entire mission of Jesus and will ultimately "consume" him in the most radical sense of encompassing his death.[9]

Let the reader decide: does Jesus' behavior as recorded here reflect one who is content with a broken-cistern type of relationship with God or one that is fueled by the free-flowing streams of living water from his throne? Now, take your answer to that question and compare it with how we might react in a situation similar to that facing Jesus at the temple; how does it make you feel when God's house is more renowned for being an emporium of merchandise than it is a place of worship? I'm sure we all feel a sense of uplifting when in the presence of those who glorify God, whether in praise, by their teaching, or through their achievements. But do we also experience pain when it is dishonored? This is the crux of what was happening to Jesus. The reproaches that were directed toward his Father fell on him, too; when God's rightful place was being denied in the name of religious enterprise, he also felt the rejection.

Streams or cisterns? What would Jesus do? I think we know the answer. The question is: Why would you do otherwise?

Relationship Versus Idolatry

Jeremiah's context was precisely the same as much Old Testament prophecy: Israel's forsaking of their covenant God in favor of the "gods" of the

---

8. Hendriksen, *John*, 123.
9. Byrne, *Life Abounding*, 61.

surrounding nations. The way they saw it, their God was powerless to help them in their troubles, whereas those who relied on stone or wooden carved images as representative of their deities had their ambitions realized. They failed to grasp—or, more likely, refused to acknowledge—that the cause was not divine impotence, but rather their own disobedience. This was the crux of the matter.

No gods but God

The kind of "gods" that were venerated by the other nations were inanimate objects, thereby utterly devoid of personality. As such, they could only ever be subject to idolatry. Yahweh, on the other hand, is a Being; the Supreme Being, but a Being nonetheless and, therefore, capable of relationship. It is also possible to be involved in an idolatrous association with a personal being, when the worship proffered is not rooted in relationship. But God's initiation of Israel was designed with relationship in mind, encapsulated in covenant terminology: "I will take you as my own people and I will be your God" (Exod 6:7a).

Perhaps unsurprisingly, it is this basis of allegiance to which Jeremiah constantly draws his listeners' attention. He also introduces an explicit condition that is only implied elsewhere, at the same time reversing the order:

> This is what the Lord Almighty, the God of Israel says . . . "Obey me, and I will be your God and you will be my people. Walk in all the ways I command you, that it may go well with you." But they did not listen or pay attention; instead they followed the stubborn inclinations of their evil hearts. (Jer 7:21–24)

Here, the prophet identifies obedience as the sole validating expression of allegiance. The more laterally observant among us might reasonably presume that the inverse is equally true: disobedience negates any claim to fidelity. But notice also how Jeremiah describes Israel's disloyalty, in terms of them following "the stubborn inclinations of their evil hearts." Substituting idols for Yahweh wasn't a hankering for better advice, wiser counsel, or more trustworthy guidance; it was Israel feigning spirituality, while at the same time shutting off their ears to any voice that contradicted their own proclivities and predispositions. Their prayers amounted to no more than a pattern of sounds, liberally infused with gratuitous supposition.

Is idolatry such a big deal, anyway? Well, even without an explanation, it should be sufficient that God considers it to be a serious issue. So much so, in fact, that it is the first and most detailed of the ten commandments:

You shall have no other gods before/besides me. You shall not make for yourself an idol in the form of anything in heaven above or the earth beneath or in the waters below. You shall not bow down to them or worship them; for I, the Lord your God, am a jealous God, punishing the sins of the fathers to the third and fourth generation of those who hate me, but showing love to a thousand generations of those who love me and keep my commands. (Exod 20:3–6)

Isn't this just an old covenant law that has no bearing on new covenant life? First of all, the law is not entirely abandoned, but rather fulfilled by the good news of the gospel. And secondly, when asked by an expert in the law which was the greatest commandment, Jesus summarized its vertical aspects thus: "Love the Lord your God with all your heart and with all your soul and with all your mind and with all your strength" (Mark 12:28–30). In the Lukan account, he added: "Do this and you will live" (Luke 10:28b).

Although many of the religious leaders of Jesus' day from a very early stage in his ministry sought to discredit him, there is no evidence that this was such a ploy. As far as we are able to discern, it was a legitimate question, posed without cunning or any hidden agenda. Indeed, Jesus' response in Mark's presentation seems to reaffirm this: "You are not far from the kingdom of God" (Mark 12:34). If we are to glean anything that is not actually recorded of the incident, then it can only be the esteem with which Jesus was held by the one who asked.

How is this relevant here? I promise I'll get to that in due course. First of all, let us backtrack a little to that first of the ten commandments. By way of introduction, God had announced himself to his hearers as the Lord their God (Exod 20:2). He then goes on to demand that they "shall have no other gods" (Exod 20:3). Notice that the choices available to the human condition are not three-fold but two-fold. There is no third option of having no gods at all. If we reject God's rightful claim to be enthroned in our lives, then we cannot help but find a substitute "god" to take his place.

I would hazard a guess that most, if not all, readers of this book will have some measure of Christian allegiance, so this may be difficult to grasp personally. That being so, think of a non-Christian friend, work colleague, fellow student, or family member who has absolutely no other religious context to their life. Not only do they not follow Christ, but neither are they adherents of Judaism, Islam, Sikhism, Buddhism, Hinduism, Rastafarianism, or—as one of my students submitted in an end-of-year Religious Studies exam—the Jedi Order. Picture them in your mind and, if possible, recall the most recent conversation you had with them. What subject dominated their speech? What posters do they have on their bedroom wall? Is there one thing above all else on which they spend every spare dime? What is their obsession? Who or what is their god?

You see, God has placed within us an innate need to relate in worship; we are also free to choose the object of that reverence. This is no figment of propaganda. If we refuse to engage in worshipful relationship toward God, then idolatry is inescapable. I apologize if this comes across as if I am attempting to patronize the reader. In all honesty, I'm convinced that most will already recognize this truth, but I am equally determined to reinforce the fact as a sound basis for what follows.

All in the mind?

Jesus' reply to the expert in the law is particularly noteworthy (Mark 12:28–30). It is reminiscent of the Jewish declaration of faith, known as the *Shema* (see Deut 6:4–5), which is still observed in the synagogue to this day. But notice that Jesus introduces the idea of loving God with the mind to the traditional heart, soul, and strength. It could hardly be an unintentional misquotation. Moreover, Ronald Kernaghan's premise that "Jesus added a fourth . . . to create a kind of supertotality"[10] is not supported by any known numerological principle; even if it was, biblical numerology is not so widely regarded as to be sufficiently recognized.

I think William Hendriksen is correct to warn against the dangers of overanalyzing, concluding that: "What is meant in all these passages is that man should love God with all the faculties with which God has endowed him." However, I also cannot ignore Hendriksen's own separate analysis of the four features, wherein he describes the mind as "not only the seat and center of his purely intellectual life but also of the dispositions and attitudes."[11]

So what is the significance of Jesus' inclusion of loving God with our minds as a summary of the greatest commandment? Before we go angling with Paul, I would like you to do something: I invite you, the reader, to take a moment to think about that question for a few minutes before you continue reading.

Where did your thoughts lead you? Have you formed an opinion yet? If so, did you take any action, even if it was only jotting down a note or two? Is your opinion such that it is beyond being challenged or are you, at this stage, still sitting on the fence? And what is the point of all these questions? Simply to demonstrate that everything we do in life, every conversation

---

10. Kernaghan, *Mark*, 236.
11. Hendriksen, *Mark*, 493.

in which we engage, every belief we hold dear, good or bad, begins with a thought: it starts in the mind. In fact, and at the risk only of increasing any unpopularity, I would contend that the largest single battleground facing the Christian is not the threat of Islam, the philosophical ideals of a postmodernist society, a Dylan-esque phobia of "lawbreakers making rules," or how to plan for the feeding of a global population explosion: it is the mind of the individual.

What justifiable reason could I possibly have for saying this? Am I out of my—now, what's the word? Ah yes, "mind"? Well, let us consider the evidence. Take a look at Paul's instruction to the church at Rome:

> Those who live according to the sinful nature [do so because they] have their minds set on what that nature desires; but those who live in accordance with the Spirit [do so because they] have their minds set on what the Spirit desires. The mind of sinful man is death, but the mind controlled by the Spirit is life and peace; the sinful mind is hostile to God. It does not submit to God's law, nor can it do so. (Rom 8:5–7)

Just a couple of things to concede before we move on: yes, I did introduce a phrase that doesn't appear in the original (in square brackets), but on each occasion it is implied by the flow of the argument; and yes, Paul is here comparing two types of minds, each dictated to by different sets of governing criteria. Four chapters later, however, he revisits the scene. Paul begins chapter 12 with: "Therefore . . . " Alternative ways to put it might have been: "Consequently . . . "; "Because of this . . . "; or "In view of all that has gone before . . . " He goes on: "Do not conform any longer to the pattern of this world." How? "Be transformed by the renewing of your mind" (Rom 12:1–2a).

A power struggle that must be engaged to be won

Perhaps it is indicative of the types of churches with which I have been most familiar, but for as long as I can remember, there has seemed to be a constant mentality of immediacy attached to becoming a Christian. Instant healing, zap-approach transformation, and on-the-spot rejection of carnal instincts have been the norm. So ingrained has this become that those who show no external evidence of having been touched in this way by God's Spirit are often made to feel shamefaced for not contributing enough or being resistant to change, while the guilt-ridden themselves are prone to blaming God for not removing the obstacles as quickly as they would deem seemly.

In truth, however, the instantaneous is the exception to the rule, and certainly so in the realm of the renewing of the mind. If it is to achieve its objective, an arrow must be drawn back before it can be sent forth. Although in a slightly different context, Paul hints at the progressive nature of mental filtration in his second extant letter to the Corinthians:

> For though we live in the world, we do not wage war as the world does. The weapons we fight with are not the weapons of the world. On the contrary, they have divine power to demolish strongholds. We demolish arguments and every pretension that sets itself up against the knowledge of God, and we take captive every thought to make it obedient to Christ. (2 Cor 10:3–5)

That is quite a responsibility. Taking a random sample of one or two thoughts might be considered radical by some, but *every* thought? That's what the man said. How practical is this in real terms? Well, that all depends on how serious we are about drinking only from God's uncontaminated stream of living waters. Or, are we prepared to settle for a second-best, broken-cistern Christian experience? To put it another way: Are we sufficiently protective of the purity of our relationship with God that we are determined to thwart any potential idols that may seek to pollute that rapport at the earliest opportunity?

If nothing else, Paul's line of thought completely dismisses the "I can't help it" mentality. What we fix our minds on (Col 3:2) is not something that can ultimately be blamed on our circumstances, our environment, our upbringing, peer pressure, or the social climate: it is entirely a matter of personal choice, the practical outworking of which requires endurance and endeavor. This is not to minimize or underestimate the sway of external factors, but those influences do not have the final say in what we opt to fill our minds with—we do!

Strange as it may seem, the practice doesn't work the same in reverse. If we want to think as the world does, follow its goals and ideals to the detriment of our Christian experience, and have every deed conditioned by a milieu that is alien to the revelation of Scripture, we must simply do nothing. Our fallen nature and the flow of the world's current will gladly take care of that for us. To conform is to passively allow ourselves to be squeezed into a mold; to be transformed requires active initiative on our part.

The stakes have never been higher than they are today. Almost twenty years ago, a number of my colleagues and I were invited to read for appraisal a then-recently published book by Alister McGrath, entitled *The Future of Christianity*. It served as a propitious warning then, and the intervening years have not served to diminish that timeliness; quite the opposite. Amongst his concluding remarks, McGrath called for an end within Evangelicalism to what he described as "the Babylonian captivity of the theologian." In order to bridge the gulf of mistrust on both sides, he proposed a wider acknowledgment of organic theology, citing David Wells thus:

> It is the task of theology, then, to discover what God has said in and through scripture and to clothe that in a conceptuality which is native to our own age. Scripture, at its *terminus a quo*, needs to be decontextualized in order to grasp its transcultural content, and it needs to be recontextualized in order that its content may be meshed with the cognitive assumptions and social patterns of our own time.[12]

A worthy goal that would surely necessitate the renewing of some lofty minds!

Free, but Not without Cost

What a strange heading! Conundrum or contradiction in terms? About a month before last Christmas, my wife made a fairly expensive purchase from our local department store. Unfortunately for me, it wasn't bought with the intention of wrapping in decorative paper with my name scrawled across an attached card in gold ink. However, because the store was at the time running a seasonal promotion, every item bought for over £100 came with a gift voucher towards a future purchase. The value of the token was determined by how much had been spent initially. My wife's new kitchen-bound music streaming device earned her £25 off her next acquisition, redeemable in-store or online for the next twelve months.

The discounted money is a free gift, but it did not come without cost. Barbara had to pay almost sixteen times its value and will have to spend again to use it. There were associated non-monetary costs, too, such as the time taken to listen to sales waffle in the store, travelling to and from the location, spending time deciding which model best fits the bill, not to mention the small matter of potential costs to our marriage in discussing whether to go for the black piano (i.e., cheap glossy plastic) or warm oak veneer finish. Apparently, none of this negates the idea that the piece of paper we received stapled to the receipt constitutes a free gift. I was aglow only in a low wattage sort of way.

Salvation itself falls into this same category of being God's free gift to humanity. It cannot be achieved by personal merit; there is no hint that we may even contribute toward salvation, let alone earn it. As Paul reminds us quite clearly:

---

12. McGrath, *Future of Christianity*, 143.

> For it is by grace you have been saved, through faith—and this not from yourselves, it is the gift of God—not by works, so that nobody can boast. (Eph 2:8-9)

Sacrificially obedient

Work is involved in salvation, but it is not our work; or, at least, not in the attaining of it. Anyone who can rightly identify themselves with the term "Christian," in accordance with its biblical definition, will rejoice that salvation is free: it is freely offered, it is freely accessible, and it is freely received. They will also know that it is not without cost, some of which can last a lifetime. If your denominational allegiance or theological proclivities cause you to balk at the use of the word "cost" in such a context, then allow me to substitute it for one that is perhaps more palatable: "sacrifice."

Many readers will be familiar with the phrase "obedience is better than sacrifice." It forms the basis of Samuel's judgment against King Saul for failing completely to destroy the Amalekites and everything belonging to them, as instructed by God's prophet (1 Sam 15:2–3). Saul had made the excuse that his soldiers had reserved the best of Amalek's sheep and cattle, so that they could be used as offerings at Gilgal (1 Sam 15:21). It was this action that prompted Samuel's response:

> Does the Lord delight in burnt offerings and sacrifices as much as in obeying the voice of the Lord? To obey is better than sacrifice, and to heed is better than the fat of rams. (1 Sam 15:22)

The principle highlighted here is as irrevocable as it is inexorable. Obedience *is* better than sacrifice. Despite the paramountcy it enjoys, however, seldom in the Christian experience is obedience devoid of accompanying sacrifice. And, having taken that initial step of faith, it is not usually long before we have first-hand experience to support the premise. The "costs" involved in following Jesus can take many forms and will differ from one person to another, both in measure and incident. Some will find the pressures of their home life take on a whole new emphasis and intensity, especially for the young still living at home with their parents. Even when mum and dad themselves belong to the faith, the initial euphoria can quickly dissipate when treasured standards are not seen in the same way. Parents who are not Christians may have been quick enough to blame the church for most things before, but now the breath of suspicion blows in only one direction.

Bombshelled by a blond

Work colleagues, school classmates, and favored cousins are just a small sample of those who seem to be queuing up to see who can treat us with the most distrust and ridicule. The level of animosity faced by many is a cost some are not prepared to pay. It had only been a matter of weeks after I had responded to the old-fashioned altar call that the taunts and derision began at my place of work. A similar period later, I was at a local church youth conference when I spotted someone I vaguely recognized. It turned out we were both apprenticed at the same colliery, he as an electrician, I as a mechanic. "Answer to prayer," I thought. We could be each other's support: us against the rest. Maybe even with prayer and gentle evangelism, others would soon join us in what I envisaged to be a growing witness underground. A potential spanner in the works was the discovery that my younger sister had a teenage crush on him, but I think that was more to do with him bearing a passing resemblance to David Soul of *Starsky and Hutch* fame.

As often seems to be the case in such matters, our paths crossed at work within a matter of days. It turned out, Peter's idea of Christian witness outside of the comfort zone of his parent church was so far underground that it barely rose to the level of Sharlston Colliery's second deepest seam. My colleague and I had been dispatched from our usual position at shaft side to a gearbox failure closer to the coal face. Another crew had also been sent from a different part of the pit, with the distinct advantage of being able to ride the belts to the location of the stoppage. By the time we arrived, the problem had been resolved, so we all joined others in the Overman's office for a cup of tea and a catch up. The district team was already in there having their lunch break, and being regaled by the raucous tales and dirty jokes of some guy holding court in their midst, the tongue of whom was so inimical that the words it formed consisted of more asterisks than letters. It was Peter.

My immediate thought was that he was the reason I had taken such a battering. I could imagine some of the conversations: "I don't know why Chris has to be so uptight about his religion; Peter's a Christian, too, and he's always good for a laugh." "Christenings, weddings, and funerals: they're the only occasions when you'd find me in church. But if I was forced into one otherwise, then Peter's brand of Christianity is the more appealing of the two." How wrong I was! They didn't even know that he made any claim toward Christianity—largely because, outside of perhaps a couple of meetings a week and the occasional special event, he didn't make any such declaration.

We could analyze the "whys" and "wherefores" until we have a social charter: What were Peter's specific circumstances? What difficulties did he face at home? What pressures was he subject to of which I was unaware?

And at the end of all potentially mitigating criteria, we would have to reach the same conclusion: he wasn't prepared to pay the price; the sacrifice was too much; the cost was beyond his willingness to fund; the broken cisterns had claimed another victim. I don't know what became of Peter. I was transferred to the surface workshop shortly after and our paths never crossed again. I would like to imagine that he got to taste of God's living Spirit at least once more. But the happiest note of which I can be certain is that he never became my brother-in-law.

Discipleship comes with a price tag

The Old Testament sacrificial system, with all its rules, regulations, commands, and prohibitions, was designed essentially to point forward to the once for all sacrifice of Christ. Those of us who acknowledge the fact are all recipients of that sacrifice, while everyone who doesn't is still a potential beneficiary. It might be argued that, even now, non-believers profit from some of the consequences of the atonement under the auspices of common grace. But the crucifixion was the ultimate sacrifice. When we talk about sacrifice, we usually have in mind the giving up of something tangible that means a lot to us. In the economy of salvation, what was given up by the Father was his Son: "God presented [Christ Jesus] as a sacrifice of atonement, through faith in his blood" (Rom 3:25a).

So, that's it, then! Once Calvary became a past event, that was the end of sacrifice within a Christian milieu (see also Heb 10:26). The only reason for other contributors to the New Testament canon to mention sacrifice would be:

- to make others aware of it having taken place;
- to remind those familiar with the fact that it had taken place, lest they forget the basis of their standing before God;
- to give instruction on the consequences of it having taken place, including personal responsibility to live in the good of the fact;
- to warn against the futility of seeking to reintroduce a system of which it having taken place was the final page in the concluding chapter; and
- to explain the foundation of Christianity to those who may currently be ignorant of its history.

For the most part, this is true. That is, until we arrive at chapter 12 of Paul's same letter to the Romans:

> Therefore, I urge you, brothers, in view of God's mercy, to offer your bodies as living sacrifices, holy and pleasing to God—this is your spiritual act of worship. (Rom 12:1)

Not only was Paul not having a temporary lapse of concentration or bout of forgetfulness concerning everything he had previously been at pains to point out to his Roman readership, but he actually linked the two: "in view of God's mercy . . . " But neither is it simply a reminder of why the apostle thinks it might be inappropriate for Christians to behave in a certain way. There is no suggestion that: "Well, God has done this for you, so the least you can do in return is occasionally show a bit of gratitude." There is much more at stake than that. God's mercy is being presented as the primary filter through which we pass the decisions we are required to make in life regarding all things generally, but specifically here relating to our conduct.

This is vitally important—so much so that what follows is not entirely unexpected. What would have arrested our attention as being out of kilter is if Paul had written something along the lines of: " . . . in view of God's mercy, you can live as you like, indulge the old nature, don't give others a second thought, and if it feels good, do it." If that were true, then it would make a complete mockery of our having been set free from Satan's clutches, thereby descending into insensibility. Set free why? Just so that we can exercise such freedom by offering ourselves once more to slavery? And yet the basis of much that passes for Christian doctrine today seems to be following just such an ideal. It is not Pauline and it is not biblical. Rather, we are confronted with the reality that we will face difficult circumstances, compromising situations, and potentially damaging conditions where questions will be asked of us that seem beyond our scope. The way we begin to address them should neither be gut instinct nor theoretical pros and cons, but by reminding ourselves of who we are.

It is not that what we do is unimportant *per se*, but what motivates those acts should be more of a concern. This is equally true of right behavior patterns that come from impure roots. If you have any doubts at all about that, just think of some of the things you do or see being done by others that on the surface give every semblance of being noble deeds. They might be acts that superficially could be regarded as contributing toward the work of the local fellowship to which you belong. Their spiritual legitimacy is not governed by necessity, measure of corporate blessing attached to them, or whether they would be accomplished to the same standard, if at all, were it not for your input, but by what conditions them. Is it an act of sacrificial service or is it like stolen stardust with which to surreptitiously sprinkle oneself in the vain hope of attracting second-hand acclaim?

Perhaps it would help us to answer honestly if we reversed the earlier substitution of the word "sacrifice" for the word "cost." This is really what is going on here. When Paul talks about offering our "bodies as living sacrifices," he is actually presenting before his Roman readership a summary on the cost of discipleship. Interestingly enough, there is a Christian classic by Dietrich Bonhoeffer bearing the name *The Cost of Discipleship*. When first published in 1937 in the author's homeland, it went by the simple German title, *Nachfolge*, meaning "the act of following."

"Oh, but my pastor proclaims a gospel without cost." Then he is not preaching the gospel of Christ; you can take it from Paul. Elsewhere, the apostle speaks of this cost in terms of us putting "to death . . . whatever belongs to [the] earthly nature," the ways in which we once lived (Col 3:5–7). Is he just taking the Colossians on a day trip to Nostalgiaville, while at the same time urging them not to leave the coach? "This is what you were like before you accepted Jesus, but now all those desires have been magically removed, like a divinely appointed sin-ectomy." Well, he introduces this chapter by establishing their credentials as believers: "Since you have been raised with Christ . . . " (Rom 12:1). But then, without changing the direction of his address by so much as a millimeter, he catalogues a whole range of expressions, the responsibility for the removal of which he places squarely at their door:

> But now you must rid yourselves [future imperative] of all such things as these: anger, rage, malice, slander and filthy language from your lips. Do not lie to each other, since you have taken off your old self [past] with its practices and have put on the new self [also past], which is being renewed [present continuous] in knowledge in the image of its Creator. (Col 3:8–10)

Paul recognizes the Colossians in the past have adopted the principle that their passive involvement in the present is continuous with their compliant submission to the sanctifying process; but they—and we—also have an active role to play in that process. And it could be costly.

Choose Life

In Christian circles, the story of Jesus' conversation with the woman of Samaria (John 4:1–26) is known and loved by all age groups, from Sunday school to *Silver Lining*. Jesus was on his way from Judea to Galilee when he stopped off *en route* at the Samaritan town of Sychar. Having borne the brunt of the day's heat, Jesus was both weary and in need of refreshment. (Yes, the incarnate Son of God was personally familiar with basic human needs and the rigors that precipitated them.) He was resting by a local well when a woman arrived to draw water, so he asked her for a drink. Noticing that Jesus was a Jew, the Samaritan woman expressed her surprise that he should even speak to her, let alone in such a casual, matter-of-fact way. Opportunity was about to knock:

> Jesus answered her, "If you knew the gift of God and who it is that asks you for a drink, you would have asked him and he would have given you living water . . . Everyone who drinks this water will be thirsty again, but whoever drinks the water I give him will never thirst. Indeed, the water I give him will become in him a spring of water welling up to eternal life." (John 4:10–14)

Keep on drinking

I am now well into my fifth decade as a Christian. Although I had produced a handful of teaching pamphlets and training manuals, I didn't submit a manuscript for publication until as recently as 2011. This text provides a classic example of why it would have been imprudent for me to have done so any earlier. I would probably have spent most of the last ten years rescinding and apologizing for my previous gaffes. Possibly conditioned by the kind of teaching I was subjected to early on, I always read this with the underlying narrative that to drink what Jesus offered was a once-only experience, simply because having done so would so quench one's thirst that further practice would thereby be rendered unnecessary.

I now believe I was at least partly wrong. In some ways, drinking of Christ's provision is a once-only experience, but only because it is a perpetual one that lasts a lifetime. We will never thirst so long as we continue to drink of him. It sounds so obvious that the reader would be forgiven for wondering how I had managed to have been mistaken for so many years. Thank God that such errors often prove to be but portals of discovery. It is the same principle in operation as when Paul advised the believers at Ephesus concerning their social habits: "Do not [keep] get[ting] drunk on wine, which leads to debauchery. Instead, be [continuously] filled with the Spirit" (Eph 5:18). I insert the square-bracketed content to create a more accurate reflection of the Greek present-continuous tense.

It is unlikely that the woman herself would have noticed this distinction. Although the immediate text allows for the possibility that she did, the fact that she was still thinking in terms of a literal drink of water with potentially mystical qualities makes it improbable. Thankfully, both for the woman and for us, her intrigue exceeded her reticence.

Although this incident records the first time Jesus identifies himself with the capacity to offer living water—and its inclusion in the Gospel accounts is unique to John—he develops the theme to a much wider audience three chapters later:

> On the last and greatest day of the Feast, Jesus stood and said in a loud voice, "If anyone is thirsty, let him come to me and drink. Whoever believes in me, as the Scripture has said, streams of living water will flow from within him." (John 7:37-38)

The first thing to notice from this is Jesus' claim to exclusivity. One of the common features during the notices section at our local church is to direct those who may want to discuss such things as accepting the invitation to come to Christ, becoming members, joining one of the regionalized home groups, volunteering to help in any of the church's ministries, or asking for clarity on what we believe doctrinally to speak to any one of the leaders who may be present on the day. Jesus didn't summon his hearers to address anyone but himself, not even the inner circle of his disciples.

Is it enough simply to come to him? Do coming to him and drinking of him constitute one and the same act? I would reply "No!" to both questions, though drinking and believing in him do appear to amount to the same thing. It is all too easy to read passages like this, or even have them expounded by a great orator, in a one-dimensional way that looks only subjectively at our personal satisfaction: "Come, drink, have your thirst quenched, be blessed, indulge yourself, take what you can, enjoy the experience, create a memory so that you can continue to enjoy the experience, keep drinking to keep enjoying." Even our response often consists of little more than, "Bless me, Lord!"

Drinking brings release

But I want to take a little time to consider what Scripture describes as some of the consequences of such drinking. Here's how Isaiah put it:

> With joy you will draw water from the wells of salvation. In that day you will say: "Give thanks to the Lord, call on his name; make known among the nations what he has done, and proclaim that his name is exalted. Sing to the Lord, for he has done glorious things; let this be known to all the world. Shout aloud

and sing for joy, people of Zion, for great is the Holy One of
Israel among you." (Isa 12:3-6)

Many commentators identify the text in speech marks as ways to drink. For example, one way would be to give thanks to God, another in singing to him, and so on. In the context of the earlier reading from John's Gospel account, however, I think it is more plausible that these are the products of having had our thirst quenched by drinking: we can only truly be a blessing to others out of the overflow of our having been blessed by God. Let us take a brief look at each of these consequences in turn:

❦ Giving Thanks to God

Judging by some of the church prayer meetings I have attended through the years, you would think that giving thanks to God was the most difficult enterprise with which to engage as a Christian. Even a ten-minute interlude given over especially for the purpose can often be like the soundtrack to a silent movie. "I find it so difficult to think of anything to give thanks for." Really! Isn't this more about being conditioned to express gratitude only when we have been the recipient of some gesture of goodwill? What about thanking him simply for who he is? Or just for the fact that he exists? If we cannot stray beyond the realm of seeing ourselves as personal beneficiaries, thank him for the cross.

To be brutally honest, I think the mindset of only being grateful for things whereby or situations wherein we are favored and not being able to think of anything at all are symptoms of the same condition. Remember my earlier submission that I believe these features from the text in Isaiah to be the supernaturally natural outcome of having drunk rather than ways by which we may drink from God's wells of salvation? Well, if I am correct, is it not therefore logical also to conclude that those who can proffer no evidence of such an overflow might have chosen instead to drink from the broken cisterns?

❦ Calling on His Name

This phrase could be subject to numerous interpretations, some of which are more tenable than others. I think that it is certainly more than merely an instruction to address God by his covenant name, Yahweh, as if that in and of itself unlocked the key to his willingness to listen to what may follow. I'm more inclined to agree with Alec Motyer, when he posits:

> . . . of all the shades of meaning . . . the most suitable here is "to invoke the Lord in worship by using his name" [that being]

shorthand for all that he has revealed about himself. Those to whom he has thus made himself known enter into a worshipping intimacy with him.[13]

Although common in the Old Testament, calling on the name of the Lord is not an exclusively old covenant practice. It should also be pointed out that on those occasions where it is either recommended or recorded as having taken place, there is no suggestion of a mere verbal recitation that is unaccompanied by faith. But neither is that faith necessarily of the goose-pimply corporate worship variety. When Stephen called on the name of his revealed Lord, it was to ask him to receive his spirit as he was being stoned to death for refusing to deny him (Acts 7:59). Even in the throes of death, he chose to continue to drink at God's living stream rather than momentarily sup from the offered broken cistern.

§ Making His Deeds Known

Evangelism, witnessing, testifying, door-knocking, street preaching, beach missions, "invite your friends and neighbors," coffee mornings, unbeliever friendly. Apart from the obvious, what these words and phrases also share in common is that in the early part of my Christian experience, the mere whisper of any one of them would strike in me such a panic that I would hastily scribble something else in my diary for whatever date was being proposed. Very often, I could barely read what I had just conjured as an excuse. It didn't seem to help someone of my naturally tentative disposition when, only a couple of weeks after having "signed on the dotted line," I was being handed a small box of tracts, a local street name scrawled on a piece of paper, and with no more instruction than: "That's your patch!" The fact that this was accompanied with a somewhat threatening: "And remember, God's watching you," hardly induced any comfort. Then again, that was not its design.

This all changed when I went to Bible College, but perhaps not in ways either that I would have imagined or that I had been led to believe God would find pleasing. One of my lecturers was the wonderful David Shepherd, and there is no doubt that the sharing both of his expertise and some of his experiences contributed toward the transformation. As I soaked in the teaching from the equally superb Jeff Cox and Ieuan Jones, I definitely became more comfortable at the prospect of answering any tricky questions.

I also became aware that God's love for me wasn't dependent upon my having to earn it. If he loved me so much to send his Son for me, then

---

13. Motyer, *Isaiah*, 124.

that love must supersede everything less than such a sacrifice, which actually amounts to everything else. All I had to do was keep drinking from the stream, uninterrupted by my practice up to that point of nipping off every so often for a sip from the broken cistern, just for old times' sake. Thereafter, I found I no longer had to nervously fabricate conversations; all that was required of me was that I take advantage of every opportunity God provided. "What are you reading?" "How do you spend your weekends away from work?" "What are you getting up to in the summer vacation?" can all introduce marvelous opportunities to make God's deeds known.

§ Reminding Others That His Name Is Exalted

Notice first of all that there is a subtle, though significant, difference between what the prophet advises and reminding others to exalt God's name. His name is already exalted; the proclamation is a reminder of that fact. This is an important distinction. When we sing of exalting him, or the Bible speaks of him being exalted on the lips of those currently alienated from him at some time in the future, any idea of "becoming" relates only to a subjective recognition of what already is an objective reality. In much the same way, light does not produce what is seen, but simply enables us to view what was always there. Moreover, our acknowledgment of that fact, when it comes, adds nothing to his perpetually exalted status, if for no other reason than that our failure to do so cannot detract from it.

Without getting into the vagaries of the Trinity, not only is God the Supreme Being, exalted beyond further acclaim, but he has also chosen to invest that supremacy specifically in the Person of his Son, Christ Jesus:

> Therefore God exalted him to the highest place and gave him the name that is above every name, that at the name of Jesus every knee should bow, in heaven and on earth and under the earth, and every tongue confess that Jesus Christ is Lord, to the glory of God the Father. (Phil 2:9–11)

The words "could," "should," and "would" are often employed as subjunctives contrary to fact: e.g., "I could tell you, but I'm afraid I'm bound by confidentiality laws"; "He should have thought more carefully about the potential consequences of his actions"; "They would probably have won more comfortably if they hadn't had a man sent off for violent conduct." Whether such ambiguity arises in the original Greek of this text (e.g., "every knee should bow [but they don't]") is not immediately clear. Translators who substitute "should" for "will" seem, at first glance, to have taken a step too far in the direction of interpreting this verse on the basis of what is known from elsewhere. However, the "what is known from elsewhere" bit is that:

> It is written: "As surely as I live," declares the Lord, "Every knee will bow before me; every tongue will confess to God." (Rom 14:11; Isa 45:23)

❦ Singing Praises unto Him

There are some examples of prayer that, when analyzed alongside some expressions of praise, might cause us to believe that they are very different concepts. Others demonstrate a much closer interrelatedness. Praise can be sung prayerfully, just as prayers may be offered up tunefully, while each has the capacity to become the foundation for the other. Perhaps the most common misconception they share, however, is that many Christians seem to imagine their sole domain to be that of the corporate gathering: "I must remember to pray for so and so next Thursday evening around eight o'clock," or "I hope we sing such and such on Sunday morning between the giving of the weekly notices and the breaking of bread." No such restrictions appear to be biblically validated.

Notice also what it is that prompts such singing. This is no mere emotional response to a worship leader's skill at supercharging the atmosphere, but the glorious things that may be attributed to God. This is not to say that our emotions are uninvolved, but they are triggered by an overflow of having drunk from God's pure waters of delight, not manipulated by an outside agency, much less one whose expertise stretches no further than to invite us to choose a personal favorite. True worship emanates from relationship; the intimacy of that relationship is governed by having spent time in the presence of the One with whom our worship is but an expression.

❦ Declaring His Greatness Joyfully

Moules marinière, pain de campagne, poulet chasseur, bûche de Noël, all neatly washed down with a *blanc Chateauneuf-du-Pape: joie de vivre*? Well, as mouthwatering a menu as this undoubtedly is, my vote for the joy of life goes to knowing the greatness of God. Throw in the small matter of being allowed also to know the God of such greatness, and how could we possibly help but declare it?

In my opinion, this is the crowning factor in the debate over whether these features create an environment in which we may drink from God's spring or they issue from having done so. To suggest the former seems more akin to an "Abracadabra!" approach to the Christian experience rather than a true heart response. Almost like we are being encouraged to twist the divine arm behind his anthropomorphic back in an attempt to force him into blessing us against his better judgment. Does that sound just a little nonsensical? And so it should!

Such an outpouring is reminiscent of some of the most exuberant declarations of the Old Testament: Moses and Miriam's songs of deliverance from the Egyptian hordes, having journeyed through the Red Sea on dry land (Exod 15:1–21); the song of Deborah and Barak, after God had pursued their Canaanite oppressor (Judg 5:1–31); David's song of victory, recognizing God's hand in rescuing him from his foes (2 Sam 22; Ps 18); and Jehoshaphat's battle cry in anticipation of God's hand in defeating the combined forces of the Moabites and Ammonites (2 Chr 20:21). As sons and daughters of the new covenant, do we not have abundantly more reason to declare God's greatness and to do so more joyously?

Summary

In typically evangelistic fashion, I'm guessing most readers will now be left with a decision to make; the rest will already have made it. Where will you source your drinking water? Broken cisterns do give the appearance of the cheaper option, but the semblance of a reduced initial outlay can prove to be a false economy. Some of the benefits and rewards that we miss out on by rejecting God's ideal are obvious: intimacy of relationship; the promise of life as intended by the Creator, in all its fullness, unpolluted and undiluted; meaningful fellowship with those who are likeminded; and a contentedness in the midst of trials that is only accessible by God's Spirit to those who choose to live in the free flow of his pure stream.

My experience is such that few Christians belong exclusively to one camp or the other, but flit from side to side as circumstances dictate their path. I close this chapter with two biblical texts, neither of which require further comment. The first was uttered by God's prophet to the people of God on Mount Carmel, having summoned also the false prophets of Baal and Asherah:

> Elijah went before the people and said, "How long will you waver between two opinions? If the Lord is God, follow him; but if Baal is God, follow him." (1 Kgs 18:21)

The second is my recommended response:

> As the deer pants for streams of living water, so my soul pants for you, O God. My soul thirsts for God, for the living God. When can I go and meet with God? (Ps 42:1-2)

3

Lamentations

BACKGROUND

The appropriate background for the book of Lamentations is in some ways governed by the reader's viewpoint regarding its author. There are two principal schools of thought: either Jeremiah wrote Lamentations or he did not. There are worthy scholars for each position, for whom I have the utmost respect. But to my mind, neither can be proven conclusively, though I am also of the opinion that the latter is the more likely.

The arguments in favor of Jeremiah's authorship just seem so unconvincing. That it is recorded that he composed laments for King Josiah (2 Chr 35:25) hardly secures the argument, and neither can any alleged similarity of literary style between the two works traditionally attributed to him, especially as there are just as many obstacles presented by marked differences. It might even reasonably be argued that there are closer stylistic affinities elsewhere, none of which attract the same conclusions. What is beyond question is that the author of Lamentations was an eyewitness to the destruction that befell Jerusalem in 586 BC and expresses grief in a most overwhelming manner, but I seriously doubt that Jeremiah would have been alone either in his mournfulness or in his capacity to put it into words. Perhaps the best we may offer is a hearty "Amen!" to these words from Gleason Archer: "If Jeremiah was not the composer, whoever wrote it must have been a contemporary of his and witnessed the same pitiless destruction meted out to Zion by its Chaldean conquerors."[1]

I would add, however, that if the identity was vital to our understanding of the message we know as Lamentations, then it would not be clouded in such uncertainty. For any readers who are absolutely adamant that Jeremiah was the author, then all I can do at this stage is to direct you to the *Historical* and *Personal Background* sections relating to the book that bears his name (pp. 40-46). Those of you who are more inclined to support my position will still find the *Historical Background* relevant here, too.

The contributors of the Septuagint were the first to place the book of Lamentations immediately after that of Jeremiah, which seems its natural position chronologically, even if no such claim may be made in relation to its authorship. They even conspired to create a *faux* introduction, presumably to add credence to their opinion, the English translation of which is:

> And it came to pass, after Israel had been carried away captive, and Jerusalem had become desolate, that Jeremiah sat weeping, and lamented with this lamentation over Jerusalem and said . . .[2]

In its original setting of the Tanakh, however, Lamentations found itself in the company of the Song of Solomon, Ruth, Ecclesiastes (or *Qoheleth*), and Esther, collectively known as *Hamesh Megilloth* (i.e., the Five Festival Scrolls), itself a component part of the *Ketuvim* (Writings). Even today, these are read out on the anniversary of the events to which they relate, Lamentations being recited each 09 Av on the Jewish calendar (i.e., mid-July) by Jerusalem's Western Wall.

Most commentaries place Jeremiah and Lamentations in one volume when presenting their findings on the two works. This is fitting, regardless of the debate about authorship, as they really do belong together. They are like the introduction and conclusion to a single Greek tragedy. Whereas the bulk of Jeremiah's prophecies anticipate the fall of Jerusalem, the writer of Lamentations looks back in anguish; from thread to threnody.

The dating of the book arouses considerably less controversy. On the basis of the internal evidence, it had to have been written after Judah's desolation of 586 BC. Even if the fifth lament was penned later than the others—and this in no way presupposes a different hand—then I am inclined to support Ronald Harrison's conclusion:

---

1. Archer, *Old Testament Survey*, 374.
2. See Guthrie and Motyer, *New Bible Commentary*, 659.

There seems to be no convincing reason for placing the extant composition later than 550 BC, whether or not portions of it were written at rather different times.[3]

Lamentations comprises five melancholic poems, all but the last one following an acrostic pattern based on the twenty-two letters of the Hebrew alphabet (see also Ps 119). The third one, at sixty-six verses, is assigned three verses per letter, each verse within the stanza beginning with the same letter in the original. There have been some creative suggestions as to the reasoning behind such structure and sequence, the most plausible being that Israel had sinned from *aleph* to *tau*, conveying the same idea as *Alpha* and *Omega*, or from A to Z. Norman Gottwald proposes that it was "to encourage completeness in the expression of grief, the confession of sin and the instilling of hope."[4] This may well be the case, and it does afford a certain dignity that might otherwise be absent, but it also seems somewhat ironic to use a device designed to inspire freedom of expression that is by its very nature so incommodious.

One can only assume that those responsible for the later application of verse markers assigned twenty-two to the final poem in an attempt to present a symmetrical whole. Some commentators insist that this, too, must have originally followed the same form as the rest, as it also contains the number of lines equivalent to that of consonants in the Hebrew alphabet, though their lilting meter is also markedly lacking. Each elegy is ascribed as a single chapter in our English Bibles.

Two final notes by way of observation before we press on, both regarding omissions. First of all, the student will search in vain for the intentional use of rhyming couplets. Any that appear are but an accident of translation. Although this book consists entirely of poetry, rhyme was not a consideration for the Hebrew prophets of this period. Indeed, the same may be said of most ancient near-Eastern people groups. Secondly, Lamentations contains no Yahwistic response. It is comprised only of the unrestrained unburdening of an anguished soul.

OVERVIEW

Lament 1: Sorrow for Jerusalem

The personification of Jerusalem proves a useful tool to describe the effects of sin. It was a tactic also employed by Jesus some six hundred years later

---

3. Harrison, *Jeremiah and Lamentations*, 201.
4. Gottwald, *Lamentations*, 28.

and with which this opening chapter bears striking comparison (see Luke 13:34–35; 19:41–44). The sense of mournfulness that so typifies chapter 1 is a thread that runs constantly through all five chapters of Lamentations, but its introduction here is the most intense. Just look at some of the phrases employed to describe Jerusalem's sorrow: bitter weeping, tears upon the cheeks, nobody to offer consolation, no resting place, despised and cruelly mocked by others. The reason may appear obvious, though it was not just the current condition of Jerusalem that was so lamentable, but that in the context of its previous state: from thriving center of commerce and industry to deserted ruin. Thus, Jerusalem is depicted not as an ageing spinster, but as a grieving widow.

Of course, all of these were consequences of her sullen indifference and, therefore, self-inflicted. But the greatest cause of her grief is neither her overthrow by tyrants nor ridicule by enemies, but "because the comforter that should relieve [her] soul is far from [her]" (Lam 1:16b, KJV). This is not a complaint regarding a perceived injustice; God's judgments are acknowledged as righteous and have been administered accordingly (Lam 1:22a). The groans may be multiplied and the heart may grow faint (Lam 1:22b), but no claim may be made that either is undeserved.

Lament 2: God's Judgment for Jerusalem's Sin

Here, the writer allows metaphor, hyperbole, and simile to vie for the most expressive means of conveying the sense of God's ire. One might be forgiven for thinking that the execution of judgment is just a general withholding of divine favor, especially in the context of the opening verse. The detail in the rest of the chapter, however, suggests something more specific, a more targeted strategy. Every facet of life was adversely affected: living accommodation (Lam 1:2a), national security (Lam 1:2b, 5b, 7b–9a), political and religious leadership (Lam 1:2c, 6d, 9b–10a, 14), and places of worship (Lam 1:6–7a) were all stripped of their potential to provide solace. In every one of these areas, it seemed that God's people imagined themselves to be the beneficiaries of divine favor solely because of the covenant relationship they enjoyed with the Almighty, regardless of whether they met the conditions thereof.

But privilege cannot be divorced from responsibility, as they had discovered. The nature, suddenness, and completeness of Judah's degradation left nobody in any uncertainty as to its author. Where there had previously been warnings that could have been written off as circumstantial or coincidental, on this occasion there was no room for doubt or misunderstanding.

The secure was stormed and smashed, the inviolable was violated, and the sacred defiled. The prophets remained silent on two counts: those who had presumed peace and prosperity had been proved false (Lam 1:14), and those who had not found that God had nothing further to say (Lam 1:9).

Lament 3: Hope amidst Affliction

The opening verse would not have been out of place introducing one of Job's responses to his "comforting" friends. Indeed, much of the language employed in this chapter is reminiscent of that used by Job in his defense (e.g., Job 9:18, 34, 12:25; 13:28; 30:13). Is it the writer's intention to inject a note of personal affliction, or is he simply identifying himself with the plight of his people? Probably both are true. There may also be an element of returning to the personification of Jerusalem that began in chapter 1.

It is astonishing to think that a heart of such anguish and desolation should inspire arguably one of the most uplifting hymns of the Christian era. Despair glimpses a shaft of light in the dungeon of gloom as the writer recalls God's covenant loyalty. Indeed, only the great faithfulness of a covenant-keeping God could proffer such hope (Lam 3:23b). And it is real hope, the brightness of which shines all the more intensely in the context of an otherwise incommodious darkness.

Such hope is possible precisely because the present condition is born of divine judgment, which is consistently just and never anything other than equal to the deficiency by which it is aroused. The mathematical equation is quite simple and intransigent: if covenant people + disobedience and disavowal of obligations = punitive judgment, then those same covenant people + obedience and acceptance of responsibility = restorative judgment. Therein lay Judah's hope.

Lament 4: God's Judicial Displeasure Is Satisfied

Perhaps the siege and overthrow of Jerusalem was the price that had to be paid to assuage the divine wrath? The devastation left behind is often compared to its previous state. Some of the horrors are described in graphic detail and some readers today may find that they offend twenty-first century sensitivities in relation to morality, wrongdoing, and justice. Why should all this befall the inhabitants of Jerusalem? Could any crime warrant such harsh punishment?

> But it happened because of the sins of her prophets and the iniquities of her priests, who shed within her the blood of the righteous. (Lam 4:13)

Until now, the reason for God's judgment had been somewhat generalized by terms like disobedience, rebellion, idolatry, and self-reliance. Here, however, we get about as close to the hub of the issue as it is possible to be, and that without much in the way of elaboration. Was it just one example plucked from the many that could have been cited, or was the author too embarrassed to elucidate further? Some commentators make the link to Jeremiah's treatment for daring to utter words that ran counter to those of the religious leaders of his day (see Jer 26:7–11), the moral scruple for whom was manipulated by self-interest. It is my belief, however, that it was related to something just as specific, but even more sinister: the abhorrent practice of child sacrifice associated with King Manasseh (2 Kgs 21:6), in contemptible contravention of Levitical law (Lev 18:21; see also Jer 32:26–35).

Lament 5: A Plea for Restoration

When the realization takes hold that Yahweh's judgment is responsible for your sorrowful condition, to whom will you appeal for renewal? This fifth lament is effectively and essentially a communal prayer for mercy. That the basis for such an entreaty was Yahweh's own name's sake was both a stroke of genius and an admission that they have nothing else with which to plead. Only the constant and consistent nature of a covenant-keeping God can be trusted to be finally merciful.

Irving Jensen cites verse fifteen as "[o]ne of the most pathetic lines in the book of Lamentations."[5] It reads: "The joy of our heart is ceased" (Lam 5:15, KJV). I would have disagreed had Jensen said "*the* most pathetic," for that award surely belongs to the final verse: "Or have you rejected us forever? Is there no limit to your anger?" Whether this was put as a genuine question in the original or as a plausible reason for rebuttal in the hope that it would be dismissed hardly matters. Is there anything more somber for theists than to contemplate that the God in whom they trust may have abandoned them completely? It is a truly lamentable thought upon which to end the book, surely prompting more than a mere glazing of the eyes. I am particularly grateful, therefore, to Harrison for the following:

> Several Old Testament prophecies conclude on a negative or inauspicious note . . . Consequently in synagogue readings it

---

5. Jensen, *Jeremiah and Lamentations*, 137.

became customary to conclude such compositions with a repetition of the preceding verse, so that under these circumstances verse 21 would be read again after verse 22.[6]

NO SHADOW OF TURNING

Look up the word "fidelity" in any English language dictionary and you will find among its primary definitions something along the lines: "faithfulness to a person, cause, or belief, demonstrated by continuing loyalty or support." In general terms, this is a perfectly accurate description. With reference to the Almighty, however, I would suggest that the person toward whom that faithfulness is primarily directed is himself. All other acts of faithfulness on God's part are but expressions of the simple truth that he is first and foremost faithful to his own intrinsic nature. Arguments that he can be no other fail to detract from that fact.

Although apparently obvious, it is of vital importance that we grasp this at the very outset. When we speak of human fidelity, whether in relationships or in relation to a commonly pursued objective, we do so in relative terms. The parameters are finite and, therefore, restricted to boundaries we are incapable of breaching. Moreover, our capacity to fully comprehend outside of such limitations is similarly constrained.

When we sing *Great Is Thy Faithfulness,* we must understand that God's faithfulness is great because its existence within him is consistent with his Person: it is absolute, its measure is infinite, and its longevity is eternal. As a perfection within him, God is perfectly faithful. Nor may we imagine him being free to scale down his faithfulness at any point, so that he would be more faithful in some circumstances or toward some individuals than others. To suggest a limitation, even one that is self-imposed, would be to imply also that he is unfaithful beyond that point. God's faithfulness extends beyond our agreement with or understanding of it.

Let us begin our journey toward a fuller appreciation of God's faithfulness by reading Lamentations, chapter 3.

God's Preparation for the Future

The key text for the whole of this chapter, especially this first section, has already been alluded to:

---

6. Harrison, *Jeremiah and Lamentations,* 246.

> Because of the Lord's great love we are not consumed, for his compassions never fail. They are new every morning; great is your faithfulness. I say to myself, "The Lord is my portion; therefore I will wait for him." (Lam 3:22–24)

As ever, readers would do well both to immerse themselves in the context before we continue and to remind themselves of it as we proceed.

Suffering at God's hand

The "I am" of verse one finds no place in the New Testament, but it is one that might legitimately have been claimed by Christ: "I am the man who has seen affliction" (Lam 3:1). What the writer of Lamentations describes in the subsequent nineteen verses is conspicuous only by its absence in the self-help guides of today's white-suited and perma-tanned health, wealth, and prosperity peddlers. But notice who the author holds responsible for his condition: it comes "by the rod of his wrath" (Lam 3:1b), the subject being a continuation from chapter 2, "The Lord . . . " (Lam 2:17–22).

Arguably, the most difficult concept to explain is that of suffering by the apparently innocent. It is the question most frequently asked during street evangelism and for which there seems no satisfactory explanation. The difficulty is made no easier for those Christians who are themselves coping with hardship and seeking to determine God's purpose in the midst of it or where it might lead. This is true not only when we ourselves are the ones who are suffering, but also when we are experiencing by proxy the difficulties faced by those to whom we are personally or covenantally related.

Often, however, our experiences can testify to God's greatness because we have found him to be faithful in the midst of suffering. (The footsteps of Christ in which we plant our feet have—and will leave—a blood-stained imprint.) This was certainly true of the writer of the Lamentations, as Irving Jensen points out: "It is interesting to observe that just as a man's hope arises out of a dark experience, so in [this] poem the stanza about hope is surrounded by two stanzas about affliction."[7] When this happens to us, we are thereby able to bring comfort to those in similar circumstances in the future. In turn, their situations will provide experiences from which they may draw to benefit others at some later date. If we—and they—are to be in a position to do so, then it is incumbent on us all to broaden our understanding of suffering by not limiting it to a narrow band that focuses exclusively on the physical element.

---

7. Jensen, *Jeremiah and Lamentations*, 133.

Anguish isn't always obvious to onlookers

I have already mentioned relational or third-party suffering, where we empathize with those close to us in their time of need. Spiritual suffering may also take many forms, some of which may be further categorized as either tests or temptations. Is this really suffering? Perhaps only those who have succumbed at the first hint of either or both would deny their inclusion. Allow me to put it this way: Do we imagine that suffering was entirely absent from Jesus' wilderness experience in the company of the devil (Luke 4:1–13)? I have heard those who concede that it was not argue that Jesus was a man of suffering and familiar with grief so that his followers wouldn't need to be. Presumably, the apostles Paul and Peter and countless thousands of others up to the present day have all been blinded to this wonderfully liberating "truth."

Although mental suffering is often discarded as being "all in the mind," its debilitating effects are more far-reaching. Even for those with no Christian conviction, there remains insufficient recognition and largely inadequate treatment beyond attempting to minimize the symptoms endured by its victims. Christians are not exempt. There is a battle for the mind and that battle must be engaged and overcome, but until it is, we are all susceptible to anxiety, fears, and personal tragedy. Even positive anticipation can induce a stress of sorts. It is but another product of the Fall, where the sweat of man's brow is as likely to include mental as well as physical toil (Gen 3:19).

There is also emotional suffering, often brought about by things like lust, anger, despair, hopelessness, and unfulfilled ambition. In an attempt to disarm their effects, we are prone either to deny their existence with mind-over-matter defense strategies or seek to indulge in forms of escapist distraction, such as virtual reality games and mentally conditioning fantasies. Again, this is true of humankind in general, but becomes no less applicable in the lives of Christians as it is for their non-believing counterparts. To permit oneself to become incarcerated by such circumstances is lamentable; to allow hope to diminish to such an extent that we fail to see beyond the prison bars is bordering on the cataclysmic.

Getting to grips with what we can grasp

Why should this be the case? I believe at least part of the reason is a shallow or inadequate theology. I would also include in that a theology that is so denominationally conditioned as to restrict the guidance of the Holy Spirit to predetermined constitutional parameters. As a young Christian contemplating Bible College, I well remember the counsel of someone who was widely regarded as a stalwart of the local church; he advised me that the seeking after knowledge would seriously damage my faith. It certainly had an adverse effect on much of what I had been taught prior to my enrolling.

One of the lessons I learned was that we cope better with those things we comprehend, even if our deeper understanding of them is no more than that they are beyond comprehension. What I was able to deduce is that God is not some ethereal Santa Claus, the sole purpose of whom is to give us an occasional bout of goosebumps. The author of Lamentations was personally familiar with suffering. I realize, of course, that this is alien territory for those whose power of positive thinking cannot extend beyond: "God has great things in store for me," "God works to bless me with an abundance of riches," and "I'll be your pastor, but God has told me to hold out for a salary equivalent to that of a high school departmental head." We need to make provision for the fact that God sometimes instigates suffering for reasons other than a failure on our part to comply.

The verses cited at the beginning of this section are reminiscent of those uttered by Job, also in the context of personal adversity: "Though he slay me, yet will I hope in him" (Job 13:15a). What was the common feature of both writers besides the intensity of their afflictions? They each recognized God's covenant faithfulness. Significantly, the Hebrew word translated "great love" or "steadfast love" (ESV) is *hesed*, employed prominently throughout the Old Testament in relation to Yahweh's bestowal of covenant mercies. As such, *hesed* in the divine plane is a continuing expression of a prior undertaking on the part of God in relation to its recipients, though there is also an implied reciprocity and mutuality that requires a corresponding allegiance in return (see 1 Kgs 3:6).

It is the apparent dichotomy between the level of protection one might expect as a beneficiary of God's covenant faithfulness and the existence of suffering that disturbs us most. The Old Testament saints were not similarly troubled. They pleaded for God's covenant love to continue (Ps 36:10), they reminded him of its basis in times of difficulty (Ps 143:12), they recognized its part in rescuing them (Ps 94:17–18), and they gave thanks for it when it had clearly provided the foundation for their deliverance (Ps 31:7–8). There is no hint, however, either in fact or expectation, that God's steadfast love extended to providing a passage that was utterly devoid of risk or danger, much less suffering. Rather, there is an understanding that deliverance in one form or another will come, but the pain associated with its arrival is never fully removed.

There may be trouble ahead

For the Christian, then, suffering is inevitable. I was tempted to add "as much as for the non-Christian," but it is probably actually more so. Why is this? Throughout this chapter, I have maintained a position of anonymity regarding the author of Lamentations. I believe it may have been Jeremiah, but remain unconvinced by the arguments that support such a conclusion. We must now turn to a New Testament book, the writer of which is shrouded in similar mystery:

> During the days of Jesus' life on earth, he offered up prayers and petitions with loud cries and tears to the one who could save him from death, and was heard because of his reverent submission. Although he was a son, he learned obedience from what he suffered and, once made perfect, he became the source of eternal salvation for all who obey him and was designated by God to be high priest in the order of Melchizedek. (Heb 5:7–10)

Jesus, incarnate Son of God, co-equal and co-eternal, in his sinless flesh was made perfect through suffering (see also Heb 2:10). Most commentators are in agreement that the specific incident referred to here was the agony of Gethsemane, culminating in the excruciating plea: "My Father, if it is possible, may this cup be taken from me" (Matt 26:39b). Jesus had already indicated the extent of his suffering by telling the disciples: "My soul is overwhelmed with sorrow to the point of death" (Matt 26:38b). He would yield, but to the pain or the Father's purpose? "Yet not as I will, but as you will" (Matt 26:39c). Perfection came through suffering, and the suffering was a direct consequence of Christ's obedience which, in turn, attracted divine strengthening that he might endure whatever he had to face. Gethsemane prepared Jesus for Calvary.

For us, there may well be moments that we call our own Gethsemanes, but there can only ever be one Calvary. But our suffering is still a preparation for the future. Prior to meeting Christ, Paul had a great deal of which to be proud by the standards of his day: Jew of Jews, Pharisee of Pharisees, zealous to the point of persecuting Christians, and upholder of the Law extraordinaire (Phil 3:3–6). By becoming a follower of Jesus, Paul had sacrificed his reputation, his esteem amongst peers, he became subject to the curtailment of certain liberties, at the time of writing this letter he was imprisoned, and he knew what it was to be desperate for his hunger to be satiated and his thirst to be quenched (see 2 Cor 11:23–29). And yet he regarded all that he had previously cherished as rubbish and all that he had suffered as of value in order to gain Christ (Phil 3:7–8).

"But Jesus was the Messiah and Paul was arguably the Apostle of all other apostles," some may object. And both invite us to follow their example (John 12:26; Phil 3:17).

God's Promises Are Trustworthy

> The Lord is good to those whose hope is in him, to the one who seeks him; it is good to wait quietly for the salvation of the Lord. (Lam 3:25–26)

A very good friend of mine privately confessed to me a short time ago that, as a recently saved impetuous teenager, he had asked God for the gift of patience. He got so bored awaiting its arrival that he asked the Almighty if he could change his request to self-control. Imagine my friend being in Jeremiah's shoes, or those of Abraham, Moses, or any of the unnamed heroes of the faith cited by the writer to the Hebrews:

> These were all commended for their faith, yet none of them received what had been promised. God has planned something better for us so that only together with us would they be made perfect. (Heb 11:39–40)

Because they are his

For over forty years, I have described myself as an Evangelical Christian, regardless of the denominational allegiance of the church to which I have belonged. In more recent times, I have considered the validity of such an label in the light of its application by those with whom I appear to have little doctrinally in common. Thus, I feel I must qualify what I mean by Evangelical. I embrace the traditional view that holds to the authority of the Bible as God's written revelation to humanity. I do not elevate Scripture to the point of believing it to be invested with inherent authority outside of the fact that it is God's word; therein lies its command.

The same may be said of God's promises. Their trustworthiness derives not from how they make us feel, how welcome their fulfilment might be, whether they receive consensus at the church annual general meeting, or if Aunt Nellie might be upset at them coming to pass. They are dependable because—and only because—the one who makes them is utterly reliable. Vine has the following to say of the New Testament use of the word *epangelia*:

Except in Acts 23:21, it is used only of the promises of God. It frequently stands for the thing promised, and so signifies a gift graciously bestowed, not a pledge secured by negotiation.[8]

Not without significance is the fact that there is no direct Hebrew equivalent in the Old Testament. The closest we have is "I will . . . " with future reference, which possibly lies behind Jesus' counsel regarding the issuing of oaths, culminating in the sagacious: "Simply let your 'Yes' be 'Yes,' and your 'No,' 'No'; anything beyond this comes from the evil one" (Matt 5:33–37).

So, do all God's promises prove true, come what may? In order to attempt to answer this, we need first to grasp something of God's perspective on the unfolding of events. We live in the now of time, with a past that partly conditions the present, and a future largely governed by both that same past and today's present, which will then be its past. God exists in the eternal now, with a perfect view of tomorrow's reality, both actual and potential. Thus, faith is not so much an act as a qualitative trait, divinely apportioned by which deeds of faith may be brought into existence. The reality of such products of faith is not determined by their tangible physicality. They are no more or less real when they enter the time/space continuum than before.

Some promises are also presented as conditional: "I will . . . if you will . . . " This is akin to me agreeing to meet my wife for coffee in town if she is outside the abbey between 11:00 and 11:30 AM. Five minutes later is five minutes too late, because I will not be there. Did I fail to fulfil my promise? No, because I met the conditions for it to be proved trustworthy; someone else did not. There may well be a justifiable reason for my wife's absence; there usually is. But whatever the cause of her delay, the agreed time slot was there for a reason, and it has been and gone. Of course, I would first check that no crisis had emerged before going about the rest of my day's business, providing I had remembered to bring my cell phone with me and charge it to capacity before doing so.

Postponing the inevitable

Some promises remain unfulfilled for years because of staunch rebellion or contra-presumption. Israel's wilderness journey would be an example of the former, taking four decades to accomplish a mission that most commentators agree could have been achieved in a fraction of the time. Others fall into the latter category. What do I mean by "contra-presumption"? Let me give you an example: I became a Christian just three months after leaving

---

8. Vine, *Expository Dictionary*, 891.

school. I had gained so few qualifications that I told my grandparents that the succession of As in red ink at the side of subject names was the highest award available when, in fact, it represented my absence from those exams so marked. There seemed no point in wasting another couple of hours doodling on the desk. Three months later, I suddenly developed an aptitude and passion for learning.

To say that I devoured the Bible is, of course, a metaphor, but I would have done so literally if I had thought that it would enable me to engage more speedily with its contents. Others described me as "a man of the word," and that could mean only one thing: I was called to be a pastor. The trouble was, I had no such inclination, but believed that those who were more experienced than I would have a better understanding of God's ways in such matters. So, for a while, I followed the path of their choosing. Its brevity was an undisguised blessing. Thankfully—and not just for my own sake—I never got to be a pastor. The truth is, whatever gift God had given me, the appointed channel for that to be expressed did not coincide until I was almost forty years of age. Why so long a wait? Largely, I believe, because both others and myself took hold of incidental component parts and presumed a promise that had no basis in reality. At the time, I was as guilty as they of being sadly lacking both in sagacity and *savoir-faire*.

The fact of the matter is that God's unconditional promises always come to fruition. The "dos" and "don'ts" as far as we are concerned are to be patient and don't pigeon-hole. When it comes to personal promises, I would add another caveat: be prepared to be tested. I used to think this meant to be assessed as to one's suitability to receive that which was promised, but I then realized that God would know that in advance of committing himself to our part in the unfolding of his purpose. A more old-fashioned—and now little used—application of the verb "test" is to prove; that is, to demonstrate the existence of a thing or quality currently concealed from public view. In the context of God's promises, I can think of no more suitable description of one's faith. It is not so much an assessment of our suitability by God and for his benefit as it is an exposure of it—even in its rawest form—lest we, or others, be in any doubt.

This "testing" or "proving" often works in conjunction with our patience. Consider Joseph: as a teenager, God revealed to him in a dream something of what he had in store for him (Gen 37:5–11). Oh, how Joseph must have thought, "I'm going to soar, I'm going to fly!" The next thing he knows, he is hurled into a pit by his brothers, while they plot to do who-knows-what with him (Gen 37:12–24). Had he got it wrong? Had he misheard or misunderstood God? Had his dreams really only been a product of some late-night cheese beyond its expiration date? No, the fulfilment of the promise awaited the character that Joseph had yet to grow into.

God's word really is his bond

When God promised the land of Canaan to Israel, Moses sent an exploratory mission to suss it out. The Numbers narrative tells us that the Lord instructed Moses to do so (Num 13:1), but the suggestion from Deuteronomy is that this was in response to the people's request (Deut 1:22–23). Twelve men were appointed for the task, one from each tribe. Ten returned with a report that there were giants in the land, while only two advised taking possession of it. I have often cited this incident as an example that democracy based on majority rule does not always lead to the correct decision.

But there is another issue at stake here. Why did the reports of Joshua and Caleb differ from those of their peers? Were they blinkered or blinded to reality? Had they not the capacity to compute the risk? Did they have some kind of hidden agenda to curry favor with Moses so that he might grant them each a position of esteem? No, it was none of these things. They saw what the others saw with their physical eyes and understood the potential danger associated with engagement. But they were also bound by a shared interest and bonded over a mutual enthusiasm to believe God, knowing then what Balak, king of Moab, came to know through Balaam just a few chapters later:

> God is not a man, that he should lie, nor a son of man, that he should change his mind. Does he speak and then not act? Does he promise and not fulfil? I have received a command to bless; he has blessed and I cannot change it. (Num 23:19–20)

In other words, the guarantee of God's trustworthiness lies in his integrity and in his immutability. His promises are, therefore, irrevocable. If God was not immutable, for example, we would have justifiable cause for distrust. This seems obvious, but the reasons are far greater than those that are immediately apparent. To be subject to change implies improvement, deterioration, or imperfection. If divine intentions are capable of improvement, then they must have been lacking in the first instance; if they are worse now than before, then why is he settling for second best? And do I really need to spell out the implications of attributing imperfection to the Almighty? Tozer put it far better than I could:

> He is immutable, which means that He has never changed and can never change in any smallest measure. To change He would

need to go from better to worse or from worse to better. He cannot do either, for being perfect He cannot become more perfect, and if He were to become less perfect, He would be less than God.[9]

Changeability is linked to becoming, whereas immutability is annexed to being. As such, God is essentially and necessarily unchangeable in relation to his being, his perfections, his purposes, and his promises.[10] Thus, we can know that God "is good to those whose hope is in him" (see below); *ergo*, it is good to wait patiently for that goodness to materialize.

God's Provision Is Never Less Than That Required

> The Lord is good to those whose hope is in him, to the one who seeks him. (Lam 3:25)

Although not the primary focus of our attention here, it needs to be said that God is good, full stop. He is good to those who do not hope in him, to those who do not seek him (see Ps 145:9). Our difficulty in comprehending this truth lies in our inability to equate goodness with anything other than aesthetic pleasantness or immediate personal advantage. The innate problem with such a yardstick is that it makes flawed finite humanity the judge of what is or is not worthy of approval. Even without the distortion brought about by the Fall, there is always a conflict of interest involved in our determining an act's goodness. A more morally upright standard is required.

Approved by God

Jesus was confronted with this very issue. When asked by a rich young man what he must do to inherit eternal life, Jesus first of all challenged the enquirer's form of address, "Good teacher" (Mark 10:17): "Why do you call me good?" Jesus answered. "Nobody is good—except God alone" (Mark 10:18). There is little evidence to support the idea that the young man was seeking to attract a favorable response by way of flattery; it is at least as likely to have been a simple term of respect. But Jesus was not about to allow the opportunity to slip by. Whether his question was intentionally rhetorical or not is unclear; neither can we know for certain how the man might have answered had he opted to do so. What we do know is that if he was to continue in

---

9. Tozer, *Pursuit of God*, 44.
10. See Berkhof, *Systematic Theology*, 58.

his evaluation of Jesus as good in the context of this new information, then at the very least he would thereby be confirming Jesus as God's delegated earthly agent.

The goodness of God, then, consists in the fact that he is intrinsically good and can be no other. But it is not a latent quality devoid of expression. Because he is good, all his actions must be invested also with that goodness (see Ps 119:68). Moreover, he is the source of all goodness that finds expression outside of himself (Jas 1:17), and it behooves those of us who acknowledge that fact to seek to imitate him in our dealings, especially with fellow-believers, but not to the exclusion of all who were made in his image (Gal 6:10), regardless of whether or not they feature too highly on our likeability index.

Arguably, the most common objection to the existence of God revolves around the problem of evil. "If God . . . then why . . . ?" begins so many questions that they are impossible to enumerate. The gist of them all is that if God really is good, then why is there so much badness in the world? On the surface, it seems a reasonable question. It is one that I have been forced to concede that I simply do not know its answer, except insofar that good things are not always manifest in happy experiences. I have been helped enormously in recent times by the work of Wayne Grudem in this regard, who has an unerring knack for coming across as erudite, but never pompous or patronizing. The real problem is not so much in the existence of evil or bad things, but in contemplating a more accurate definition of goodness. It is inadequate to speak of goodness in terms of sensual gratification or even moral satisfaction when such things are subject to relative inclinations. In God, the standard is—and must remain—absolute. Grudem writes, "The goodness of God means that God is the final standard of good, and that all that God is and does is worthy of approval."[11]

Whose approval? It certainly cannot be ours; we are no better equipped than the rich young ruler. If God himself is the final standard, then he alone is qualified to give his own approval of an act, thing, or other being in relation to that standard. All else that falls below that standard is not approved, but merely allowed—for reasons ultimately known only to himself. I could continue to unpack the doctrine in further detail, but we would all be better served by reserving the rest of this section to look at its practical application. Suffice to say, we may legitimately assign the word "good" to nothing that fails to carry with it God's seal of approval. Jim Packer goes even further by reminding us: "Woe, then, to those who invert the divine scale of values,

---

11. Grudem, *Systematic Theology*, 197.

giving the name of good to what God calls evil, and vice versa."[12] This is why "[t]he steps of a good man are ordered by the Lord" (Ps 37:23a, KJV). I used to think this meant that the blessing followed the qualifying condition; that is, those who were good men would thereafter find their life unfold in accordance with divine direction. This is not the case, however. What the Psalmist is really saying is that willingly yielding the direction of our steps to the Almighty is the criterion by which they are thereby determined to be good.

Fulfilling the conditions

What, then, may we learn from the goodness of God? The question almost answers itself, for the goodness of God is the perfect model of goodness. If God is especially good to us because our hope is in him, should we not all the more extend that goodness, inasmuch as it resides in us, to those who share the same hope? It is perhaps significant that of the two Greek words translated "goodness" in the New Testament (*agathosyne* and *chresotes*), Paul's use of *chresotes* is often seen alongside *philanthropia*. Commentators seem unable to find agreement regarding the distinguishing features of each word, some believing that one is an umbrella term that includes the other. Although both may also be translated "kindness," it would appear that, while *agathosyne* indicates a readiness to do good, its release is usually predicated on strict moral standards having first been met. *Chresotes*, on the other hand, is lavish in its expression of kindness, with no such qualifying criterion attached.[13]

One of the most oft-quoted verses relating to God's provision is to be found in Paul's epistle to the Philippians: "And my God will meet all your needs according to his glorious riches in Christ Jesus" (Phil 4:19). No amount of mistranslation can escape the fact that there is a great blessing in store, but for whom? The word "[a]nd" at the beginning is a conjoining word, linking it to what has gone before. This can be as an addendum to a list, as a suddenly remembered afterthought, or as a consequence of conditions having been met. The context is all-important in helping us to determine which:

> Yet it was good of you to share in my troubles. Moreover . . . in the early days of your acquaintance with the gospel, when I set out from Macedonia, not one church shared with me in the matter of giving and receiving, except you only; for even when I

---

12. In Douglas, *New Bible Dictionary*, 433.
13. See Trench, *Epistle to the Seven Churches*, 248–9.

was in Thessalonica, you sent me aid again and again when I was in need ... (Phil 4:14–18)

No other church received the same promise because no other church met the same criterion. The promise is often used and abused in similar measure by those who seek to excuse their extravagant lifestyles, and yet for truth to be true truth, it must be the whole truth. Truth is never more itself than when it is not interfused with selectivity. Guile may very well be the truth; it can even be championed as nothing but the truth. But by its very nature, it must never lay claim to being the whole truth. Only when read in isolation from its context can this text remotely be seen to sanction the idea that God's generosity may be anticipated by the less-than generous.

Out of the abundance of God's wealth

For those whose claim is not grounded in gratuitous living, however, the blessing of God is far greater than is immediately evident from the text. God's promise is not that he will meet our needs in accordance with the nature or extent of those needs, but "according to his glorious riches in Christ Jesus" (Phil 4:19b). In other words, God's provision is in direct correlation to his unlimited resources.

When I was at College, second-year students would often be invited to preach at one of the many local churches. It was quite an experience, having prepared earnestly to deliver God's word in these vast two-hundred seater Welsh chapels, to then find a scattered congregation of no more than a dozen faithful souls. A friend of mine received such an invitation, but he seemed less than excited by the news. It turned out that his only suit had fallen victim to the damp hostel walls to such an extent that its trousers were now unfit to be worn except for gardening chores. His misery was compounded by the fact that he couldn't borrow clothing from one of his fellow students without giving the impression that he was mimicking Charlie Chaplin's portrayal of his most well-known character, the Tramp; he was a good six inches taller than any of us.

Prayer is often employed as a desperate last resort and it became my friend's. He frantically pleaded with the Almighty to save him from embarrassment. A couple of days earlier, another student had received a check from the Inland Revenue, in lieu of overpaid taxes for the previous financial year. In relative terms, it was quite a sum. At the time, none of us knew of our colleague's windfall; he simply asked to see his struggling fellow student, whereupon he handed over sufficient funds to pay for a new suit with accompanying shirt, tie, and shoes. What had he done? He had met his brother's need in accordance with his own riches, however temporal, rather than doing so in accordance with the need itself.

I was neither the benefactor nor the prime beneficiary. But I did learn quite a few vital lessons that day:

- God's provision is never less than that required;
- God's blessing is never in the nick of time, but always perfectly on time;
- God almost invariably employs us to be the channels through which he chooses to meet the needs of his children;
- we are only stewards of all we claim to possess; and
- if I suddenly acquire unexpected wealth, there is every likelihood of a coming need to be met, of which I might presently be unaware.

Because of the issue at hand, it is easy to read Paul's words as addressing exclusively materialistic requirements, but "all your needs" is all-embracing. The principles we have looked at are, therefore, universally applicable. In whatever way we find ourselves impoverished, out of the abundance of God's gracious resources in Christ Jesus, we may expect to be enriched. Do we lack understanding? It is ours for the asking. Are we deficient in humility (or confidence)? Do we feel that our faith is not up to the task before us, or our compassion for others not as Christlike as it should be? These, too, are included in the "all" of our needs. And the same remedy awaits each one of them. Why should we be so bold? Because we are in Christ and they are available in Christ Jesus.

God's Presence Endures

The greatness of God's faithfulness is also to be seen in his abiding presence. Or is it? Normally, when I pose such a question, the answer is "Yes and No!" depending on the circumstances. This time, I offer a slight variation: "Yes, immediately," "Yes, in hindsight," and "No, not always!" The key to understanding the latter two responses lies in our being able to appreciate the difference between the presence of the Lord and having a sensory awareness of that presence.

I doubt that anyone reading this will be unfamiliar with the footprints-in-the-sand analogy. At one time, I could barely attend a Sunday evening meeting without either someone employing it to drive home a point or someone else alluding to it in prayer. But we should not allow our familiarity with such examples or anecdotes to breed contempt within us for their veracity. Often, God is with us in the midst of difficulty without our necessarily having been consciously mindful of it at the time. Is such a confession shameful? Does an admission of our incognizance render us also spiritually deficient? I don't think it does. Even if I'm wrong, it didn't lessen God's desire to attend to our need in difficult times.

What is so "omni" about God's presence?

This should hardly come as any surprise to us. One of God's incommunicable attributes is his omnipresence, which means that he is all-present. But I wonder if we have ever really come to grips with the implications of such a truth; or, at least, as far as our finite intellects will allow. This is not merely that God has the capacity to be anywhere in the Universe at any time of his choosing, nor that he is capable of being more or less present as the need arises, like some divine genie that exists only to respond to the whims of his creatures. As with his omnipotence and his omniscience, his omnipresence is absolute. My early introduction to Christian theology was through the works of Louis Berkhof, but I think Wayne Grudem puts it best when he defines God's omnipresence thus: "God does not have size or spatial dimensions and is present at every point of space with his whole being, yet God acts differently in different places."[14] This all sounds very convincing and as if it should be true. But in all honesty, if I heard this kind of thing for the first time from someone standing behind a pulpit, however persuasive the argument or inflection, I would also need some supporting biblical evidence. The first comes to us by inference: as Creator of everything that is in the material world (Gen 1:1), it is unthinkable that he could possibly thereafter be subject to anything within that creation. The only plausible exception I can imagine would be if he voluntarily opted to yield his authority which, of course, he did in the person of his Son and in the act of the incarnation. Even then, the Father did not abdicate his responsibility to sustain creation.

The trouble with inference, however, is that it has so much in common with implication, not least of which is their shared subjective dependence: I may infer the wrong thing from your actions and you might imply—deliberately or otherwise—something that is not entirely factual. Thankfully, the scriptural evidence for God's omnipresence is more explicit:

> Where can I go from your Spirit? Where can I flee from your presence? If I go up to the heavens, you are there; if I make my bed in the depths, you are there. If I rise on the wings of the dawn, if I settle on the far side of the sea, even there your hand will guide me, your right hand will hold me fast. (Ps 139:7–10)

---

14. Grudem, *Systematic Theology*, 173.

David seems to be expressing an occasional desire to get away from God, perhaps in the aftermath of episodes in his life where he feels he has let God down. He concludes that it is impossible to do so, though as a truth acknowledged with gratitude rather than complaint. Interestingly enough, after one such episode, having been confronted by the prophet Nathan over his illicit relationship with Bathsheba, David had pleaded with God: "Do not cast me from your presence or take your Holy Spirit from me" (Ps 51:11). Had his understanding developed between the two Psalms? Or is this an example of biblical contradiction that literary critics are fond of citing?

An absence of awareness

The former is possible, but a more likely explanation is that the ancient Hebrew language suffered in the same way as does our English for lack of vocabulary to distinguish between the concept of presence and a sensory awareness of that presence. The Hebrew phrase is *mille paneka*, literally meaning "from before your face." On the one hand, nothing we do can ever be anything other than "before his face"; on the other hand, we are not always gifted with the same level of consciousness of that fact. Prayerful pleas on our part and heartfelt invitations by the choirmaster to "come into his presence" imply that it is possible to step out of it. I guess we all know that what is really meant is that we be not excluded or exempted from the subjective thrill of it.

Matters become only a little clearer in the New Testament (chiefly *prosopon* and *enopion*). Here, the concept of divine presence includes both its objective reality and subjective cognizance. A further element is also introduced, relating to one having sight of a physical appearance (that is, *parousia*). Moreover, we are now presented with the eschatological possibility of being "shut out from the presence of the Lord" (2 Thess 1:8–10). It would be strange indeed to add this to the foregoing "everlasting destruction" if such destruction means annihilation, as some propose. What concerns us here is this apparent contradiction of God's enduring omnipresence.

Without addressing the matter full on, perhaps Hendriksen gets closer to the mark by contrasting this fate of the wicked with that of the faithful. Having first established that the everlasting nature of their respective destruction or life must be entirely consistent (i.e., never ending), he then insists that if "everlasting life manifests itself in the blessed contemplation of the face of the Lord, sweet fellowship with him, closeness to him . . . a most wonderful togetherness, [then] everlasting destruction . . . is the very opposite."[15] Thus, as far as we may reasonably deduce, to be "shut out from the presence of the Lord" surely consists at least in being deprived of that "blessed contemplation," "sweet fellowship," "closeness," and "wonderful togetherness."

God is with us

It can be no coincidence that the revelation of God through Scripture begins and ends with the presence of the Lord (see Gen 3:8; Rev 21:1–4). It might even be argued that the whole of the redemption story that fills the pages in between is concerned with the restoration of the manifestation of God's abiding presence with humanity. This should not astonish us. After all, the central figure in the intervening narrative is the One in whom that paradise lost becomes paradise regained: the Redeemer, the Restorer, the Reconciler. "'[a]nd they will call him Immanuel!'—which means God with us" (see Matt 1:23; John 1:14).

Matthew's citation of this text from Isa 7:14 was to demonstrate Christ's fulfilment of the promised Messianic expectation. It is reminiscent also of the covenant motif, with which the Old Testament saints were especially familiar: "I will be your God and you shall be my people" (see Gen 17:7; Exod 6:7; Ezek 36:28). If we are to learn anything at all about the manifest presence of God with us, then we can have no better schoolmaster than the Gospel accounts of Jesus' earthly sojourn. What did "God with us" mean for that generation with whom, in Christ, God came to dwell? He was present:

- with the sick and the infirm (Matt 14:13–14; 20:34);
- with those afflicted by demons (Matt 8:28–34; Mark 9:26–27);
- with the poor in spirit, the mournful, the meek, the merciful, the unblemished, the persecuted, and the wrongly accused (Matt 5:3–11);
- with the desperate and the needy (Matt 9:36; Mark 6:34);
- with the hypercritical and the hypocritical, if only to teach them to be otherwise (Matt 7:1–5);
- with the disenfranchised and the downtrodden (Luke 17:11–19; John 7:53—8:11);
- with the hungry, both physically and metaphysically (Matt 15:32; 5:6); and
- with the disadvantaged (Mark 10:21–22; 12:41–44).

15. Hendriksen, *1 & 2 Thessalonians*, 160.

Most importantly of all, God was present for those who were prepared to acknowledge that they could afford to absent themselves from his company no longer (Luke 7:36–50). There seems to be so much unnecessary debate about the episode recorded here in Luke, which serves only to detract from the lessons we may truly derive from it. The assumption by some that the woman was a prostitute may well be unfounded, but I remain equally unconvinced that it would be such an offensive claim. That there are similarities between Luke's recording here and that of the other Gospel writers (Matt 26:6–13; Mark 14:3–9; John 12:1–8) could mean that they are different accounts of the same episode, but it is also by no means certain. What we do know is what her lavish expression of love produced: forgiveness, salvation, and peace (Luke 7:48–50).

So, the effects of God's abiding presence are often immediately obvious; someone who is hungry today requires an instant solution. At other times, we only become consciously aware of his involvement in our lives retrospectively. Although I can never remember a time when I doubted the existence of God, I didn't become a Christian until the age of sixteen. It wasn't long afterwards before I began to recognize God's hand in safeguarding me through some of those earlier childhood experiences.

But what about those occasions of God being present with us of which we never become mindful? Consider the danger we didn't face, the risk we didn't have to endure, or the trauma that failed to materialize because the level of protection was such and God's faithfulness so great that they were kept from us. That everything we do is not only with God's knowledge, nor even simply in his sight, but also in his presence is one of the most sobering truths I know. His presence may not always be manifest, but he is never absent. His faithfulness is great, and I am grateful.

God's Peace Is Always Accessible

> You heard my plea: "Do not close your ears to my cry for relief."
> You came near when I called you, and you said, "Do not fear."
> (Lam 3:56–57)

I have intentionally lifted these verses out of their immediate context so that we may view them initially in isolation. The principle that lays behind the citation remains valid, regardless of the context, but we will return to it in due course.

Offenders beware

Arguably the single greatest contributing factor toward anyone being at dis-peace is fear. Whether the apprehension is well grounded or not is largely immaterial. It may or may not be life threatening. Oftentimes, the most relatively inconsequential matters can induce within us a measure of anxiety that is wholly incommensurate with the actual danger. A short time ago, I was driving along a road that is very familiar to me, not far from my home. I was on my way to church one Sunday morning and had just entered a stretch of road that is both straight and uncluttered with risk for about three miles of its length. The vehicle I was driving had only been in my possession for a couple of months. There were amongst its features some that I needed quickly to become accustomed to, not least of which were its automatic transmission and 50-percent extra brake horse power.

My mind having been temporarily elsewhere, about halfway along the road in question, I suddenly remembered there was often a police patrol car parked up just ahead with a speed camera trained on both carriageways. I cannot say with any certainty what I did first, but I did spot that the expected mobile unit was in position about four hundred yards ahead. A brief check of the instrument panel revealed that I was travelling over the speed limit for that road. It was not excessively so, but beyond the margin of tolerance before a mandatory fine is sent your way. I quickly discovered just how effective the brakes were. The thing that really mattered now was, had I managed to come below the target speed before I was in range of the camera? I was not optimistic.

Unfortunately, the only way to know for sure was to wait. Offenders will typically receive a brown envelope through their letter box within a couple of weeks or so, inviting the recipient to part with a fixed penalty, which includes a sum of points on their license and an involuntary contribution towards the road safety benevolent fund, also known as a speeding fine. I have known it take more than three weeks to arrive if there are Bank Holidays to delay administration and delivery. I was unintimidated, but inhibited nonetheless. Every day, I irreligiously, yet anxiously, checked the front door mat for news. Only when a month had passed could I genuinely relax, thank God that he had allowed me to get away with it, and pray for more important matters.

In the grand scheme of things, a three-point penalty and a seventy-pound fine are not such a great price to pay for a minor lapse of concentration, though I could think of better ways to spend such a sum without personal benefit. But the sense of dread every time I heard the rattle of the letter box was utterly unbefitting of such a "crime." And yet I don't think I am alone in such experiences: we often have a tendency to fear the relatively unfearful.

Trusting the trustworthy

Now, the incident I have described, whatever the circumstances, was an error of judgment on my part. I guess some might even say that I deserved to be penalized for it. What about the writer of Lamentations? To discover that context I mentioned earlier, we need retrace our steps only a few verses. If we go back just one verse, we learn: "I called on your name, O Lord, from the depths of the pit" (Lam 3:55). These appear to be circumstances in which there was genuine cause for concern, but perhaps he had deserved to find himself there? Apparently not:

> Those who were my enemies without cause hunted me like a bird. They tried to end my life in a pit and threw stones at me; the waters closed over my head, and I thought I was about to be cut off. (Lam 3:52–54)

The author was not only justified in feeling fearful, but he also had reasonable grounds to believe that the cause of his distress was entirely unwarranted. It was a real crisis and he experienced real anguish. It is into such situations where we may anticipate God calling out to us: "Do not fear." Jesus said a similar thing in equally trying circumstances for his closest disciples. Having given them final instructions about his coming betrayal and the prediction of Peter's denial, he immediately goes on to offer succor: "Do not let your hearts be troubled. Trust in God; trust also in me" (John 14:1). A more accurate translation might be: "Let not your hearts be troubled any longer. You trust in God; continue also in your trusting of me."

A quotation often attributed to Ernest Hemingway is that "the best way to find out if you can trust someone is to trust them." It is actually a misquotation, but it has more of a ring of truth to it than the original: "The way to make people trustworthy is to trust them."[16] Trust is essential to human social relations; their level of intimacy depends upon it. The disciples had placed their trust in Jesus. For some, it had not been entirely steadfast, nor would it be wholly unshakable in the future. That probably had more to do with trusting their own judgment than in having found Jesus to be anything less than completely trustworthy.

---

16. See Hemingway, *Selected Letters*, 805.

The disciples' emotions at this time may have been mixed, but they were varied in precisely the same negative direction. William Hendriksen elucidates further:

> They were sad because of the gloomy prospect of Christ's departure; ashamed because of their own demonstrated selfishness and pride; perplexed because of the prediction that one of their own number would betray the Master, that another would deny him, and that all would be ensnared because of him; and finally, they were all wavering in their faith . . .[17]

This is the context into which Jesus spoke the words: "Do not let your hearts be troubled. Trust in God; trust also in me" (John 14:1). One of those who needed to hear such counsel, at least as much as any other, was Peter. "Sad," "ashamed," "perplexed," "ensnared," and "wavering": he experienced them all. As the promise made to him about his denial began to unfold in the realm of reality, Peter's sense of disgrace and bewilderment were only compounded (John 18:15–18, 25–27). Nevertheless, keep trusting, Peter! All through Jesus' arrest in the garden, the meeting before the religious officials, being handed over to Pilate, his reluctant sentencing, the soldiers' mocking, the crowd being whipped into a frenzy to demand Jesus' death, the cries from the cross, and the crucifixion itself, all Peter and his colleagues were required to do was to keep on trusting, which would eliminate their fear.

From humiliation to humility

When Jesus died, it must have seemed to the disciples that their trust had been misplaced. They couldn't have been more wrong. If God truly is God, death cannot hold him. The resurrection took place and Peter could add folly to the growing list of emotions. As far as Jesus' time on earth was concerned, there were just a few loose ends to tie up, not least of which was the restoration of Peter's trust in his own judgment (see John 21:15–17).

Many years later, Peter wrote his first letter, addressed to those who recognized that their residence upon God's earth was but temporary (1 Pet 1:1). It is a letter of encouragement, its themes taken from around thirty years of experience since the author first encountered Christ. There are subtle reminders throughout, none more reminiscent of Jesus' words considered here than Peter's advice to "Cast all your anxiety on [God] because he cares for you" (1 Pet 5:7). What a beautiful text! How nice to see it adorning the homes of believers on framed posters, signs on church office doors, coasters

---

17. Hendriksen, *John*, 263.

on which we place our hot coffee mugs, and the like! But how easy also both to misunderstand the phrase in isolation and to disregard its dependence upon the previous verse!

The verb translated "cast" (Greek *epiripto*) appears only here and in Luke's Gospel account (Luke 19:35) in the whole of the New Testament. It means "to throw upon" or "to deposit with," and is used metaphorically, as here, to denote the relieving oneself of a burden by allowing or enabling another to take it; it is not a sharing, but a complete giving over. At least as important, however, is Peter's use of it here as a participle. There is a requirement demanded of us that we may thence find ourselves able to cast our burdens Godward. What is it? "Humble yourselves . . . under God's mighty hand" (1 Pet 5:6).

Although not mentioned specifically, this same prerequisite of humility is implied by Paul in his letter to the believers at Philippi, and with the same promised result:

> Rejoice in the Lord always. I will say it again: Rejoice! Let your gentleness be evident to all. The Lord is near. Do not be anxious about anything, but in everything, by prayer and petition, with thanksgiving, present your requests to God. And the peace of God, which transcends all understanding, will guard your hearts and minds in Christ Jesus. (Phil 4:4–7)

At the risk of stating the obvious, "anything" and "everything" preclude all exceptions. Whatever the circumstances, anxiety is usually born of a perception of futility. As such, for the Christian believer it displays a lack of confidence in the care and capability of the Father. There is nothing so beyond him that should cause us to be anxious, and there is nothing so great or so insignificant to exempt it from being brought prayerfully before him.

But notice also that it is not by following the command to not be anxious that ushers in God's peace, but the presenting to him of those things that would give rise to anxiety. How best to understand the peace of God? It is but a continuation of the stillness that reigned in the heart of his Son. It was always accessible to Jesus because he brought everything to his Father in prayer.

God's Protection Sustains Us at All Times

> "You have seen, O Lord, the wrong done to me. Uphold my cause!" (Lam 3:59)

A word at the outset about this section heading: it is not *God Protects Us from Injury at All Times*. If we, as Christians, fail to honor our obligations, behave in ways that are contrary to our profession of working toward Christlikeness, or act unjustly in the way we relate to others, then we must be prepared to accept the natural consequences of such conduct. Indeed, according to Peter, our response to ill treatment for wrongdoing and unjust hardship should be precisely the same:

> ... it is commendable if a man bears up under the pain of unjust suffering because he is conscious of God. But how is it to your credit if you receive a beating for doing wrong and endure it? But if you suffer for doing good and you endure it, this is commendable before God. To this you were called, because Christ suffered for you, leaving you an example, that you should follow in his steps. (1 Pet 2:19–21)

I realize, of course, that the immediate context of Peter's counsel is specifically addressing the issue of slaves' submission to their masters, but the principle he expatiates is not so limited. The key is endurance, the divine protection we can expect comes in the form of being sustained that we might endure, and our example is Christ. This last point is particularly noteworthy given some of the erroneous teaching I have encountered on the subject in recent years.

On the basis of presumed lateral thinking, some have taken Paul's teaching on generosity to the church at Corinth and extended an imagined precept to include the negation of suffering for the believer. If Jesus became poor so that we might become rich (2 Cor 8:9), they argue, then surely everything connected with the humiliation of Christ (Phil 2:6–8) was that we might now "reign in life" (Rom 5:17) in the good of his subsequent exaltation (Phil 2:9–11). All this really demonstrates is the potential for heresy by the uninformed, their ponderings being the products of a fertile imagination and the random throwing together of dissociated Scriptures.

Taking it on the chin (or spine)

According to the above verses from Peter, not only is the unjust suffering of believers possible, it is to this we have been called. There is no hint of lobbying our governmental representative, organizing a banner-wielding demonstration outside Parliament, or crowdfunding for a prime-time slot on Trinity Broadcasting Network so that we may invite the international family of God to vent their collective fury against such injustice. Prayers were summoned by apostolic letter, the design of which was to enable the afflicted to persevere in the heat of spiritual battle (see also Eph 6:10–20). Thus, God's protection may or may not shield us, but it will always sustain us.

In what way do we imagine that the endurance of suffering for doing good is commendable before God (1 Pet 2:19)? More precisely, what form do we understand that commendability to take? Other English translations have alternative renderings for the Greek, which include "thankworthy" (KJV), "finds favor" (NASB), "a gracious thing" (ESV), and "is what counts" (MSG), all of which seem to point by degrees in the same direction as "God will bless you for this" (GNT). The original, however, is no more substantial than *touto gar charis*, meaning "for this [is] grace." This may be understood in a number of ways, the distinction between some of which is admittedly fine:

i. it is a gracious act;

ii. it is an act that warrants appreciation;

iii. it is an act that occasions favor; or

iv. it is an act that precipitates a gracious experience.

Of the four possibilities, the first requires translation only, whereas the other three must be subject also to a certain amount of subjective interpretation. That being the case, I am most comfortable with the first item—it is a gracious act—the rendering of which thence becomes something like: "If believers suffer because their consciences convince them that, motivated by a desire to remain obedient to God, they are behaving righteously, then their suffering itself becomes an experience of divine grace."

When we equate the suffering alluded to by Peter with the kind of wrong that was done to the writer of Lamentations, we must acknowledge that, though always personal, it is by no means necessarily physical. Affliction can take many forms, and very rarely do we experience any of it in isolation. A little over twenty years ago, I worked as an ambulance paramedic and had to retire from service, having suffered a serious back injury on duty. The elevation mechanism on one of our trolleyed stretchers failed to engage with a patient *in situ* and I took most of the falling weight. For three weeks, I could barely move and not at all without incredible pain.

My injury was primarily physical, but not exclusively so. As I began to ponder the possibilities associated with only limited improvement, other aspects entered the equation. My mental health suffered, relationships with those closest to me slowly began to deteriorate, my trust in God was at an all-time low, and, as a consequence of all that, my reputation with others—such as it had been—grew steadily worse. The point is that not all symptoms of suffering are obvious to the naked eye.

The cumulative effect

But then again, the sustaining hand of God is not always as immediately apparent as some might have us believe. Moreover, though the major incidents cause the most traumatic impact, it is often a culmination of minor setbacks that have a knack of evoking the most anguish. My only consolation in confessing this to be my Achilles' heel is that it is even more so for my wife. Just last week, she had arranged to meet a friend in town for a coffee and a chat. Barbara is now of an age that entitles her to free bus travel at certain times of the day, which is all well and good when published timetables can be relied upon. Her scheduled bus had either been early or hadn't arrived at all; she had a twenty-minute wait for the next one, which came ten minutes late. By the time she arrived at her rendezvous point, her friend was on her second drink and the last of the morning cakes had been replaced by the first lunchtime sitting.

Throughout what was left of the morning and well into the afternoon, everything that could possibly go wrong did go wrong. The refund department of the store that seems to specialize in wrongly sized garments was closed due to staff illness, the purchase that required her loyalty card for a cash discount had to be abandoned in recognition of the fact that said card was in a different handbag, the three-for-two offer was useless given that there were only two of anything that qualified, and the sole secluded part of the city where we often go to gather our thoughts had been taken over by the York branch of The Let-Us-See-How-Loud-and-Unmelodious-We-Can-Make-These-Instruments-Sound Brass Band.

By the time my wife had boarded the homeward-bound bus, she'd had a catastrophe-free day. But the miniscule measure of distress attached to so many little niggles had combined to produce such anguish that all she could look forward to for the rest of the day was her bed. When she arrived home, I had painkillers at the ready, the kettle filled with water, and the TV on to catch the local news. Cameras were trained on our local bypass from Selby to York, where there had been a serious road traffic accident that morning. Had the bus Barbara had taken on the first part of her journey been on time, it is likely she would have been involved. God had preserved us a while longer from the world of tributes and obituaries.

Seeing the unseen and the unseeable

God not only sees the actual wrong done to us as it unfolds, but he also sees that potential for harm that runs counter to his plan for us and upholds our cause, sometimes without our having ever been aware of it. I believe therein lies the key. God upholds the cause of the faithful when that cause is aligned with his purpose. Conversely, he also allows what we might otherwise perceive to be calamitous when he considers that to be the best way of causing us to realign with his purpose. David was subject to both kinds of experience.

As God's chosen king, David was constantly a prime target for ungodly foes outside and jealous would-be competitors within. As a young man, he had demonstrated a covenantal commitment beyond his years in the episode with the uncircumcised Philistines (1 Sam 17), and God had honored David's dedication. It was thus that he could address the Almighty with boldness:

> Hear, O Lord, my righteous plea; listen to my cry. Give ear to my prayer—it does not rise from deceitful lips. May my vindication come from you; may your eyes see what is right. Though you probe my heart and examine me at night, though you test me, you will find nothing; I have resolved that my mouth will not sin. As for the deeds of men—by the words of your lips I have kept myself from the ways of the violent. My steps have held to your paths; my feet have not slipped. (Ps 17:1-5)

He continues in similar vein, claiming divine justice on the basis that his actions have been nothing but just. The incident with Bathsheba (2 Sam 11) provoked a completely different response. Not content with the guilt associated with having committed adultery (2 Sam 11:4), he compounded the issue by arranging to have Bathsheba's husband placed where his death was almost guaranteed (2 Sam 11:14-17), as if that would absolve David of all responsibility. Bathsheba's orchestrated widowhood was to David what the ship bound for Tarshish had been to Jonah (Jonah 1:1-3): "Ooh, look! It's all working out just as I had hoped."

How less full of bravado David was when he stood before God's prophet:

> This is what the Lord says: "Out of your own household I am going to bring calamity upon you. Before your very eyes I will take your wives and give them to one who is close to you, and he will lie with your wives in broad daylight. You did it in secret, but I will do this thing in broad daylight before all Israel . . . You are not going to die. But because by doing this you have made

> the enemies of the Lord show utter contempt, the son born to you [by Bathsheba] will die." (2 Sam 12:11–14)

It was not a capricious act, but one designed to bring David back to his senses and restore him to God's purpose, thereby protecting him from a path of unknown misery (see Ps 51).

God's Pardon Testifies to His Abiding Goodness

> Because of the Lord's great love we are not consumed, for his compassions never fail. (Lam 3:22)

It is a constant source of amazement to me how so many Old Testament saints were able to demonstrate such faith outside of a wittingly Christocentric context. The writer to the Hebrews sums it up perfectly, having commended Abel, Enoch, Noah, Abraham, Sarah, Isaac, and Jacob:

> All these people were still living by faith when they died. They did not receive the things promised; they only saw them and welcomed them from a distance. And they admitted that they were aliens and strangers on earth. (Heb 11:13)

It is at least as astonishing that they had such an appreciation for the greatness of God's love when the full extent of that love had still to be expressed. And yet, the underlying principle behind their confidence and ours remains precisely the same: God's abiding goodness.

How great a love!

We have already seen that true goodness is that which finds approval with God, and so his own goodness is effectively self-achieving. In many ways, it is also self-revealing, but he has chosen to unveil it in other ways outside of his Being, yet within the confines of his government. For example, creation testifies to his goodness, both in that which has been created and in the act of it having been brought into being (Rom 1:18–22). Why is this evidence of divine goodness more than merely providing testimony to God's existence? Simply because each environment is perfectly suited to sustain the life of that which inhabits it.

Indeed, it might be said that every means by which God's existence is revealed, both general and special, unveils him also to be a God who is good. Scripture exposes him to be a God who chooses to enter into covenant relationships with fallen and finite creatures for their benefit alone; the retention in humankind of basic human morality and conscience is evidence of our having been created originally in his image, which attracted divine approval; history provides a documented record of God's establishing of righteous and overthrowing of tyrannical regimes; and the church, despite its many frailties and, at times, questionable motives, has often been a conduit through which God's goodness has found expression toward both those most ignorant and those most needful of it.

However, just as the progression of divine self-revelation concerning God's existence found fulfilment in the incarnation of Christ, so it is to him that we must look for the full and final manifestation of God's goodness. That this was annexed to the unveiling also of God's pardon for humanity is no random occurrence. It is also more than just a happy coincidence that the Hebrew phrase translated "great love" in our text is indicative of Yahweh's loving faithfulness to his covenant promises, all of which find ultimate fulfilment in Christ's initiation of the new covenant.

Mercy, not merit

Many translations speak of this "great love" as God's mercies, that is, his unmerited favor. The sense thus becomes: "we are not consumed, though we deserve to be; his compassions never fail, though we could hardly blame him if they did." I remember being part of a group who were set the task of discussing the difference between grace and mercy by one of our College lecturers. As an enthusiastic but relatively ignorant twenty-one-year-old, I had already embarrassed myself by imagining that I had been endowed with knowledge on such matters. On this occasion, I mustered sufficient wisdom and self-discipline to remain silent, while others contributed to the debate, opting only to nod sagacious agreement when it seemed appropriate. (I didn't even get that quite right.)

The consensus settled on grace being what God extends toward us, his mercy being the reason he does so. I wasn't sure of the legitimacy at the time and am even less so now. I have since discovered a far better way of defining grace, employing the well-known acronym: God's riches at Christ's expense. To help us remember the essence of mercy, a fellow student related to us the story of Napoleon being approached by a mother, whose son had been sentenced to hang. It was the young boy's second offence and there was not a hint of doubt regarding his guilt or that the punishment to be meted out was in just accordance with the law. "But he deserves to die," reasoned the

Emperor. "He does," replied the sobbing mother, before continuing, "otherwise I would not be pleading for mercy, but justice." Her son was spared.

We have Paul's letter to the Romans to thank for reminding us that: "There is nobody righteous, not even one . . . for all have sinned and fall short of the glory of God" (Rom 3:10, 23). We, like the boy whose release was in Napoleon's gift, deserve only death. God would be perfectly just in passing such a sentence. Indeed, such justice was demanded of him by his own nature. And yet, his mercy also could not be ignored. How to reconcile the two, while giving satisfaction to each? Paul speaks further about all those who sinned:

> . . . and are justified freely by his grace through the redemption that came by Christ Jesus. God presented him as a sacrifice of atonement, through faith in his blood. He did this to demonstrate his justice, because in his forbearance he had left the sins committed beforehand unpunished—he did it to demonstrate his justice at the present time, so as to be just and the one who justifies those who have faith in Jesus. (Rom 3:24–26)

God's pardon toward us is not the turning of an anthropomorphic eye to some petty misdemeanor or a divinely orchestrated sin-ectomy procedure. Nor does redemption consist in the Father reluctantly giving in to the pleas of the Son on behalf of humankind. "Propitiation" is a word that does not find favor with many modern theologians. It is an ugly word, and a word that is absent from the vocabulary of too many Christians. But it is a necessary word; or, at least, the doctrine represented by it is necessary to our understanding of how the chasm between humanity in a state of sin and warranting only alienation from God could be bridged so that humanity can now find reconciliation with him. It is the essence of what links verses 23 and 26 in the above reading. Martyn Lloyd-Jones put it this way:

> Propitiation carries this notion that there is Someone who has been offended, someone who has done the offending, that there is an offence, and that something is necessary on both sides. Something has got to be done from the side of the One who has been offended as well as from the side of the offender; and this great and glorious doctrine teaches us that the very God whom we have offended has Himself provided the way whereby the offence has been dealt with. His anger, His wrath against the sin and the sinner, has been satisfied, appeased, and He therefore can now thus reconcile man unto Himself.[18]

---

18. Lloyd-Jones, *Romans*, 78.

By Christ and in Christ

Let us be quite clear about two things. First of all, God was under no obligation to find a way to reconcile humanity to himself. He is subject to nobody or anything that resides outside of his own Being. His only limitation—if it may be so identified—is to behave consistently within the framework provided by his own nature, which is infinite in all its perfections. Secondly, the act of offering humanity the means by which to be reconciled with him was not to meet any need within himself. He did not require a relationship with humanity in order to retain perfection, nor did its absence diminish him in any way. Neither am I convinced by arguments that God had to demonstrate his goodness for its existence to find fulfilment. He is inherently good for he can be no other.

According to the NIV, the basis of our redemption comes "by Christ." This is perfectly true and is an acceptable translation of the original, though doctrinally incomplete. It is the same as saying that sin came into the world by Adam. Yes it did, but personal responsibility is attributed to each of us because we all sinned "in Adam" (Rom 5:12–21). In the same way, redemption/justification/righteousness with God/reconciliation comes "in Christ Jesus" (Rom 3:24, KJV, RSV, NASB, Wycliffe, YLT).

This is an important concept that we ignore to the detriment of our understanding. To be "in Christ" is a particularly Pauline motif, often symbolizing the union to be found by Christian believers with Christ and, thereby, with each other as co-members of his body (e.g., Rom 12:4–5). In the context of the cross as the way by which we are introduced to that corporate setting, however, it includes not only what Christ has done as our penal substitute, but also our participation in it through faith.[19]

The idea that the gulf between God and humanity exists only in the minds of those who believe it to be true is a devilish delusion. Otherwise, it renders the cross unnecessary and the Mediatorial aspects of the work of Christ nonsense. It would also make Scripture unreliable and God a liar, all of which is as unthinkable as it is untenable. The fact that such drivel is often peddled by those who claim to be representative of Christianity does nothing to remove its impiety, exposes its perpetrators to be presently devoid of faith, and, therefore, remaining in their inherent state of sin.

Such an evaluation may seem harsh to some, but I am unable to draw any other conclusion. Faith is not unreasonable. A number of years ago, a leading bishop in the North of England gained a measure of notoriety for denying the need for and the actuality of the resurrection of Jesus. He was

---

19. See Moo, *Letter to the Romans*, 230.

not alone; nor was it an idea exclusive to the twentieth century. This was the apostle Paul's conclusion on the matter:

> If there is no resurrection of the dead, then not even Christ has been raised. And if Christ has not been raised, then our preaching is useless and so is your faith. More than that, we are then found to be false witnesses about God, for we have testified about God that he raised Christ from the dead. But he did not raise him if in fact the dead are not raised. For if the dead are not raised, then Christ has not been raised either. And if Christ has not been raised, your faith is futile; you are still in your sins. Then those who have fallen asleep in Christ are lost. If only for this life we have hope in Christ, we are to be pitied more than all men. (1 Cor 15:13–19)

Thank God the apostle doesn't leave us to wallow in the horror of such an alternative (1 Cor 15:20–28). Why was it that Jesus came, died, and was raised again? "Because of the Lord's great love . . . for his compassions never fail" (Lam 3:22).

Summary

God is great! In fact, there is some merit in the argument that we do him a disservice by attaching the idea of greatness to anything or anyone but him. He is great in the whole of his Being, which means that everything about him is great, both infinitely and perfectly so. He is great in power, great in majesty, great in splendor, his love is great, his mercy is great, his justice is great, his kindness is great, his purposes are great, his patience is great, his forgiveness is great, and his faithfulness is great. His goodness is not just good, nor even very good, but great. In fact, so great is he that it is impossible to exhaust the list. Moreover, every expression of each of his attributes cannot help but reflect its source, thereby making them also great.

I have looked here at only a few areas of God's greatness in relation to his faithfulness. Mostly, I have considered the implications of those areas doctrinally while offering the odd anecdotal reference to reinforce the theology. But we must be careful that we do not restrict our understanding or our appreciation of God's faithfulness thus. Rather, allow Scripture to be our guide, especially in the examples it provides. The most common feature elicited by those who are recorded in the Bible as beneficiaries of God's faithfulness is praise. That was their priority. Could there be a more fitting response? Or one more likely to generate its further exercise?

4

Ezekiel

HISTORICAL BACKGROUND

Although Ezekiel is numbered amongst the post-exilic prophets, he was a contemporary of Jeremiah. Because Jerusalem did not fall until nineteen years after the first wave of exiles had been carried off to Babylon, Jeremiah's warning to those still in Judah coincided with that of Ezekiel to the already exiled. The kings of Judah under whom Ezekiel lived were identical to those under whom Jeremiah lived. Ezekiel himself was a member of the second phase of exiles in 597 BC (Ezek 40:1), a twenty-five-year-old amongst the ten thousand carried away at the same time as King Jehoiachin, the queen mother, palace officials, and leading citizens of the land (see 2 Kgs 24:11–18).

It is not without significance that all Ezekiel's messages are calculated from this point. That he omitted to identify Zedekiah as king implies that he understood Jehoiachin to have retained that right. The discovery and translation of a series of cuneiform tablets in the early part of the twentieth century suggests that the Babylonians shared Ezekiel's conviction, Zedekiah's appointment being a temporary but necessary measure.[1]

Nebuchadnezzar had been quite content to allow Jerusalem to remain intact, as long as his appointed puppet, Zedekiah, towed the line. When Zedekiah rebelled, however, the Babylonians laid siege to Judah's capital. Two years later, in 586 BC, the city walls were breached, Jerusalem was

---

1. See Taylor, *Ezekiel*, 34.

plundered, and the temple razed to the ground. Judah's monarchy was effectively and terminally ended, the City of David would be left crumbled and derelict, while the former site of the Lord's temple served only to remind onlookers of what might otherwise have been. All the hallmarks of past glories were now gone: royal, political, and spiritual.

We'll take a more in-depth look at Ezekiel's contribution in due course, but it is worthwhile noting here how his messages were shaped by changes to the political landscape. The cross of Christ six hundred years later became the hinge upon which the door of history turns. For God's people of the sixth-century BC, and Ezekiel in particular, that catalyst was the fall of Jerusalem. The first part of Ezekiel's ministry is concerned solely with relaying to his fellow exiles the uncompromising and unrelenting word of divine judgment that was about to unfold (Ezek 1–24). During the siege, almost as if to divert his own attention, he proclaimed a series of judgments against Israel's traditional enemies (Ezek 25–32). Once news began to filter through and it was subsequently confirmed that Jerusalem had fallen, his focus became directed toward the hope of restoration (Ezek 33–48).

It must also be noted that the Jews fared reasonably well in exile; Babylon was certainly a more sympathetic captor than Assyria had been. There was neither the same degree of cruelty nor the insistence that their detainees should honor astral deities. Thus, the potential for religious reawakening was not inhibited by possible accusations of rebellion against their captors. Indeed, once the dust had begun to settle, Judaism as a religion positively thrived under Babylonian—and later, Medo-Persian—supervision. It might reasonably be argued that it was only occasions of prosperity and self-government that seemed to cultivate impurity and corruption. Rich and powerful kings were seldom harbingers of national godliness for either the northern kingdom of Israel or Judah to the south. Perhaps bizarrely, it was at such times that neighboring religions were at their most appealing. In this context, it is not quite so baffling to learn that many of the exiles chose to stay put when finally given the opportunity to return to their homeland.

Although the conditions of captivity—and the circumstances that led to it—enabled Judaism to flourish by comparison with its years of independent governance, the transformation was by no means an overnight event. Irving Jensen takes up the narrative:

> The idolatry which Ezekiel saw as Judah's blight before he left Jerusalem was the same condition he faced in the settlements of Jewish exiles in Babylonia. The judgment of captivity did not stir the first contingents of exiles to repentance. In fact, they found it very hard to believe, as Ezekiel was prophesying, that

Jerusalem would actually be destroyed by the Babylonians. They were loath to believe that Jehovah had given world dominion to Babylon, and that His will was for Judah to submit to this enemy. Hence, it was necessary for Ezekiel in Babylon—and Jeremiah in Jerusalem—to show the people how unfounded were any expectations of immediate deliverance.[2]

For both men, the task was as thankless as it was arduous, but neither was ill-equipped, nor were they seeking the gratitude of others. The responsibility of the prophet is simply to discharge that with which he has been entrusted; both Jeremiah and Ezekiel were fully aware of this.

It has long been my conviction that repentance, according to the New Testament pattern, involves three key features: recognition of sin, remorse for wrongdoing, and a redirection of lifestyle on the part of the individual. All three components involve the co-operation of the Holy Spirit and are only possible because of Christ's finished work of atonement. We look to Immanuel (God coming down to us), not to Israel (our struggle to attain). For those held captive in Babylon, however, there was a further stumbling block. It was one with which all of God's prophets of the period were confronted, none more so than Ezekiel: How could a covenant God use an unclean instrument with which to chastise his covenant people? They perhaps needed to realize two things: God is God and therefore requires nobody's permission concerning how he chooses to bring about his purposes; and a more apt description of them might have been that they were a covenant-forsaking people. To spin the two around, we might even say that God's sovereignty is just that, and therefore not dependent upon or governed by either the frailties or fortitude of his people.

Given the contemporaneous nature of their ministries and that both were effectively products of the same historical background, the apparent lack of mutual acknowledgment between Jeremiah and Ezekiel has not passed without comment. Did such an absence equate to a commensurate dearth of respect? I think not for the following reasons:

- by the same token that we search in vain for any acknowledgment of one by the other, so too there is no evidence of animosity between them;
- the messages they proclaimed, though to vastly different audiences, were both complementary and demonstrate shared values, often remarkably so; and
- other prophets who shared the same time platform failed to acknowledge their contemporaries without attracting the same conclusions.

2. Jensen, *Survey of the Old Testament*, 360.

PERSONAL BACKGROUND

Whenever I am working on a manuscript, at least one of my fellow home-group members will ask for a fortnightly progress report, which often amounts to little more than how many words I have managed since our last gathering. While putting together the initial draft for my last publication, one of the guys asked which minor prophet is my favorite. My response then, as always, was that it happens to be whichever I am reading at the time. When it comes to the major prophets, however, the answer is quite different. So, Tim, if you're reading, it's Ezekiel.

If I was asked for a single reason for this, I'm not sure what it would be. Perhaps he is the one I would most like to mimic if I was faced with the same set of circumstances, and if it wasn't for my natural proclivity to be more Jeremiah-like. Ezekiel's name means "Yahweh strengthens," and I can certainly identify as one who has been constantly aware of the Lord's bolstering. Such occasions have usually revealed themselves when I have been most in need of divine intervention, and often when I have exhausted any natural resources at my disposal. Those who are similarly disposed will also testify that such strengthening is not entirely for personal edification, but that by being so uplifted, the individual might be better equipped to enable others. This was unquestionably true of Ezekiel: he was fortified by God's grace, and by God's grace he sought to fortify his fellows.

Ezekiel was born in 622 BC, spending the first twenty-five years of his life in his homeland before being exiled to Babylon in 597. This means that he would have been a babe in arms when Josiah found the Book of the Law, though Ezekiel's childhood and early teenage years would surely have benefited from the reforms its discovery evoked. He was called to be a prophet five years later at the age of thirty, six years before Jerusalem fell. The last recorded utterance from Ezekiel was in 570 at the age of fifty-two. There is no conclusive data allowing us to determine how long he lived after this.

Ezekiel is frequently numbered amongst that small group of Old Testament prophets who were also priests. The basis for doing so is that he is so ascribed in most translations of the early verses of his first chapter, from which we also learn the name of his father: "the word of the Lord came to Ezekiel the priest, the son of Buzi" (Ezek 1:3). However, this could just as readily be translated: " . . . Ezekiel, son of Buzi the priest," which would in itself account for the broad knowledge of temple ritual he displays in the work that bears his name. This would not have been unusual for one so fervently dedicated to his religion. He demonstrated a similarly wide understanding of international affairs and local industry, though I am unaware of any commentators who would thereby presume him to have been either a leading politician or master shipbuilder.

We learn also that he was married, but that his wife died suddenly, shortly after Nebuchadnezzar's final siege of Jerusalem began (Ezek 24:16–24). Arguably the two darkest features of his entire life were separated by only a few hours, at the most. Thus, though already in exile, he spent the majority of it as a widower and presumably childless. In common with many prophets of the period, Ezekiel's personal circumstances became prophetically symbolic of the message with which he was entrusted. From them we are also able to conclude that he led a relatively relaxed existence; he was captive only in the sense that he had been forced to leave the comfortable surroundings of his homeland against his wishes. This was far from unusual. Ezekiel and others like him will not have been allowed unlimited movement, but it was hardly the prison ghetto scenario imagined by some preachers of our day. Indeed, it would have been regarded as a useful propaganda tool on the part of their captors to permit these "guests" to see the alleged benefits of a multi-faith society compared to what their own brand of monotheism had produced for them.

Ezekiel has often been nominated as the father of Judaism. It is usually intended as a compliment. Certainly, we can see from the contents of his book that the visions he shared could well have formed the catalyst for Judaistic development, such as the vivid imagery that became prevalent in later apocalyptic circles. He also seems to have crystallized some of the cultic ideas that had long been peripheral to Yahwistic religion, such as personal accountability. Many of the features we see in seed form in Ezekiel became bastardized as the centuries unfolded, in much the same way that some elements of Calvinism are now so far removed from their sixteenth-century AD setting. But it would be grossly unfair to hold either man responsible for the subsequent dilution or concentration by others of their original ideas.

One feature sometimes attributed to Ezekiel borders unnecessarily on telepathy and clairvoyance. The meticulous accuracy with which he "knew" details concerning Jerusalem's plight *in absentia* need not resort to claims of the paranormal. If the knowledge of future events was not beyond the remit of the prophets of old, in some cases down to the precise minutia, then why should distance be restricted in a way that time was not? To deny this of Ezekiel is surely tantamount to refuting that he was a prophet. And if he was not that, then with what conclusion are we left? Moreover, even in the natural realm, we know from other examples that written communication was not restricted between Jerusalem and Babylon during this period (Jer 29:1–23). We also know that Ezekiel's reputation was such that he attracted those with confidential information either to seek him out or to be taken to him (e.g., Ezek 33:21).

What single word best describes the Ezekiel with which we are presented by the pages of the Old Testament? Priest? Prophet? Pastor? Visionary? Statesman? Physician? Theologian? He was quite possibly all of these, and none to the necessary exclusion of any other. But no noun adequately describes his impact without an accompanying adjectival qualification. If he was a priest, he was a God-fearing one, he was a fearless prophet, a caring pastor, a graphic visionary, a dedicated statesman, a soothing physician, and a pragmatic theologian. This is what I see of the man; but, then, I am biased.

OVERVIEW

Chapters 1–24: Before the Siege of Jerusalem

Ezekiel's commissioning (chapters 1–3)

There are those of my acquaintance who have cited the mystery entangled in the vivid imagery of these opening chapters as the prime reason they have postponed further inquiry. If you presently fall into the same category, content yourself for the time being with the simple message that God was calling Ezekiel to be "a watchman for the house of Israel" (Ezek 3:17). Although I have separated these chapters dealing with Ezekiel's commission from the others in this section relating to Judah's judgment, there was a temptation to leave them together. The reason I considered doing so is that even God's calling of Ezekiel was a pronouncement of coming judgment upon Judah.

On balance, however, I decided to treat these opening chapters independently, as there are lessons we may glean from them that set the tone for the whole book. Chief among these, in my opinion, is one for which I must extend a debt of gratitude to the scholarly skills of Irving Jensen for the following:

> Like the other prophets, Ezekiel received a vision of God which put him on his face in the dust before his Maker (Ezek 1:26–28). Compare Isaiah's vision (Isa 6) and John's vision (Rev 1:10–18) ... and observe the different ways in which the Lord manifested himself. To Isaiah, His *holiness* was emphasized; to Ezekiel, His *power, majesty,* and *government*; and to John, His *love*.[3]

---

3. Jensen, *Survey of the Old Testament*, 369.

Judah's judgment (chapters 4–24)

Prophetic signs, dramatic enactments, parabolic illustrations, and scorching rhetoric abound as Ezekiel employs every device at his disposal to leave his audience in no doubt as to the certainty of God's judgment upon his unruly people. The fact that any hope is reserved for Ezekiel's later chapters has the effect here of forcing the reader to wince in revulsion at the sheer relentless onslaught of judgment upon sorrowful judgment. It wasn't just the fact of Jerusalem's coming siege and final falling into enemy hands, though that was surely sufficient to arouse sympathy in all but the most hardened of hearts; it was also the famine conditions that would accompany Judah's careworn state. Some, no doubt, would have to make the choice between dietary prohibition and siege starvation.

Why such severe punishment was reserved for God's covenant people is often shrouded in controversy. Perhaps the fact that they were betrothed to God by divine election and were made fully aware of their obligations and penalties for disobedience is reason enough. But we must also consider the purpose of that election, further ratified in God's promise of restoration for Israel through Isaiah: to be "a light for the Gentiles, that [they] may bring [God's] salvation to the ends of the earth" (Isa 49:6). Each nation would be judged in accordance with the measure of light by which they conducted their affairs. Judah had not even lived by the relatively dim glimmer of the nations that were around them, let alone the radiant luminosity that shone through the corpus of God's revealed will to them (Ezek 5:5–7).

Chapters 25–32: During the Siege of Jerusalem

This whole section is concerned with pronouncing judgment on the nations surrounding Judah, all of whom at one time or another had proven themselves to be enemies of God's covenant people:

Ammon	Ezek 25:1–7;
Moab	vv. 8–11;
Edom	vv. 12–14;
Philistia	vv. 15–17;
Tyre	26:1—28:19;
Sidon	28:20–26; and
Egypt	chapters 29–32.

Even a casual glance at the above table reveals that most of Ezekiel's attention is focused on Tyre and Egypt. Closer inspection of the text shows that the judgment for each is concentrated on their respective leaders: the king of Tyre (Ezek 28:1–19) and Pharaoh of Egypt (Ezek 29:1–12). Of course, each man was targeted partly as representative of all Tyrians and Egyptians respectively, but this should not mask the very personal nature of God's words through Ezekiel. There are notable similarities between the two, all of which extend beyond expressions of cruelty against God's covenant people to a single root cause: pride. Moreover, it was not just the self-satisfaction or smugness of their own achievements in having realized their ambitions, but to be so self-opinionated as to think of themselves as gods.

There is a strong Christian tradition that the king of Tyre whom Ezekiel cites (Ithobal II) is also an allusion to Satan's fall from heaven. Certainly, some of the prophet's choice of imagery is reminiscent of the Genesis narrative, though at the same time more elaborate in parts. The description of an Edenic role cannot apply to the human Ithobal, but if the details supplied in that regard do belong to the creation account, then they are not known from any other extant source. Divine revelation of this kind is not beyond the scope of the prophetic, and it would be dangerous to imagine that it is. But we must also be careful that we do not read what isn't there. Ezekiel is not presenting the king of Tyre as a demon or personification of the devil; it is simply that he recognizes the author of the sin he displays.

Chapters 33–48: After the Siege of Jerusalem

The restoration of Israel (chapters 33–39)

Arguably the key feature to the fulfilling of the promise to restore God's flock is the removal and replacement of those he holds accountable for failing in their delegated duty of care:

> For this is what the Sovereign Lord says: I myself will search for my sheep and look after them. As a shepherd looks after his scattered flock when he is with them, so will I look after my sheep. I will rescue them from all the places where they were scattered on a day of clouds and darkness. I will bring them out from the nations and gather them from the countries, and I will bring them into their own land. I will pasture them on the mountains of Israel, in the ravines and in all the settlements in the land. I will tend them in a good pasture, and the mountain heights of Israel will be their grazing land . . . I myself will

tend my sheep and make them lie down, declares the Sovereign Lord. (Ezek 34:11–15)

Even as a stand-alone passage, this is incredibly encouraging. For its full effect, however, it must be read in its original context. It was a pastoral style that Israel simply wasn't used to, where previous shepherds had:

- exalted themselves at the expense of the flock (vv. 2–3);
- failed to bring comfort and healing to the feeble and the sick (v. 4a);
- displayed a cavalier attitude toward the vulnerable and the disorientated (v. 4b);
- demonstrated an utter lack of compassion in their leadership (v. 4c);
- and treated their potential loss as mere collateral damage (vv. 5–6).

Can those who have been subjected to such treatment be restored? Can dry bones live (Ezek 37:1–14)? We shall see.

The restoration of the Temple (chapters 40–48)

Just as the restoration of Israel involved God himself replacing the worthless shepherds, so too the restoration of the Temple necessitated the return of his glory as an expression of his abiding presence (Ezek 43:2–5). In this sense, it might well be argued that the restoration of the Temple is more concerned with the vindication of God's honor than it is the revitalization of hope for God's people, except insofar that the latter benefits from the former. We must not forget, however, that if chronology may be deduced from their order of presentation, then the restoration of Israel precedes that of the Temple. In the words of George Beasley-Murray: "In a land purged of uncleanness, the ideal worship in an ideal Temple is set forth for the observance of an ideal people."[4]

Neither can it reasonably be inferred from these chapters that Ezekiel was parochial or narrow minded. First of all, he was speaking only as God's mouthpiece; but secondly—and, from a subjective perspective, just as importantly—the prophetic references to the Temple should not be interpreted temporally only without also seeing them in their eschatological context, any more than we would the restoration of Israel.

---

4. Guthrie and Motyer, *New Bible Commentary*, 666.

A MATTER OF DEATH AND LIFE

I'm not sure whether this gives away too much about the kind of company I keep, but there seems to be a constant clamoring amongst Christians of my acquaintance for what is perceived to be "the now word of God." This is hardly a new phenomenon. It is one with which I have been familiar for almost the whole of my Christian experience, and often been party to it. Neither is it one that is entirely devoid of merit. After all, who would not want to receive a word from God that is specifically designed to meet their particular needs at the moment of receipt?

There is a sense, of course, in which God's word is always his "now" word. How could it be any other? Thus, the responsibility is largely ours—though guided by his Holy Spirit—to find application of that word in such a way that affords due respect to its authority, vibrancy, and illuminatory values, while at the same time retaining as much of its original intent as the passage of time and events will allow. Even those of us who find some difficulty in acknowledging this perpetually prophetic element of God's word must at least concede that what they presently regard as the "then" word was very much the "now" word to its original recipient(s).

Certain texts lend themselves easily to given conditions. Some lead favorably to the emotional altar call or the final night's rallying cry of the week-long series. Familiarity with such verses does not necessarily breed contempt, but it can rob us of a more balanced contemplation. In an attempt to reverse that trend, I would ask you to put aside for one moment the direction your mind might be accustomed to taking as you consider the following passage: Ezekiel 37:1–28.

Decay in a Decadent Environment

Life and death have one thing in common: the process of each begins at birth. It also should go without saying that the longer one lives, the closer he or she is to dying than they have been at any other time. Death is a unique experience: "[I]t is appointed unto men once to die . . . " (Heb 9:27, KJV). But true spiritual enlightenment can only come about if natural birth is followed by what the Bible calls being "born again" (see John 3:3). It might reasonably be argued that without this rebirth, we can never enjoy life to the full as God intended, even if our experience seems to suggest otherwise. It is possible, however, both to hasten the day of our natural death and to quicken the process of decay during life.

Visions and parables—or, at least, the interpretation of them—also share some features. Prominent amongst these is that they should not be treated as allegories, where we are invited to imagine symbolism where it does not exist. Nor should we be so free as to create a past or future backdrop unless that is specifically provided in the text. That said, however, I had always regarded the valley of Ezekiel's vision as some sort of deserted cemetery for the unburied dead. This, of course, may well be a legitimate conclusion to draw. But neither should the possibility entirely be dismissed that the valley was in some measure responsible for bringing about the premature deaths of those who ventured there.

To a church familiar with corrupt practices and corroding influences, the apostle Paul wrote these words: "Do not be misled: 'Bad company corrupts good character'" (1 Cor 15:33). Some commentators suggest that Paul may have had the words of the Proverbialist in mind:

> The righteous choose their friends carefully, but the way of the wicked leads them astray. (Prov 12:26)
> Whoever walks with the wise becomes wise, but the companion of fools will suffer harm. (Prov 13:20)
> Do not make friends with a hot-tempered man, do not associate with one easily angered, or you may learn his ways and get yourself ensnared. (Prov 22:24–25)

It is a plausible assumption. What is not open to question is that Paul's motivation was for a positive outcome. Commands that begin "Thou shalt not" are often portrayed as the dictates of a killjoy, but rather they are designed to encourage sound thinking and godly conduct. Bruce put it this way: "Paul's aim is not to humiliate [the recipients of his counsel] but to bring them to a better frame of mind."[5]

Moreover, it is not just the tendency of another's inappropriate influence that concerned Paul and the writer of these Proverbs. Friendship with those who are prone to such excesses can often blind us to their extent and the harm they cause. There have been times—thankfully few—when I have had to dissociate myself from fellowship with individuals whose persistent inclinations toward expressed views and deeds have lay outside the parameters of those befitting an ambassador of Christ. I dare say some have done the same with me; there have certainly been times when my walk may have warranted separation. The price can be costly and the immediate consequences difficult to overcome, but the prize is surely worth it. If it only avoids finding ourselves trapped side by side in a valley of dry bones, then the temporal discomfort of pruning was surely worth undertaking.

5. Bruce, *1 & 2 Corinthians*, 150.

We should also be aware that concurring ideas do not necessarily imply kindred spirits; they may just be the random bullets of opinion falling occasionally upon the same target. There are countless examples, both in Scripture and in the history of the church, where God's people have been swayed by the behavioral patterns of those with whom they have mistakenly chosen to align themselves. During the early part of King Joash's reign, the chronicler records that "he did what was right in the eyes of the Lord" (2 Chr 24:2a), but only while he was subject to the influence of the godly priest, Jehoiada (2 Chr 24:2b). Jehoiada was a wise man, but he was also an old man. The two often go hand in hand. Jehoiada eventually died at the age of one hundred and thirty years (2 Chr 24:15). Such was his reputation that he was honored by being buried alongside Israel's most worthy kings (2 Chr 24:16). There was now a vacuum, and look how it was filled:

> After the death of Jehoiada, the officials of Judah came and paid homage to the king, and he listened to them. They abandoned the temple of the Lord, the God of their fathers, and worshipped Asherah poles and idols. (2 Chr 24:17–18a)

There then followed a sequence of events that culminated in the regicide of Joash, though his burial was not afforded the same respect as that bestowed upon Jehoiada (2 Chr 24:25). It is arguable whether there is a more tragic phrase in the Old Testament than "he listened to them." It is not one solely applicable to Joash, nor can it lay claim to being the first such recorded episode (see 2 Chr 11–12), but is there a more apposite reminder of the danger of giving ear to the voices of the ungodly?

Of course, Judah's officials didn't begin by offering advice. They had to gain the king's ear before they could control his mind, so they told him what they knew he wanted to hear: they "paid homage to [him]." In modern parlance, they tickled his ears, they buttered him up, they curried the king's favor, and they were not to be disappointed. This is not an uncommon strategy as far as the enemy of our souls is concerned. "It's time people began to respect you for who you are," "You deserve better than this," "You're too good for them," "Did God really say . . . ?"

The danger is there for all to see. It was certainly not lost on the writer of the epistle to the Hebrews:

> Let us hold unswervingly to the hope we profess, for he who promised is faithful. And let us consider how we may spur one another on towards love and good deeds. Let us not give up meeting together, as some are in the habit of doing, but let us encourage one another—and all the more as you see the Day approaching. (Heb 10:23–25)

A dear, elderly lady in the church into which I was saved would often refer to this portion of Scripture (i.e., from Heb 10:19 on) as the Christian salad diet, by virtue of the recurring phrase, "Let us . . . " It certainly dispels any notion of independency as a means of effecting pilgrims' progress. But neither should we imagine the writer to be advocating a corporate walk without qualification. Joash listened to advice, as had Rehoboam before him, and in each case it proved their undoing. The writer provides four conditions for drawing near to God (Heb 10:22). We can do no better than to harness ourselves to those who meet the same criteria:

A sincere heart

To be sincere is to be without guile, pretense, or deceit; to be of a sincere heart is for the outward appearance to be a true reflection of the inner condition. British television viewers of a certain age may remember a program that was possibly the very first amateur talent show, where acts of varying aptitude displayed their gifts in the hope of attracting sufficient viewer votes to be recalled the following week. More public exposure also meant an increased likelihood of being noticed by those able to further their careers. It was called *Opportunity Knocks*, first aired in the UK in February 1949 (well before my time), and was hosted by Hughie Green. His catchphrase, usually following the contrived desire to see the previous act do well, was: "I mean that most sincerely, folks." That it was expressed after every act hardly added to the value of his proposed sincerity. Details that emerged later regarding the host's private life suggest that he may not have been a stranger to those qualities against which sincerity is the polar opposite. Claims to sincerity and true candor are not the same things at all. It is first and foremost a matter of the heart.

Full assurance of faith

Is the writer guilty of pleonasm? In other words, is the modifier "full" unnecessary and, therefore, redundant? After all, are we not dealing either with assurance of faith or something altogether different? Perhaps the original Greek will help. The noun *plerophoria* indicates an entire confidence without hesitation, or conviction with no room for the slightest of doubts, in that to which it is attached. In general terms, to be full of one thing is to be entirely devoid of anything that, by its nature, would dilute that of which one is filled.

Such confidence is not only a product of faith, but can come by no other means. While it is possible to have a measure of assurance by way of previous experience, either personal or historical, or even as a result of a carefully reasoned thesis, having considered all potential arguments for and against, the assurance of which Scripture speaks in these types of contexts has no odds stacked contrary to it. Moreover, objects of faith may only be realized when the one in whom such faith resides is fully assured of the outcome. This kind of faith is not presented as an optional extra or the exclusive domain of the spiritual elite, but the way by which the just of God are repeatedly commanded to live (see Rom 1:17; Gal 3:11; Heb 10:38).

Cleansed from a guilty conscience

Do you believe you are saved? You do? Good! Do you know what it is you are saved from, who paid the price, and how it was paid? Yes to all three? Even better! You understand that, because of all this, forensically before God you are now guiltless? Excellent! Now, has your mental assent to this convinced your conscience of its reality or do you still play games of mind over matter with yourself, whereby you endlessly repeat phrases like, "I'm not a sinner, I'm a saint; I'm not a sinner, I'm a saint," in the hope that one day your conscience will catch up experientially with what you know to be true existentially?

It should not startle the reader to discover that the remedy for a guilty conscience is precisely the same as for guilt: the blood of Christ. Does that mean it is like a second blessing? I don't think it is so much that as allowing the work of the atonement to take deeper effect and recognizing the full extent of what Jesus' death actually achieved. There is perhaps a clue in Paul's counsel to the believers at Rome: "Likewise reckon ye also yourselves to be dead indeed unto sin, but alive unto God through Jesus Christ our Lord" (Rom 6:11, KJV). The "likewise" links back to the previous verse, and conveys the senses of: "In similar fashion": "The death [Jesus] died, he died to sin once for all; but the life he lives, he lives to God" (Rom 6:10). It has absolutely nothing to do with feeling guiltless or deserving, but reckoning it to be so and commanding our consciences to get in line with that reality. But what if our consciences bear true witness and are an accurate reflection of a guilty condition? The remedy remains unaltered: nothing but the blood of Jesus.

Washed with water

There seems to be some disagreement as to whether this refers to water baptism. In so far as I am able to judge such things, the arguments against revolve almost exclusively on the fact that it would be too obvious a conclusion to reach. It is almost as if the most obscure interpretation is somehow invested with the most legitimacy, which is nonsense—or is it? The act of washing is a recurring theme in both Testaments of the Bible. Prior to entering the Holy Place to offer their sacrifices, the priests were ritually required to wash their hands and feet as a symbol of their representative responsibilities. The consequences of not having done so were far more grim than merely being left with unclean extremities (see Exod 30:17–21).

The outer cleansing was symbolic of inner purification, the instruments used representative of the power of God, and the whole ritual a reminder of the cost of entering into God's holy presence. Fast forward to the New Testament and we find the same ritual being fulfilled in the sacrament of baptism. I say "fulfilled" rather than replaced because that is the correct terminology to show the relationship between type and antitype. But it is not really the same ritual as the effects are now more permanent, based on what the writer to the Hebrews had earlier described as "a better sacrifice" (Heb 9:11—10:17). The waters of baptism represent the cleansing blood of Christ.

Thereafter, we are called to interact with those who both need to receive the gospel and are presently unclean. In so doing, we must remind ourselves that whatever seems unsavory to us is not unsaveable to God; the irreligious are not irredeemable. But how do we ensure that our engagement with unbelievers will not leave us muddied by the influence of their social habits and godless ways? By daily cleansing, of course. This is not to promote any notion of repeated baptisms, but Jesus has made further provision: "Christ loved the church and gave himself up for her to make her holy, cleansing her by the washing with water through the word" (Eph 5:25b–26). It is the word of God that continues to cleanse us. And it is the word of God that will keep us from sharing the destiny of the decadent. Indeed, it is no coincidence that these words appear in a section devoted by the apostle to transformed relationships. The death of Christ made us holy, thereby transforming our relationship toward God (justification), and his cleansing work thereafter through the word of God (sanctification) enables us not only to maintain fellowship with the Father, but also radically to alter our relationships elsewhere. By way of example, Paul cites our marriages (Eph 5:22–23), the home (Eph 6:1–4), and the workplace (Eph 5–9).

This link between cleansing and the word of God (both written and spoken) is not exclusively Pauline. Note Jesus' allusion to it in his priestly prayer on behalf of the disciples: "Sanctify them by the truth; your word is truth" (John 17:17). But notice also the immediate context of the previous verse: "They are not of the world, even as I am not of it" (John 17:16). We are strangers; we are aliens; we do not belong in a valley filled with dry bones.

Where Are You?

I was sixteen-years-old when I came to Christ. It was the perfect time for me to do so. This is not true because I was sixteen, but because that is when God chose to arrest my attention. Whenever it had been would have been the perfect time. But even on the natural plane, conditions were just right. I had recently left school and started my first adult job at the local colliery. We had only moved to the area twelve months prior, so I'd had little opportunity to develop any strong high school friendships, nor had I yet become entangled by the worldly-wise pit mentality.

A sense of belonging

There were, however, some other deep-rooted issues, which were to cause me a little heartache during those first fledgling years as a believer. One or two have even left their scars all these years later. From about the age of eight, I had become increasingly interested in football. I had some talent for the game and dreamed of the day when I would score the winning goal at Wembley stadium. I was far from unique in that regard, though I also knew it was a dream unlikely to be realized.

Where my real passion lay was in supporting my local professional football club, the (then) mighty Leeds United. I longed for the day when my own funds would allow me to buy a season ticket so I could be there to watch every home game. I had finally managed to do just that only three weeks before giving my life to Christ. Alternate Saturday afternoons were as exciting as I had hoped they would be. Church involvement meant that the rest of the week was pretty good, too.

But then I realized a bizarre phenomenon beginning to take shape: the more I gave myself to the latter, the less I enjoyed the former. Stranger still was the fact that it had nothing to do with the play on the pitch, but was exclusively concerned with the atmosphere being created by my fellow fans, both *en route* and inside the ground. Whereas I had previously enjoyed arriving early to join in with the singing of players' names, shouting abuse at the opposition (more often than not liberally laden with expletives), questioning the referee's parentage, and loudly cheering any misfortune that befell an opponent, whether that meant being sent off for misconduct or carried away on a stretcher with a career-threatening injury, I now found the whole thing repugnant. What had happened? I no longer belonged there.

There is a world of difference between being and belonging. Where we find ourselves is not always where we should be. I didn't belong at Elland Road in the company of forty-thousand football fanatics, but that is precisely where I was, and I had a choice to make. Would I continue to resist the prompting of God's Spirit until the conviction became an unbearable burden or, worse still, would God decide I wasn't worth the effort (remember, this is how I was thinking as a sixteen year old), or would I do as I had promised in the words of all those songs I now sang with gusto three or four times a week? I have not seen a live football match since, and I haven't missed it in the slightest.

Am I saying that Christian believers should abandon all worldly pursuits? No! Should we all turn our backs on everything we cherished prior to our coming to Christ? Not at all! God has not entrusted me with the task of being either your convictor or your confessor. But if the one who has been appointed with that responsibility is putting his finger on issues for which reading this now serves to confirm the matter in your spirit, then you, too, have a choice to make. And let us be clear precisely what that choice is. Once highlighted, we may no longer claim ignorance. Neither are the options before us obedience, delay, or disobedience. Postponed obedience, for whatever reason, remains disobedience for as long as the delay persists. We must choose either to yield to the urging of God's Spirit or to continue to go our own way.

No hiding place

Historically, men and women do not have a good track record where making the right decision is concerned. The issue goes back as far as our first parents (Gen 3:8–9). The background is familiar even to those who regard it as little more than a myth or a fable. Even for those of us who consider the Fall of humanity in the garden to be factual, it is easy to miss the full significance of God's question to Adam: "Where are you?" The context tells us that, having eaten the forbidden fruit, Eden's first couple saw their own nakedness, hastily attempted to cover their shame, and hid from their Maker when they heard him approaching (Gen 3:6–8). "Where are you?" seems a natural enough question to ask by someone who is searching for those in hiding.

Let us just think about this for a moment. God, the Creator of all that exists, the sustainer of life in all its forms, both provider and provision, the resources of whom can never be exhausted, who not only knows, but is the source of all knowledge, who is not only powerful, but whose power is beyond limitation, real or imagined, who is not only present with us, but fills every space with his presence, both known and unknown. This God asks, "Where are you?" and we imagine it has anything to do with him being unaware of our whereabouts? Really? David knew the futility of such thinking:

> Where can I go from your Spirit? Where can I flee from your presence? If I go up to the heavens, you are there; if I make my bed in the depths, you are there. If I rise on the wings of the dawn, if I settle on the far side of the sea, even there your hand will guide me, your right hand will hold me fast. If I say, "Surely the darkness will hide me and the light become night around me," even the darkness will not be dark to you; the night will shine like the day, for darkness is as light to you. (Ps 139:7–12)

I think the real gist of the question is more along the lines of: "Why are you where you are?" or "What are you doing there?" The same kind of divine rhetoric occurs in the following chapter after Cain's envy of his brother, Abel, finally got the better of him, and he killed him (Gen 4:1–8). Whether Cain's attack was with the intention of terminating Abel's life is neither clear nor relevant: Abel was no less dead and Cain was no less guilty. "Where is your brother Abel?" the Lord asked. As the narrative unfolds, it becomes clear that God knew precisely where Abel was and who was responsible for him being there. Where Abel was physically was a product of where Cain was spiritually; neither would be without consequence.

The same question reverberates as an echo down the corridor of time. To Israel of old, king and peasant alike, God asked, "Where are you?" To his creation today, with technological advancements aplenty, a secular morality that scoffs at the perceived depravity of previous generations, and lifestyles where in relative terms still the needs of the many are sacrificed on the altar of the wants of the few, he says, "Why are you here?" As Christians, of course, we wouldn't dream of trying to hide from God, much less disobey him by being in the wrong place at the wrong time. I mean, how foolish would that make us?

Getting back on track

I'll take a wild stab in the dark here and guess that anyone reading this will be doing so in the privacy of their own company. No reputations are at stake and no confidences likely to be broken (unless, that is, you are still trying to pretend otherwise to God). So, who amongst you has not shared Jonah's experience of running in the diametrically opposite direction to God's instruction, and then having the gall to "spiritualize" the prevailing circumstances of one last ticket to Tarshish by suggesting that God's hand was in your disobedience after all? And God says, "What on earth are you doing here?"

For the most part, being in the wrong place can easily be remedied, though its effects are potentially far greater than we might think. To consider some of these for a moment, we must temporarily lay aside our understanding of God's supremacy and look through purely natural eyes. If we are not where God wants us to be, no amount of effort on our part will compensate for the fact of our disobedience. In my younger years, I used to enjoy taking part in local car treasure hunts. Various churches in the area would get involved, each taking turns to host the annual event, which invariably culminated in a buffet supper and the awarding of prizes.

The idea was that each car would be the vehicle for a team of up to five entrants, the non-drivers all acting as navigators by following a series of cryptic clues designed to lead from one location to another. One particular year, it became obvious after about an hour or so that Team Woodall was in some difficulty. Nothing of our surroundings seemed to fit the description of where we were supposed to be. Truth be told, the last couple of clues weren't an exact match, either. They had been like jigsaw pieces from another puzzle, beaten into shape against their will. What to do? Logically, we could either plough on regardless in some vain hope that it would all come right, or we could abandon the race altogether, return to base and face the humiliation of disqualification. I was all for the latter option when I became aware of a third possibility: "Go back to the place where you knew you were right."

Nobody is an island

To return to our friend Jonah for a moment, God's command was that he should go to Nineveh and preach against its wickedness. There was no room in the plan for a detour or a miraculous intervention in order to return his agent to the correct path. Joppa docks were not part of the itinerary. The lives of those sailors were needlessly placed in peril (Jonah 1:1-6). It is not beyond the realm of possibility that there would have been other seafaring vessels in the vicinity, and the lives of those on board will have been subject to similar danger. Jonah's guilt stretched to his responsibility for bringing about the distress they now faced. By being where we shouldn't be, we run the risk of inadvertently affecting the lives of those we have no business meddling with. Or, to put it another way: all sin is personal, but no sin is private.

I have known great blessings withheld from congregations on account of the sexual impropriety of just one of its members. On occasion, the guilty party has been numbered amongst the church's leaders. More often than not, however, the evidence unearthed has pointed to someone otherwise inconsequential and to all intents and purposes unnoticeable. Remember, nobody would have known who Achan was were it not for him taking that which had been forbidden. His confession points the blame at nobody but himself: "I have sinned . . . I saw . . . I coveted . . . [I] took . . . " (Josh 7:20–21). But look where the judgment fell: "So the Lord's anger burned against Israel" (Josh 7:1). There is corporeality in covenant.

Toward the end of Paul's epistle to the Romans, he seems to sum the whole thing up perfectly when he says: "For none of us lives to himself alone and none of us dies to himself alone" (Rom 14:7). The immediate context specifies that such living and dying is "to the Lord," so it would be easy to imagine that it is his company alone to which the apostle refers. The key verse, however, follows a little later:

> Therefore, let us stop passing judgment on one another. Instead, make up your mind not to put any stumbling-block or obstacle in your brother's way. (Rom 14:13)

Paul was dealing with a specific issue—liberty or otherwise based on personal conscience—but the principle is surely more widely applicable. Moreover, and as one might expect, it is perfectly consistent with Jesus' teaching in the Gospel accounts (see Matt 18:1–9; Mark 9:42–48; Luke 17:1–4). A couple of matters are not clear from the NIV rendering. They are minor, but they are not entirely unimportant. First of all, the same Greek word is used for both "judgment" and "make up your mind" [*krino*]. The sense of it is: "stop passing judgment . . . make a judgment not to . . . " Secondly, though the English "stumbling-block" and "obstacle" are sufficiently close to be rendered almost synonymous, the original sentence structure suggests not being a stumbling-block or placing an obstacle with the deliberate design to ensnare.

But the converse is equally true. By not being where we are meant to be, it is highly likely that we are thereby failing in our duty to bring blessing to those with whom we were supposed to engage. This is not always as obvious as it may seem, and the enemy is a shrewd tactician when it comes to diverting the focus of our attention from the real battles we should be facing. His attempts to distract Jesus proved wholly futile, but only because the Lord's gaze was aligned to nothing but his Father's will (e.g., Luke 9:51).

One of my closest friends is a retired minister. He continues to preach two or three times a month by invitation, but no longer has any direct pastoral responsibility. He was minister at a Congregational church in the Welsh valleys for almost forty years, and told me quite recently that his biggest regret was his failure to discern those who were out to drain his resources from those with genuine needs. The former were constantly demanding with their barrage of relatively minor complaints, for which he was often regarded as little more than an all-too-willing dumping ground. There are few things I find more enervating. Prior to a work accident, I spent almost twenty years as an ambulance paramedic. My colleagues and I would occasionally be called out to motorway incidents, where there were often multiple casualties. We soon learned how to prioritize the most urgent cases: they were usually the quieter ones.

Fulfilled in Part

I must concede at the very outset that I am not entirely happy with the title of this section: it is something of a misnomer. For something to be fulfilled is for the object to be filled out to its fullest potential. Anything less is not fulfilment in the truest sense of the word. Perhaps a better way to consider what I have in mind is the initial unfolding of that which was promised, a token—if you will—of the fullness that is to come.

Some things never change

People of a certain age often say that if you can remember the 1960s, you weren't really there. Well, I can remember some of them most vividly and I was really there. Although born at the very beginning of 1960, my earliest memory is of going with my father to the local maternity hospital to bring my mother and newly born sister home. This was October 1962. Much of the rest of the decade was turbulent, to say the least, both personally and politically. Life at home seemed little more than a hamster's wheel of funerals, beatings, and betrayal; the world at large offered little comfort, with social instability brought about by nuclear threats, war-scarred victims continuing to struggle to find their place once again in society, and the constant battle between a generation of heroes and their sons and daughters clamoring for a more permissive society.

Many of the threats of yesteryear have gone, only to be replaced by new ones. Civil rights remain an issue for many, but certainly not to the extent they were fifty-odd years ago. Calls for further sexual freedom causes many—myself included—to wonder where it will all lead. The panic produced by the Cold War has long since disappeared, but to say that we are now fearless as a result is to deny the peril posed by militant Islamists. Is it politically correct to describe them as terrorists? Allow me to put it this way: Do they terrorize?

During the course of my lifetime so far, the world has been transformed beyond recognition. It would be naïve to imagine that all changes have been beneficial. While some unsavory traits have thankfully been consigned to the pages of history, legislation has allowed others to emerge to the surface where they previously were enjoyed only by a seedy minority behind locked doors. Other issues vanished for a while, such as nationalism, only shamelessly to reappear with precisely the same potential to divide and conquer. Through it all, the face of anti-Semitism grows ever uglier.

Will we ever learn?

Christmas here in the UK is a unique time of year: it's when bishops talk about politics, politicians talk about morality, and the Queen talks about Jesus. At the time of writing, we are facing the first December election in ninety-six years. Since its announcement, the public has been treated to an *à la carte* main course of fable, with a generous side order of fibs. Manifesto promises aside, the main issue is concerned with which party can deliver what the majority of the public wants regarding our formal association with the rest of Europe. One party will press ahead with Brexit, another has vowed to remain part of the EEC, while yet another pledges to hold a further referendum to allow the people to decide (four years after they had already done so). On this issue alone, the latter party would seem to have the upper hand. What might dissuade voters, however, is its recent history of perceived anti-Semitism.

The apparent re-emergence of anti-Semitism is a global concern. Whether that rise is commensurate with the world growth of Islam may well be a matter of conjecture, but it is one worth considering. It certainly cannot easily be dismissed. Surely those countries with a distinct Christian *ethos* should be able to provide something of a safe haven? It would seem that this has not always been the case, as we shall soon see. Before we press on, it might prove helpful to consider the term itself, under what circumstances it was first employed, and how the history of the church is often regarded by some as one of unbridled anti-Semitism.

Anti-Semitism can be defined as an act, expressed physically or orally, of hostility or oppression directed against Jews as a religious or racial group.

It is rooted in the belief of Jewish inferiority and, as such, is perhaps better described as anti-Jewish prejudice. Coined as recently as 1879, the phrase "anti-Semitism" originally designated the coordinated campaigns of resentment-fueled persecution of European Jews of the mid-to-late-nineteenth century. This is not to imply that acts befitting the description did not take place before that date. It has even been argued that anti-Semitism has always existed wherever and whenever Jews have lived outside of Palestine, though there is currently also a measure of it inside its borders.

One possible reason for this—though it can hardly be posited as a justifiable excuse—is the proclivity amongst Jewish people to opt for self-inflicted social segregation. This is hardly unique: it is often the way when a large people group with a shared history suddenly find themselves thrust together in alien territory. The significance here, however, is that the motivating factor is not cultural or, strictly speaking, ethnic, but religious. Whether in captivity during the Old Testament period or governed from afar in their homeland, sooner or later their perception of Yahweh's requirements of them as a covenant-keeping people would clash with the demands of the imperial power or social infrastructure (or both) to which they were expected to subject themselves.

Other nations that were similarly subordinate often found less difficulty in incorporating yet another "god" into their polytheistic pantheon. The *Shema* prayer dissuades true Israelites from such a comfortable passage: "Hear, O Israel: the Lord our God, the Lord is one. Love the Lord your God with all your heart and with all your soul and with all your strength" (Deut 6:4–5). Its importance can be seen in the instruction that follows:

> These commandments that I give you today are to be upon your hearts. Impress them on your children. Talk about them when you sit at home and when you walk along the road, when you lie down and when you get up. Tie them as symbols on your hands and bind them on your foreheads. Write them on the door frames of your houses and on your gates. (Deut 6:6–9)

Christianity and Judaism enjoy a shared heritage, though they rarely celebrate the fact. Acknowledgment (or refusal) of Jesus as God's promised Messiah has seen to that. When Pilate washed his hands of the responsibility for Jesus' death (Matt 27:24–25), the *de facto* outcome was that Jews were thereafter often branded as Christ killers. In the very infancy of the Christian church, its leading theologians were swift to elevate the status of this new spiritual Israel at the expense of the old natural Israel. So much so, in fact, that many advocated the position that God was now done with the Jews, since they had served their purpose of ushering in the arrival of God's promised world Savior. Their continued existence was not only an embarrassment to others, but it was widely regarded as an act of willful insolence on their part. Every misfortune that thence came their way was seen as a token of divine disfavor for their rejection and subsequent crucifixion of the Son of God. It is an alarmingly short step from Constantine's curtailment of Jewish freedoms to Hitler's death camps.

Forever a son

So, where does this leave natural Israel in the context of Ezekiel's prophetic vision? One of the key hermeneutical principles in our approach to any biblical teaching, prophecy, or instruction is to try and understand what it would have meant to its original audience or readership. For that, we need momentarily to step into the shoes of any one of Ezekiel's fellow exiles. Imagine that you are there by his side. As a member of the corporate body of God's people, you share the burden of divine discipline. God's glory has been removed from the temple and you have joined your compatriots in the tiresome and wearying journey into captivity. You are now resting on the grassless banks of the Kebar river. Its still, murky waters reflect the mood of everyone around you.

Many are sitting, exhausted more by the guilt that brought them hence than by the journey itself. Your captors, not content with the fact of their victory, continue to taunt you: "Where now your songs of joy?" they mock. Singing? For what prospect there is of ever having cause to sing again, you may as well cast all instruments aside (Ps 137:1–4). Acrimony gives way to anguish only for rancor and torment to succeed them both. Some are weeping as they remember the good old days and their own part in bringing about their end. All you have left are your memories, good and bad, yet even the bad are tinged with feint fondness—anything to cling to in the present that will postpone having to contemplate a forlorn and forsaken future.

But then a note of hope echoes from the lips of one man, Ezekiel. Promise after promise fills chapter 36: Israel's enemies will suffer scorn (Ezek 36:7), and Israel itself will once again be fruitful (Ezek 36:8–10), even more so than in former times (Ezek 36:12). For his own name's sake, the Lord will demonstrate his holiness to the unholy through his holy people (Ezek 36:22–23). Having been cleansed from impurity, Israel will be brought back to its own land (Ezek 36:24–25), there to receive "a new heart and . . . a new spirit" (Ezek 36:26), God's own Spirit. The basis of all this was the covenant relationship that existed between Israel and their God: "You will be my people and I will be your God " (Ezek 36:28b).

How could this possibly be? Well, if a picture (or parable) has the capacity to paint a thousand words, then God gave Ezekiel just the image to convey the truth of his promises to the people. There are many lessons we can glean from this passage concerning God's relationship with Israel at that time, some of which are more widely applicable. If we learn only one thing, then let it be to avoid making the same mistake as Israel's enemies: discipline is not synonymous with dismissal, nor is reprimand the same as rejection. From this side of the time divide, we know that chastisement is a token of divine sonship: "My son, do not make light of the Lord's discipline, and do not lose heart when he rebukes you, because the Lord disciplines those he loves, and he punishes everyone he accepts as a son" (Heb 12:5b–6; see also Rev 3:19a). But notice that the writer to the Hebrew Christians was quoting from a passage that would have been all too familiar to the readership's forbears: "My son, do not despise the Lord's discipline and do not resent his rebuke, because the Lord disciplines those he loves, as a father the son he delights in" (Prov 3:11–12). I doubt whether there is a Christian brother or sister reading this who has not, at one time or another, experienced God arresting their attention by means of some form of discipline. The writer to the Hebrews makes their intention clear: "[T]hat it might produce a harvest of righteousness and peace for those who have been trained by it" (Heb 12:11). Although presented here in a New Testament context, it seems highly unlikely that the same principle is not also annexed to the quotation's original usage.

God's word is trustworthy

However we may adapt or reinterpret Ezekiel's vision of the valley of dry bones to give it a contemporary Christian setting—and we are free to do so—let us not forget that God's direction to his prophet was that he should tell his people of that generation:

> I am going to open up your graves and bring you up from them; I will bring you back to the land of Israel. Then you, my people, will know that I am the Lord . . . I will put my Spirit in you and you will live, and I will settle you in your own land. Then you will know that I the Lord have spoken, and I have done it. (Ezek 37:12–14)

There is no indication anywhere in Scripture to suggest that this promise has been repealed. On the contrary, Paul reminds his readers in Rome of the glorious future God has in store for natural Israel:

> I do not want you to be ignorant of this mystery, brothers, so that you may not be conceited: Israel has experienced a hardening in part until the full number of the Gentiles has come in. And so all Israel will be saved, as it is written: "The deliverer will come from Zion; he will turn godlessness away from Jacob. And this is my covenant with them when I take away their sins." (Rom 11:25–27)

Paul was quite a guy. He had an uncanny knack of presenting truth in such a way that was perfectly suited to his target audience. On this occasion, he went for the "iron fist in a velvet glove" approach. Underlying the words: "I do not want you to be ignorant" is the intent: "Stop being stupid!" The inference is that to believe contrary to what follows would be folly. "All Israel," both natural and spiritual, "will be saved." Does this mean that the grounds for the salvation of natural Israel will be different from that of spiritual Israel? Absolutely not! Jesus remains "the way and the truth and the life," the sole means of access to the Father for all, without exception (John 14:6). Are those of a Jewish heritage thereby empowered to conduct themselves without either moral compass or repercussions for illicit behavior? No more so than they have ever been and no less so than any other covenant child of God.

So, in what way has the prophecy embraced within Ezekiel's vision of the valley of dry bones been "partially" fulfilled? We need first to look at the condition of the valley itself and the mountains either side that constitute the making of that valley. In the previous chapter, Ezekiel had been commanded to prophesy to the mountains of Israel. Their enemies had coveted them for their own, principally because of their extraordinary fertility. But the valley became a desert place and the mountains were devoid of growth during the period of foreign possession. This situation persisted for hundreds of years. Today, however, the mountains and valleys are once again a forest of arboriculture, as promised (Ezek 36:8). Moreover, the culmination of God's promise to Israel at the end of Ezekiel's vision of the valley of dry bones is given a little more detail in this earlier chapter (Ezek 36:9–12).

There is a principle of prophetic unfolding: "first the natural, then the spiritual" (see 1 Cor 15:46). I believe the natural fulfilment of Ezekiel's vision took place over seventy years ago when modern Israel was granted nationhood once more, on May 14, 1948. It is difficult not to recognize that event as a political resurrection. Their spiritual resurrection still awaits, though it remains as sure as God's promise.

(A Prophetic Cop-out?)

I would like to introduce something of a parenthesis here, by taking a brief look at Ezekiel's initial response to God's opening question, and then pose another of my own:

> The hand of the Lord was upon me, and he brought me out by the Spirit of the Lord and set me in the middle of the valley; it was full of bones. He led me to and fro among them, and I saw a great many bones on the floor of the valley, bones that were very dry. He asked me, "Son of man, can these bones live?" I said, "O Sovereign Lord, you alone know." (Ezek 37:1–3)

Interpreting the evidence

Most English translations omit the word "alone," opting simply for "O Lord God, you know" (e.g., NASB, KJV, ESV). Pardon my irreverence, and if this despoils your image of the holy prophets, then please forgive me again, but I always picture Ezekiel here with a cheeky grin and a twinkle of mirth in his one open eye, as he winks knowingly with the other. But my question is this: What do we make of Ezekiel's response? More specifically, what do we imagine motivated him to answer in the way he did? To simplify matters, allow me to proffer three possible solutions. Was Ezekiel's reply the product of:

i. skeptical unbelief;

ii. confused faith; or

iii. a clever abrogation of responsibility?

For many years, I assumed the latter, largely because I perceived something of Ezekiel's image in myself (or *vice versa*) and that is precisely what I would have done: created some sort of cunning non-answer that would betray neither my ignorance nor my lack of faith. Perhaps Ezekiel had a previous, unrecorded experience of embarrassment when faced with a similar line of questioning. The fact that it is unrecorded suggests we are not at liberty to speculate.

I have an unhealthy and apparently illogical suspicion of telecommunications devices. It all stems from a series of incidents as a small boy related only by their source, which led me to believe that the all-seeing, omniscient Being and our house telephone were one and the same. I would come home after playing with friends to see my grandfather standing beside the antiquated machine with a stern expression adorning his battle-hardened features. After a deep sigh: "What business had you in Mrs. Daniel's orchard this afternoon?" he would demand, his right hand already slipping toward the buckle end of his belt in a manner suggesting that honesty might well be the best policy. I was a mere conversational hop, skip, and a jump from regretting my earlier adventure. Or, "Straight to bed for you, my lad, and without any supper tonight or pocket money at the weekend; you've been throwing stones in the vicinity of the recently glazed windows on the new housing estate in the village."

How did it know? And just as importantly, what sinister pact existed between the phone and my grandad that compelled it to reveal all? As I grew older and just a little wiser, I learned two things in relation to all of this. First of all, Dean Hunter's dad owned a crimson version of our ivory model. Secondly, though evidence is vital in deducing the truth of a matter, a proper appraisal of that evidence is equally not to be sniffed at.

A pregnant pause

Now, I'm not so sure that Ezekiel was guilty of revoking his responsibility, as none of this really fits with what we may otherwise garner of his profile. At first glance, however, neither do the other two options. Time, I think, for a second glance, this time in the direction of the New Testament. By way of example, I want to draw your attention to two distinct, though not entirely unrelated, incidents at the beginning of Luke's Gospel account. The first concerns Zechariah the priest:

> Once when Zechariah's division was on duty and he was serving as priest before God, he was chosen by lot, according to the custom of the priesthood, to go into the temple of the Lord and burn incense. And when the time for the burning of incense came, all the assembled worshippers were praying outside. Then an angel of the Lord appeared to him, standing at the right side of the altar of incense. When Zechariah saw him, he was startled and was gripped with fear. But the angel said to him: "Do not be afraid, Zechariah; your prayer has been heard. Your wife Elizabeth will bear you a son, and you are to give him the name John." (Luke 1:8–13)

There then follows a lengthy and quite detailed account of the task to be undertaken by this promised forerunner of God's Christ (Luke 1:14–17). First of all, notice with me Zechariah's response: "How can this be? I am an old man and my wife is well on in years" (Luke 1:18). Now see the immediate consequences for Zechariah: "The angel answered . . . 'And now you will be silent and not able to speak until the day this happens, because you did not believe my words, which will come true at their proper time'" (Luke 1:19–20).

We need only to move on a few verses to arrive at our second example:

> In the sixth month [of Elizabeth's pregnancy], God sent the angel Gabriel to Nazareth, a town in Galilee, to a virgin pledged to be married to a man named Joseph, a descendant of David. The virgin's name was Mary. The angel went to her and said, "Greetings, you who are highly favored! The Lord is with you . . . Do not be afraid, Mary, you have found favor with God. You will be with child and give birth to a son, and you are to give him the name Jesus." (Luke 1:26–31)

There then follows a shorter and slightly less detailed account of what awaited the promised Messiah, to which Mary replied: "How will this be . . . since I am still a virgin" (Luke 1:34)? "How can I be sure of this?" and "How will this be?" Almost identical sentiments being expressed, you might think. And you would be correct: almost, but not quite. Look now at how Gabriel answered Mary: "The Holy Spirit will come upon you, and the power of the Most High will overshadow you. So the one to be born to you will be called the Son of God . . . For nothing is impossible with God" (Luke 1:35–37).

There are a number of comparisons to be made between the two incidents, but there are far more notes of contrast, this being one of them. Why is it that Zechariah was temporarily punished, while Mary received nothing more severe than a gracious explanation? Did the Almighty exercise more leniency toward Mary because of her relative inexperience? Was it because the shame brought about by her condition was regarded as sufficient for her to contend with? I remain unconvinced it was either.

At the risk of taking one too many detours, I believe the answer lies in God's response to Samuel when choosing Saul's successor from among the sons of Jesse: "The Lord does not look at the things man looks at. Man looks at the outward appearance, but the Lord looks at the heart" (1 Sam 16:7b). Having already made that mistake, you would think that Samuel would have learned how deceptive appearances can be without being further advised. But even with Scripture as our guide, can we guarantee that we would have conducted ourselves any differently?

During my time as an ambulance paramedic, I was temporarily seconded to a senior position at another station in the district. During my watch, I was called upon to investigate an allegation of gross misconduct against a patient by a crew member. The problem was that the party bringing the claim could not be conclusively sure which of the two-man crew was responsible. Before I had begun any examination of the evidence, I made a snap judgment based on what I otherwise knew of the two individuals, which was very little. Thankfully, I confided my suspicions in only one other person, who proved far more trustworthy than I had any right to expect. Together we engaged a due process of exploring the facts, and made our findings known to the appropriate panel for such grievances, who acted accordingly. I could quite easily have had the contract of an innocent colleague terminated.

A question of faith

The responses of Zechariah and Mary on the occasions cited reflected their heart condition at that time, and each was dealt with fittingly. William Hendriksen is in no doubt where he would place them:

> For [Zechariah's] reaction there was no excuse. It was definitely the response of unbelief . . . [his] response almost amounted to, "I don't believe you, for people as old as we are do not become parents" . . . Mary, on the other hand, is not guilty of lack of faith. She believes (see verse 45). But she is befuddled, bewildered, mystified. She has correctly interpreted the angel's message to mean that without the assistance of a husband she is about to conceive a child. So far so good. But how was this possible? Among humans conception without insemination was unheard of.[6]

Although I must acknowledge that Ezekiel's response was unlike that of either Zechariah or Mary, the motivation that lay behind it shared certain features with the latter. He, too, was "befuddled, bewildered, [and] mystified." But more than that, I believe there is also a hint of understanding for which Ezekiel is seldom given credit. Ezekiel, you may remember, probably fell into that uncommon category in the Old Testament of fulfilling both prophetic and priestly roles in Israel. As such, he will have been well-versed in the Hebrew Scriptures. I find it difficult to read his reply to God's question without thinking also of those verses that speak of God's self-appraisal as the ultimate source of life, and I seriously doubt whether Ezekiel would have been any less attentive: "See now that I myself am He! There is no god beside me. I put to death and I bring to life, I have wounded and I heal, and nobody can deliver out of my hand" (Deut 32:39)[7]

---

6. Hendriksen, *Luke*, 74, 88.
7. See also 1 Sam 2:6; Isa 45:7.

Of course, it could equally be argued that Zechariah should have been just as mindful. The narrative demonstrates that perhaps he was less alert than he might have been, however, for he had clearly forgotten how God had fulfilled a similar promise to Abram. Abram, too, had questioned God, but his "How can I know?" (Gen 15:8) was akin to that of Mary, whereby his faith—such that it was (Gen 15:6)—required strengthening. Calvin even goes so far as to suggest that Abram's "questioning with God is rather a proof of faith, than a sign of incredulity."[8] Given faith's primary determinant factor (2 Cor 5:17), I am not persuaded by Calvin's argument on this occasion, as Abram heard God's word directly. I think Derek Kidner is nearer the mark, where he compares Abram here to the father who cried out for Jesus' healing touch on behalf of his demoniac son (Mark 9:14-29):

> Abram's "how am I to know . . . ?" reveals the strain he was under, for his faith was nothing facile: its spirit was that of "Lord, I believe, help thou my unbelief"; not that of Zacharias's retort in Luke 1:8, for it earned no rebuke, only reassurance.[9]

To be lacking in sufficient faith and to be devoid of faith are not the same thing at all; neither is beyond remedy, though one is more easily attained than the other. However, a distinction must also be made between forgetfulness and ignorance. Zechariah was certainly not lacking in knowledge. Like Abram before him and Mary afterwards, Ezekiel was bereft of neither understanding nor faith. But we must remember that, at the time of the question, God had not yet given a word of promise to which Ezekiel's faith could be applied; it was merely a matter of possibility: "Can these bones live?" In purely human terms, the answer could only have been a resounding "No!" Even allowing for God's omnipotence, the most Ezekiel could have mustered would have been: "Maybe; it all depends upon your will, and you have yet to disclose it." Isn't this pretty much what he did say: "O Sovereign Lord, you alone know"?

It is also important that we do not separate the symbol from that which it was designed to signify, wherein the comparison was surely well made. For this, we need to consider not so much the possibility as the probability of each event. Thus, are we not forced to conclude that the likelihood of Israel's restoration was on par with the reanimation of the "very dry" bones that Ezekiel beheld? Of the three alternatives I proffered earlier, we almost immediately dismissed any notion of skeptical unbelief on the part of Ezekiel. Having owned a previous inclination to believe him guilty of a little

---

8. Calvin, *Genesis*, 411.
9. Kidner, *Genesis*, 135.

cunning, I admitted my folly in that regard, too. Now, all of a sudden, even the evidence that accuses him of confused faith is beginning to look more than a trifle flimsy.

I find that many modern commentators are too eager to consign Ezekiel to the naughty step for his reply in this one instance. A latter-day diet of triumphalism can shape one's thinking in that way. But Ezekiel was guilty of neither refutation nor revocation: he was simply conveying, in the only way he knew, his recognition that the accomplishing of something so astonishing resided exclusively in the gift of his God. Oh, that we might be more similarly disposed!

Reinvigorate Us, O Lord

So, where does all this leave us? Before we rush headlong into a misapplication of the text to any and every situation that we feel requires a reversal from demise, desolation, or decline, we must understand precisely what is going on here. Words that are often employed to describe the scene in the valley are resurrection, restoration, and revival. They are all valid terms, but not without further qualification. The Hebrew word *rua'h* appears nine times in the opening fourteen verses of Ezekiel's thirty-seventh chapter. It may not be so obvious in our English translations, because it is variously translated as wind, breath, or spirit; it is, in fact, the life-giving breath of God.

Defining the terms

The prefix "re-" conveys the meaning of "to do something again," that something being defined by the verb it precedes, often with the design of bringing the object back to a former condition. This is why, in my opinion, great numbers of people becoming Christians in a specific location over a relatively short period of time is the product of revival, rather than revival itself; we may only anticipate the revival of that which has previously enjoyed the blessing of God's invigorating Spirit or breath. *Dry* bones become that way after a prolonged period of absence of life. This is true both naturally and spiritually.

It might also aid our appreciation of the contrast between life and death if we allowed our understanding to be shaped more by the Spirit of God than by the spirit of the age. Metaphorically speaking, if a friend describes their experience of a church they visited on vacation as being dead, what sort of image does that present in your mind? Unfriendly? Lacking in warmth? Prescriptive? Non-experimental? Deficient in both vision and direction? Staid? So cold you feel you could almost skate down the aisles? What if they had said it was a lively church? How do you picture it now? Vibrant? Welcoming? Focused? Relevant?

I can think of many local gatherings that would fit either description, but are any of the adjectives employed appropriate for the types of churches to which we assign them? For example, what do we mean by saying that a church is relevant? Relevant to whom? The community it seeks to serve? The whims and wants of an immature congregation? My friend's needs as a one-time visitor who is prepared to invest no more than that ninety minutes on a particular Sunday morning when he happens to be in the area? That church—or any other church, for that matter—has an obligation only to maintain its relevance to the word of God and to follow the flow of the Spirit of God at any given time. Similarly, when we say that it is vibrant, do we mean only that sinners who are prepared to transfer their weekend night club mentality to a Sunday morning can have a seamless transition, without being made to feel too uncomfortable, and the worship leader is regarded as little more than a deejay for the redeemed?

To the manor reborn

It is difficult to imagine anyone having more cause to be animated than our first parents before the Fall. To suggest that they were less than perfect because of their capacity to sin ignores the fact that, unlike everyone since, they also had the capability not to sin. Their perfection consisted at least partially in that choice being a real one. What is irrefutable is the fact that Adam—again, quite like no other after him—enjoyed the *rua'h* of God in his lungs: "The Lord God formed the man from the dust of the ground and breathed into his nostrils the breath of life, and the man became a living being" (Gen 2:7). Girdlestone has the following to say:

> As long as this breath is sustained in a man, he lives (Job 27:3); when it goes forth, he returns to his earth (Ps 146:4). The most remarkable passage in which the action of breath and wind is identified with the source of life is the vision of the dry bones in Ezek 37. In this, as in some other passages, it is not easy to distinguish between the physical and the superphysical breath, both of which are gifts from God.[10]

It is the breath of God that resides in all human beings and, thus, gives them life. With a solitary exception, nobody since Adam has experienced that

---

10. Girdlestone, *Synonyms*, 74–75.

breath outside of a sin-conditioned body. The reviving of those who had experienced life, but are currently spiritually dead, is reminiscent of Jesus' imperative command to Nicodemus: "You must be born again" (John 3:7b). Words that are familiar to every Christian I know—even those who have known Jesus only a matter of days. But has their familiarity robbed us also of a little understanding?

There are some important lessons to be gleaned from this episode, but they do not become clear to us by isolating texts from their context. Again, there are both comparisons and contrasts to be made. In terms of natural birth, there is very little involvement by the one to be born except just that: to be born. It might well be argued that during the nine-month process of incubation, the fetus engages with the host mother's provision to ensure that when the day arrives, the birth itself is as uncomplicated as possible. In retrospect, the period immediately preceding my spiritual birth was one in which I met certain conditions that paved the way for a singular act of accepting Christ on September 20, 1976. It, too, was a period of some months, during which the Spirit of God precipitated crisis after crisis, so that I would desperately seek a solution to my ills. My ignorance was hardly blissful, but I was entirely unaware of what was happening at the time.

For the starkest of contrasts, we need backtrack only one verse: "Flesh gives birth to flesh, but Spirit gives birth to spirit" (John 3:6). Some have interpreted this to mean nothing more significant than that the circumstances of one's physical birth afford the subject no favor in relation to salvation. This, of course, is true and should certainly be included in our deliberations. But I believe it points to a far more meaningful principle of (re-)generation: "Then God said, 'Let the land produce vegetation: seed bearing plants and trees on the land that bear fruit with seed in it, according to their various kinds'" (Gen 1:11). Thereafter, the whole of the creation process adopted this law of reproducing after its own kind (see Gen 1:12, 21, 24–25). Regeneration is no different: sinful human nature can only ever produce after its own kind, however well intentioned. But so, too, the Holy Spirit can never initiate anything that is devoid of his own essence.

Believing is seeing

Retreat a few verses further still and we find a startling declaration: "[N]o-one can see the kingdom of God unless he is born again" (John 3:3), says Jesus. The English translation leads us toward a single conclusion that may not be in keeping with the original intent. Accurate identification of these three component parts is vital to our understanding. We have seen that to be born again is to be given birth by God's Spirit, necessarily subsequent to our natural birth (see also John 3:5). I have also pointed out elsewhere that the kingdom of God is essentially the rule of God in action.[11] Although this is unrestricted in both locus and extent, our knowledge of it is at best limited to personal encounters and corporate experiences. But is this what Jesus had in mind by his use of the verb to "see"? In other words, was he saying that without this new birth, the experience of or an encounter with God's kingdom rule is beyond anyone, because it doesn't otherwise exist for that person? Or, that without the condition of new birth having been met, it is impossible to perceive the rule of God in action even where it does exist?

I indicated earlier that in the immediate prelude to me coming to Christ, I was entirely unaware of what was happening in the heavenly realm. I knew that I had no explanation for some of the things that were beginning to take shape, both in actual events and the way I was beginning to think about those things. But my ignorance of them did not negate their existence or that of their source. In fact, I can now point to much of the sixteen years prior to me becoming a Christian where the kingdom rule of God was very much in evidence, but my appreciation of it only surfaced after my rebirth had taken place.

Because of the realms to which each belongs, natural life and spiritual life (in the contexts under consideration) are not necessarily co-terminous, the one extending beyond the temporal reach of the other into eternity. Ezekiel's vision of the valley of dry bones demonstrates that they are also not mutually co-dependent, though they each share the same source of dependency. The same cannot always be said of their fruit. The products of natural life cannot help but be despoiled by sin, even if such tainting amounts to no more than diminished understanding or perspective.

Reawakening the past to good effect

But what of spiritual fruit? We know that the honorable bearing of fruit on earth is of potentially great benefit in eternity, but the sowing and reaping principle demands that the seed of it is also of value in the temporal realm. Allow me to be more specific: That which has its origin in God, but now shows signs only of death and decay, can it be revived? Let me be more explicit still: Can dead dreams live?

Before I answer in the affirmative (which I will), let us be quite clear that the "dreams" in question are those of divine origin; they come from a good God, not a bad cheese, much less from wishful thinking or youthful

---

11. Woodall, *Kingdom*, x.

exuberance. I thank God that the "dream" he gave me almost forty years ago and I thought had died was given life again and continues to grow, bearing its own fruit. I am equally grateful that he quickly put to death a great number of fantasies that were born of my own sinful nature, though dressed in the garb of religious hypocrisy.

How can we know the difference? It requires faith, but maybe not in the way you have been led to believe. Faith doesn't allow circumstance to determine what we know to be true in God. That is not unreasonable. If anything, it is *supra*-reasonable. When you know, you know that you know; when you don't know, you only think that you do. As I write this, we are approaching Christmas. My wife has spent all year making a whisky advent calendar for me. Each 50 cl bottle is unlabeled, enclosed in a red drawstring bag, with a number stamped on the screw top, ranging from one to twenty-four. On a miniature Christmas tree beside them are pegged twenty-four labels, each stamped with a letter (A–X). A typed list has twenty-four single malt whiskies named with a corresponding letter. My task each day—arduous as it may be—is to identify what I think that day's offering is by placing a letter tag around the neck of the bottle I have most recently emptied.

So far, I have done quite well; certainly better than many Christians of my acquaintance deem appropriate. Some of this, I must confess, has been down to a process of elimination. Yesterday was the half-way point. Of the thirteen names left, I could be sure that what I had just drunk was not eleven of them, so on the spin of a coin . . . For the most part, however, I have either known or thought that I did. I have not committed to any where I only thought I knew which one it was.

Some Christian friends, even leaders, will try to convince us that such doubts need to be overcome by faith. Those who do so are guilty of treating faith as a mechanism for mind over matter, which is utterly alien to the biblical presentation of how faith comes (Rom 10:17). If you have heard and God has not spoken, then you have heard a different voice, perhaps no more sinister than your own imagination, but another voice nonetheless.

But what if God has, indeed, spoken? You received the promise with immediate gratitude, but then things didn't work out exactly as you had imagined—or as quickly. So disillusioned did you become by the fact that nobody seemed to recognize your obvious gift, that invitations didn't flow, that people weren't overawed by your capacity to give meaningful insight to the most otherwise insipid of texts that the dream was in danger of becoming something of a nightmare. What you do next will determine what becomes of the dream and whether or not it will one day be in need of restoration. Do you abandon it altogether in favor of something that will attract more instant recognition or do you re-evaluate precisely what it is that you claim to have heard?

Often, the latter is all that is required, while the former reveals that you are nowhere near ready, even if the dream is genuinely attributed. The danger with dreams and visions of this nature (and prophecy, too, for that matter) is that we allow our imagination to run farther than the revelation given. Perhaps we don't think others would be as excited as they should be, so we embellish the facts a little. Sometimes it might even be that the unveiling to us precedes the unfolding of events to which they relate by weeks, months, or even years. As one who had been given such a dream in my early twenties, I shortly thereafter listened to a preacher speak on the life of Moses. He divided it into three periods of around forty years each (see Acts 7:23, 30, 36) and emphasized how many years elapsed between God's promise to him and its fulfilment. I remember getting quite shirty afterwards and telling everyone who would listen that I wouldn't need to wait forty years. I was right; I waited twenty-five. And when it came, I wasn't thrust into the limelight, thank God!

Playing our part

So, is there anything we can do to precipitate the resurrection of apparently dead dreams? Although I have personal experience on which to draw, thankfully there are also a number of biblical examples willing to lend support. Jacob (Gen 28:10-15; 31:10-13), Solomon (1 Kgs 3:5-15), Daniel (Dan 7:1-14), and even Joseph, Jesus' father by proxy, received confirmation of the task before him by virtue of a divinely appointed dream (Matt 1:20-21). But it is another Joseph to whom our minds almost involuntarily turn when we link dreams with biblical characters. Here is what the Psalmist had to say of Israel's favorite son:

> [God] sent a man before [his people]—Joseph, sold as a slave.
> They bruised his feet with shackles, his neck was put in irons, till
> what he foretold came to pass, till the word of the Lord proved
> him true. (Ps 105:17-19)

Welcome to *Dreamland*, Joseph! At first glance, that concluding section appears to be a repeating couplet, typical of Hebraic poetry. On this occasion, however, perhaps the Amplified Bible gives a rendering closer to the original: "Until [Joseph's] word [to his cruel brothers] came true, the word of the Lord tried and tested him." Is there anything we can do to co-operate? How about the following:

- don't boast to all and sundry; rather, confide only in those who are known to be trustworthy and who have perhaps seen a dream of their own come to fruition;
- don't try to run away; it is futile and serves only to prolong the process;
- expect obstacles; that way, you won't be disappointed when they come along;
- allow God to work things out according to his plan and timescale;
- remain faithful in all things, not just those that are instantly recognizable as contributing toward the realization of the dream;
- don't try to negotiate with God for what you currently perceive to be a more attractive dream;
- in conjunction with the above, don't envy the dream of another;
- seek to serve those whose dream is being fulfilled;
- recognize God's purpose in all things; nothing is entirely pointless;
- don't jump to ill-advised preconceptions or hasty conclusions; the damage they have the potential to cause is more far-reaching than your own little bubble;
- practise today for tomorrow; the fulfilment of the dream will materialize from what you are doing when the time is right for it to be unveiled; and
- cultivate an attitude of respect and interdependency with others.

Summary

Ezekiel's vision of the valley of dry bones is a classic example of the preacher's favorite sermon. Our familiarity with it can often mask the richness of its content. How often I have heard the text announced, knowing full well that what followed its reading would invariably be an exhortation for the church to arise Phoenix-like from its dormancy to become more vibrant, more evangelistic, more socially conscious, more charitable, and—above all else—more concerned that the minister's stipend accurately reflects the fact that "the laborer is worthy of his hire" (Luke 10:7; 1 Tim 5:17–18)! While none of these are entirely invalid, neither do I believe that they should necessarily be at the forefront of our thinking whenever we are reminded of what Ezekiel saw.

The votes of the UK General Election I mentioned earlier have now been counted, and it turned out to be significant in a number of ways. Apart from being the first December election for almost a century, the controlling party gained its highest majority for over thirty years, while those now required to form a Shadow cabinet suffered their heaviest defeat in living memory, losing control of some seats held since the year of my mother's birth. Some have pointed to the unpopularity of Labour's leader as a major contributing factor, while others argued that it was the absurdity of their pre-election manifesto promises. Millions of pounds were to be pumped into every enterprise imaginable as if some magic money tree had been discovered. "Impossible!" the electorate cried, with almost one voice.

Some of the dreams God gives us can appear that way. Unlike the leader of the opposition party, "with God all things are possible" (Matt 19:26b). The impossible dream you only recently abandoned for your staunchly atheist parent or partner to come to Christ, or for your rebellious teenage child to rediscover the faith of their earlier years, or for the long-desired pregnancy that will not come, are all presently consigned to the valley of dry and drying bones. Two questions with which to conclude, and the first is as important as the second: Has God spoken concerning them? If so, can these bones live?

5

Daniel

HISTORICAL BACKGROUND

Just as Ezekiel's ministry among the exiles in Babylon mirrored that of Jeremiah back in Judah, so that of Daniel coincided with them both in the temple courts of their overlords. Daniel's uniqueness as a major prophet, however, lies primarily in the fact that he saw both the beginning and the end of the seventy-year exile (see Dan 1:4; 10:1). He was a resident in the land of Judah's exile under four important rulers and during two world empires: Nebuchadnezzar (605–562 BC) and Belshazzar (553–539), of the Babylonians; and Darius and Cyrus (539–530), of the Medo-Persians.

There are a number of things to note from these dates (or lack thereof). First of all, the years between 562 and 553 BC were largely filled with a succession of kings, Evil-Merodach (562–560), Neriglissar (560–556), and Labashi-Marduk (556). None of these played a role significant enough to merit mention by Daniel, or at least, not in the context of his purpose for writing. The last of these was only a child when he succeeded to his father's throne and was murdered nine months later in a courtly conspiracy that saw a change of dynastic rule for Babylon.

The main beneficiaries of this collusion were Nabonidus and his son, Belshazzar. Nabonidus immediately took the throne in 556 BC, but his archaeological interests (especially as they related to the moon god, Sin) took him to Tayma in modern-day Saudi Arabia, leaving Belshazzar to rule in his stead until around 542. At this point, Nabonidus returned to the Babylonian court, but it is unclear precisely what role was performed and by whom for the three remaining years of his reign. Indeed, if such uncertainty was experienced at the time, then it would not be implausible to suggest that this played a part in Babylon's downfall at the hands of the Medo-Persians.

It would be remiss of me simply to airbrush the rulership of Darius the Mede without at least passing comment. The reader will notice that I have failed to ascribe any dates to his reign. This is not an oversight. The fact cannot be disguised that, outside of the biblical record, there is no conclusive reference to such an individual. This in itself would not necessarily be problematic. After all, arguments made from silence are at best posited with extreme caution. The world has been filled with lives and events for which there is no extant historical documentation. But we are dealing here with one who allegedly ruled arguably the most significant empire of its age. Let us at least consider the possibilities.

We must first look at the only evidence we have of the man, all gleaned from the book of Daniel: he was the son of Ahasuerus (that is, Xerxes; Dan 9:1), assumed rulership of Babylon on the death of Belshazzar at the age of sixty-two (Dan 5:30–31), was known by the regnal title (Dan 6:6–25), and the Babylonian calendar at this time was annexed to that reign (Dan 11:1). There are those who deny the existence of this Darius altogether, the less hostile being prepared to concede that Daniel's account must be a muddled amalgamation of traditions. What a bizarre cocktail of confusion and elaborate detail that would be! At the other extreme, some are so insistent on the verbatim representation of Scripture as it stands that every other historical account must thus be flawed. I am of the opinion that the truth of the matter lies somewhere between the two.

One such theory is that Darius the Mede was, in fact, Cyrus the Great. This would account for the apparent smoothness of transition (in dates, at least) between the reigns of Belshazzar and the other Cyrus. Cyrus the Great was also around the age attributed to Darius the Mede. He was not, however, the son of Ahasuerus, unless this was a royal ascription with a non-literal meaning. If so, it is otherwise unknown. It is also claimed, however, that Cyrus was the maternal grandson of the Median king, Astyages, though this is as unverifiable as claims attached to other theories. What is also beyond our understanding is why Daniel would choose to identify the same person by two different names. It would not be an uncommon device, but there seems to be no immediately obvious reason for doing so. Moreover, they are each listed by their ancestry, Darius the Mede (Dan 5:31; 11:1) and Cyrus the Persian (6:28), sometimes in close proximity.

Another possibility is that the man known to Daniel as Darius the Mede was Cyrus' appointed governor-general over Babylon, an official otherwise known as Gubaru.[1] This also presents as many difficulties as it seeks to resolve, though they are all related to a lack of supporting testimony rather than conflicting evidence. He was not a king but he could have been known locally by this title in recognition of his proxy status (i.e., royal authority was invested in him); we do not know that his age was around sixty, but it could have been; we do not know that he was a son of Ahasuerus, but we have nothing to suggest that he was not. Even if he was not, the same condition could apply as mentioned above under Cyrus. What we do know is that this Gubaru (Greek *Gobryas*) both had the authority to appoint subgovernors and that he took advantage of such authorization.

Suggestions based on a work by the fourth-century BC Greek philosopher-historian, Xenophon, that Darius was the throne name of Cyaxares II fall foul of precisely the same objections as Daniel's account: there is no evidence of Cyaxares' existence outside of this one source. So, whodunnit? Well, any defense counsellor might reasonably expect their client to be acquitted on the basis of such fragile evidence, relying as it does on so much suspicion and supposition. But that wouldn't necessarily render them innocent. It is unlikely that we shall ever be able to say for certain who Darius the Mede was, nor is it necessarily vital to our understanding of the text of Daniel, except insofar that it might impinge upon any claim to inerrancy. That notwithstanding, however, the apocalyptic nature of Daniel's writing makes that our primary concern. What I will add is that no inference may be drawn from the text of an independent Median overthrow of Babylon prior to its own takeover by Persian forces. Beyond that, all I am able to conclude is voiced pretty well by Joyce Baldwin:

> While it is true that the identity of Darius cannot be established for sure on the present state of our knowledge, there is too much evidence of him as a person in history for its total rejection. It will no longer do to dismiss him as fiction.[2]

PERSONAL BACKGROUND

The name Daniel means "God is my judge." This particular Daniel was probably born of noble beginnings during the reign of King Josiah. His birth most likely coincided with Josiah's reform policy, around 622 BC. From

---

1. See Whitcomb, *Darius the Mede*, 8.
2. Baldwin, *Daniel*, 32.

such an encouraging start to life, things soon began to decline, and he was amongst the first wave of exiles taken by Nebuchadnezzar into Babylon as a teenager in 605. What may at first have seemed like an irrevocable downward spiral—and actually was for many of his compatriots—began to plateau for Daniel; some might even say that he experienced a steady uplifting of fortunes.

As far as we are able to tell, Daniel remained close to the court throughout the whole of the seventy-year exile, occupying a number of senior government positions in an advisory role. That he was regarded so highly is as much a testament to the grace of God with him during such inauspicious a time for the covenant people as it was to Daniel's natural sagacity. Scripture itself provides a sterling appraisal of the man, speaking of him in nothing but positive terms. One of his fellow exiles cites Daniel on three separate occasions as an example of righteousness (Ezek 14:14, 20; 28:3), while he also earns the heavenly recognition of one who was "highly esteemed" (Dan 9:23; 10:11, 19).

I have already mentioned that Daniel's primary focus was his fellow Jews, not just in exile, but also at court. Subsidiary to this, but no less real, was his evangelistic effort directed toward the Babylonians themselves. An example of this might be that, despite being compulsorily renamed Belteshazzar (i.e., "prince of [the pagan god] Bel"), Daniel continued to identify himself with his given name, thus recognizing Yahweh as the source of his wisdom. But his voice was heard not just because of the words he chose or the fine-sounding arguments he employed. Rather, it was Daniel's character that paved the way. Meticulous and methodical, he was trusted because he had shown himself to be trustworthy; he was listened to because his words had proved to be true; he was generally looked upon with kindness because in him was acknowledged a tender civility in his dealings with others.

Because of his experiences, especially those that were fraught with danger, we immediately think of Daniel as a man of extreme courage: "Dare to be a Daniel, dare to stand alone." It is an easy assumption to make, but would it be an accurate one? I'm not entirely convinced. Of what I am certain is that any fears he may have had were met with faith, any qualms or reservations about meeting danger head on were overcome by a more urgent desire to place himself unreservedly in the hands of his covenant God. He was not so much compulsive as compelled. Even his unwavering commitment to the Law of Moses was no mere ritual (Dan 1:8), but a recognition that in so doing he was honoring the decrees of Yahweh. In fact, so unblemished was his character that the only way his enemies could cause him to "stumble" was to create a law with which his religious dedication found itself in direct contravention (Dan 6:4–5).

This personal background for Daniel assumes the integrity of Scripture's presentation. That is always my position and I make no apology for it. However, objections based on reasoned arguments cannot utterly be ignored. The principal dispute invariably involves the date of writing. This may be further subdivided into those who insist on a later date based on the internal linguistic evidence and those who do so as an expression of their opposition to the idea of such detailed long-term prediction. Let us take a brief look at both in turn.

First of all, the book of Daniel is comprised essentially of two languages: Hebrew and Aramaic, with around twenty words borrowed from other sources in the case of the latter. Why the author chose not to consistently employ one language is not particularly relevant to the question of dating, but I believe it was a reflection of the different intended target audiences. Fluctuations in the Hebrew are so minimal and developed so slowly as to render it impossible to date with any accuracy (or to contradict a dating on its basis).

Aramaic is known to have been widely used as early as the ninth-century BC, and was recognized as the official language of the Persian empire. However, it was previously thought that changes in Aramaic were more easily detectable and some words used by Daniel were not known until some time later. For this reason, it was posited that the book of Daniel must belong to around the second or third-century BC at the earliest. More recent studies refute this in the light of archaeological evidence from other sources.[3] They do not confirm the earlier date for Daniel, but no longer can they rule it out with such flagrant dogmatism.[4] Joyce Baldwin concludes thus:

> It is becoming an accepted fact that the date of Daniel cannot be decided on linguistic grounds. And that the increasing evidence does not favour a second-century, western origin.[5]

Arguments against an earlier dating based on incredulity toward prediction would presumably also apply to other Old Testament prophets, but this appears not to be the case; or, at least, not with the same degree of venom as in relation to Daniel. There is also some inconsistency in the armory of those who contest the earlier dating: the latest they lay claim to is around 165 BC, though a widely accepted interpretation of the "prophetic" fourth beast, "terrifying and frightening and very powerful" (Dan 7:7–8),

---

3. See Seboek, *Current Trends*, 400–403.
4. Wiseman, et al, *Notes on Some Problems*, 31–79.
5. Baldwin, *Daniel*, 39.

would still leave Rome's ascendancy a hundred years in the future. Even the decisive Battle of Corinth was almost twenty years away.

It would be both incorrect and misleading to suggest that only those who are hostile toward the Christian message oppose an earlier dating for the book of Daniel. Equally, it cannot be overlooked that there was no doubt cast until the third-century AD by the neo-Platonist philosopher, Porphyry. That his attack featured in the twelfth of a fifteen-volume series entitled *Against Christians* is perhaps no accident. Porphyry's target was not Daniel, *per se*. He probably reasoned that if he could demonstrate a flaw in this strategic pillar of the Christian faith, then the whole infrastructure upon which it was perceived to be built (i.e., Old Testament prophecy) would crumble. Moreover, if sufficient uncertainty could be brought to bear upon Daniel's claim to sixth-century BC authorship, then the shadow of that doubt would fall also on the one who bore witness to such a "pretender" (see Matt 24:15; Mark 13:14).

OVERVIEW

Chapters 1–6: Daniel's Personal Experiences

Introduction (chapter 1)

As is the case in many works of this size, chapter 1 acts as a prologue for all that follows. Much of the information we have regarding the author is contained here. Daniel's background and circumstances are introduced to us, including his initial rise to prominence in the esteemed circles with which he would become familiar while in captivity. Here at the outset, we are struck by Daniel's resolve to honor his God by choosing to abstain from Babylon's luxuries, if he could not partake with a clear conscience (Dan 1:8–16). It is unclear from the text whether such delicacies contravened Jewish food laws or if they had previously been offered to idols; what matters is the commitment of Daniel and his friends to their covenantal responsibilities, for which they were rewarded (Dan 1:17–19).

Nebuchadnezzar's dream (chapter 2)

Nebuchadnezzar's challenge to the wise men in his realm seems more than a little unfair (Dan 2:5). The only apparent explanation is just how troubled the dream had made him (Dan 2:3); we see a little later precisely how susceptible he was to mental disturbance. Amazingly, however, Daniel is blessed with details both of the dream and its interpretation (Dan 2:19), the result being his further elevation in the provincial court (Dan 2:48). Daniel's role is not dissimilar to that experienced by Joseph in Pharaoh's court (see Gen 41:1–3), but the events spoken of here are not of the immediate future; they relate to the unfolding course of world history over the next six hundred years.

Confidence in God (chapter 3)

One of the problems I have discovered with genuine revelation is the tendency by some to honor the subject or site of that revelation, rather than the One who unveils such things. Jesus was confronted with the same kind of mindset after the Transfiguration (Luke 9:28–33). Shrines and idols are not so unalike. The difference on this occasion was that Nebuchadnezzar's rashness was potentially costly for others (Dan 3:6). There is no evidence that Shadrach, Meshach, and Abednego were sole abstainers from amongst the Jews; only that they were the ones named by the authorities (Dan 3:8–12). Nor was there any guarantee that their faithfulness toward Yahweh would save them (Dan 3:17–18).

Another dream, another place (chapter 4)

Nebuchadnezzar's second dream to be recorded by Daniel is more personal in nature than the first. Moreover, it is fulfilled twelve months after having been dreamed (Dan 4:28–33). If the dream itself was worrying enough, then the interpretation will have served only to compound Nebuchadnezzar's alarm. But not, it would seem, of sufficient intensity to cause him to heed Daniel's warning (Dan 4:24–30). Only the predicted boanthropic experience and subsequent restoration would cause Nebuchadnezzar to "praise and exalt and glorify the King of heaven" (Dan 4:37). His words indicate due reverence, even if the context seems to fall some way short of true repentance (Dan 4:36).

The writing is on the wall (chapter 5)

The narrative now moves forward apace, to the co-regency of father and son, Nabonidus and Belshazzar. Daniel was no longer a young man, but his wisdom and reputation have remained perfectly intact (Dan 5:10–12). When called upon to succeed where others had failed (Dan 5:8), he did not disappoint (Dan 5:25-28). Belshazzar's sin had been that of his ancestor (Dan 5:18-23). He, therefore, had Nebuchadnezzar's example from history as a warning, but failed to give it heed (Dan 5:22). No other notice would be forthcoming. Before the night was out, Belshazzar was dead (Dan 5:30). His demise brought with it also the end of the Babylonian empire (Dan 5:28).

No Sunday school outing (chapter 6)

How the images of boyhood stay with you! And how utterly devoid of accuracy they often are! I can still see the impression in my mind of a strapping juvenile surrounded by lions. Except by now, Daniel is probably in his eighties. Not as agile as he once was, perhaps, but every bit as much an asset to the royal household (Dan 6:3), and every ounce as big a nuisance to those who envied the high regard with which he was held (Dan 6:4). Scripture is not short of accounts whereby the enemies of God's people set a trap only to find themselves hoisted by their own petard (see also Esth 7:9-10; Dan 3:22). Daniel persisted to place his trust in God (Dan 6:10), and God continued to deliver Daniel from danger (Dan 6:24).

Chapters 7-12: Daniel's Prophetic Visions

Four beasts (chapter 7)

Although the imagery is quite different, those things symbolized are precisely the same here as in Nebuchadnezzar's earlier dream:

Chapter 2	Chapter 7	Identification	Commencement
Head of gold	Lion	Babylon	Contemporary
Chest and arms of silver	Bear	Medo-Persia	539 BC
Belly and thighs of bronze	Leopard	Greece	330 BC
Legs of iron and feet of iron and clay	Terrifying beast	Rome	63 BC

There is one notable addition in each case:

> In the time of those kings, the God of heaven will set up a kingdom that will never be destroyed, nor will it be left to another people. It will crush all those kingdoms and bring them to an end, but it will itself endure for ever. (Dan 2:44)

> In my vision at night I looked, and there before me was one like a son of man, coming with the clouds of heaven. He approached the Ancient of Days and was led into his presence. He was given authority, glory and sovereign power; all peoples, nations and men of every language worshipped him. His dominion is an everlasting dominion that will not pass away, and his kingdom is one that will never be destroyed. (Dan 7:13–14)

The ram and the goat (chapter 8)

The ram and the goat of chapter 8 are widely recognized to correspond to the bear and the leopard of chapter 7. They, therefore, represent Medo-Persia and Greece, respectively. The change in language from Aramaic back to Hebrew suggests a switch of emphasis to Israel's position as the remnant people of God under these two empires. The unfolding of historical events demonstrates a remarkable accuracy of detail. Anyone even remotely acquainted with the period will be able to identify the big players: the Medo-Persian empire (Dan 8:3a, 20), Persia's dominance signified by the longer horn (Dan 8:3b); the emergence of Greece, led by Alexander the Great (Dan 8:5–7, 21); the division of the Greek empire upon Alexander's death between his four principal generals (Dan 8:8, 22); the rise of Antiochus Epiphanes (Dan 8:9, 23), who was responsible for the desecration of the Jewish Temple (Dan 8:11, 24), thus provoking the Maccabean revolt in 167 BC which, in turn, led to the reconsecration of the Temple (Dan 8:14).

Seventy weeks (chapter 9)

Although the bulk of this chapter is concerned with Daniel's prayer on behalf of God's people, it closes with a heavenly response: Gabriel being sent with further revelation. Daniel, realizing that the seventy-year exile was approaching its end, besought the Almighty for his people's deliverance. What he received in return was insight into a divine timetable of events where the number seventy also featured prominently. This would culminate in a deliverance of an altogether different kind: far greater in magnitude, far broader in scope, and of inestimably more significance than merely temporal—the coming of Messiah (Dan 8:25).

What follows is familiar territory for twenty-first century Christians; it would not have been so for Daniel's original Jewish audience. "The Anointed One will be cut off" (Dan 8:26—literally, suffer a violent death under sentence)? Surely not! Remember, they did not have the advantage of the early disciples: "unless a grain of wheat falls to the ground and dies, it remains only a single seed. But if it dies . . . " (John 12:24).

Conflicting kingdoms (chapters 10–12)

Daniel's final vision gives further details about that period of Israel's history between the Testaments. Those reading now who are also familiar with the intertestamental years for God's people will immediately recognize such figures as Cambyses, Xerxes, Alexander the Great, various Ptolemies (Egypt) and Seleucids (Syria), Berenice, Antiochus, Laodice, Scopas, and Cleopatra. Hardly a who's-who of mediocrity!

Almost without warning, we find ourselves in apocalyptic territory, the first of its kind in Hebrew literature. Daniel's final chapter could have been written almost seven hundred years later on Patmos. Here is also the first time we see clues of a universal resurrection to judgment (Dan 12:2), and the phrase "everlasting life" finding its solitary Old Testament usage, though the idea of it is present elsewhere. The timescale of events implied by Daniel has wrought more consternation than clarity amongst scholars of eschatology. Perhaps the instruction to Daniel to "close up and seal the words of the scroll" (Dan 12:4) should be understood in a similar way to that given by John regarding the adding to or subtracting from the words of God's revelation to him (Rev 22:18–19).

LOYALTY REWARDED

As you might imagine, I have heard a number of one-off sermons that employed texts from the book of Daniel. I have even benefited from a three-message series derived from its contents. On one occasion, I eagerly anticipated a detailed verse-by-verse exploration through the book, only for the incumbent pastor at the time to announce at the end of chapter 6 that he would temporarily be suspending our studies for more urgent matters to be addressed. The gathered faithful were assured that we would be returning to Daniel in due course. We never did.

I can now see why. The latter stages of Daniel's contribution to Scripture make wonderful reading. This is in spite—or perhaps because—of a certain enigmatic quality that leaps from every page. Some passages are incredibly difficult to understand. Others seem relatively straightforward until you realize there has been a subtle shift of emphasis or a different person has taken center stage almost unnoticed part of the way through.

It is not my claim to have cracked the code, received hitherto unheralded revelation, or to have successfully navigated the intricacies of every nuance in the book of Daniel. But neither do I believe that we should abandon the struggle, much less sacrifice what we may learn to our benefit on the altar of present unfathomability concerning the rest. Let us allow the complexity to be a challenge.

Now, please read Daniel 10:1—11:1.

Too Young to Dream

> In the third year of Cyrus king of Persia, a revelation was given to Daniel (who was called Belteshazzar). Its message was true and it concerned a great war. The understanding of the message came to him in a vision. At that time, I, Daniel, mourned for three weeks. I ate no choice food; no meat or wine touched my lips; and I used no lotions at all until the three weeks were over. (Dan 10:1–3)

The first part of this opening sentence dates the events it describes at 536 BC, that is, three years after Cyrus' conquest of Babylon. This being the case, Daniel would by now be well into his eighties, having arrived almost seventy years earlier as a teenager. Although I am not suggesting that such information should color our interpretation of what follows, it is certainly something we should not ignore. This, I believe, is the reason for the parenthetical aside. The recipient of the revelation was Daniel, and just in case you were toying with the idea of mistakenly identifying the subject with a different Daniel, it is the one who was also previously known as Belteshazzar: "I'm still alive, I remain in Babylon, and Yahweh continues to speak to me."

Good news for the elderly

Political correctness demands that we should refer to people like Daniel at this stage in life as mature persons, of advancing years, or young at heart. Let me be quite blunt: he was old. He was not young; he could only be described as middle-aged if the norm was for his peers to live to be two hundred. Daniel was nearer the end of his life than he was to its beginning—much nearer. He had experienced turbulent times in his people's history, not just as an interested bystander, but as one close to the hub of the action. In the time that had elapsed since he last saw his birthplace, most of those with similar memories would have died. Those who didn't had taken up the new king's offer to return and look once more upon their homeland before they breathed their last.

Through all that Daniel had faced in Babylon, the trials, the tests, the responsibilities, the decisions, and the accusations, he had remained—and continued to remain—steadfast. There was no hint of scandal, no documented evidence to hush up, no diminishing of either his faith or his felicity, no trace of bitterness for his lot in life. He persisted to the end, in post and in position. Not for him a dotage of pensive tranquility and dusty tomes. He had not returned to Palestine with the first deportation under Zerubbabel, because his work in Babylon was not yet complete.

I have always had a soft spot for the elderly. Perhaps this is due in no small measure to the fact that I was brought up by my maternal grandparents. Not only did I become acquainted with their ways and idiosyncrasies, but I also became used to the company of others who were of a similar age. My grandfather's family was not only a large one, but a significant proportion of his siblings lived to enjoy retirement. It was the exception if any failed to reach their three-score years and ten. I was blessed with great aunts and uncles aplenty: three Franks, a couple of Phoebes, an Olive, two Georges, a Gertie, a Shem, a Lucy, a Jack, a Millie, a Harry, and a Doris all vied for the accolade of most preferred. I was actually named after my mother's favorite, but he had died shortly before I was born, an exception to the norm.

When I was at College, my familiarity with the much older generation stood me in good stead. By the time I arrived in 1980, many of the staff responsible for the day-to-day running of the grounds and amenities were of pensionable age. But they only ceased from what they considered to have been their God-given tasks when the services of the local funeral director were required.

While studying in South Wales, I befriended a fellow student whose parents ran a Pentecostal Eventide home in a neighboring county to my Yorkshire home. During my first Christmas break, I was invited to spend some time with them and was asked to speak at a couple of the residents' daily morning meetings. There were about twenty or so in attendance, with one centurion, a couple in their nineties, perhaps three octogenarians, with the rest at sixty plus. They all had some Christian background: retired local ministers, former missionaries, ex-church librarians, and the like. Of those in their sixties and seventies, many were younger than the staff at College, few of whom were particularly infirm. And yet, they had opted for retirement, to see out their days reminiscing, squabbling, and otherwise enjoying their surroundings. For them, daring to be a Daniel was to be identified only with what had or might have been their earlier experiences.

Perhaps it is a little unfair to compare people or events across such widely differing timescapes. What cannot be denied, however, is that despite Daniel's age, he was not too old to become envisioned. I have a number of friends in my local church for whom that will be refreshingly good news. I trust their response will be symptomatic of that of a wider audience.

Truth with integrity

First of all, the message contained within the revelation is declared to be true. Whether this is a statement proleptically applied after the events had unfolded is not clear. The fact that it was the subject of divine revelation would make it true, but I'm not entirely sure why such an acknowledgment would require further comment; it would surely have been taken as read. Given Daniel's reputation and renown, he is unlikely to have been suspected of deception or error in such matters. The Hebrew word used is *emeth*, the essence of which is reliability, security, and fidelity, the measure of guarantee being commensurate with the character of its source. Thus, the recipient's appraisal is secondary. This is not Daniel's opinion but absolute veracity, the emphasis being akin to Francis Schaeffer's use of the phrase "true truth."[6] It is truth that corresponds to eternal reality and is, thereby, devoid of the influences of relativism or subjective presupposition.

There will always be those who deny the truth of Christianity's claims for a host of reasons. Objections may range from, "My husband's sister-in-law was badly let down by what can only be described as cultish behavior," to those who point to some of the leading scientists or philosophers of the age who overwhelmingly allege their processes have debunked religion's myths. The implications are clear: you'd either be foolish to fall into the same trap or expect to be ridiculed for doing so. Evidence and interpretation, however, though obviously connected, are not synonymous terms. What we allude to as hard evidence often turns out to be nothing more persuasive or convincing than our finite understanding of it, which is often conditioned by confirmation bias.

Unfortunately, Christians are not entirely exempt from this. We hold a predetermined position and interpret facts accordingly. Some of my most cringeworthy moments have been experienced not in the company of the myopic atheist, but having to listen to ill-informed Christians, the words of whom serve only to provide critics with ammunition and truthseekers with their hunger unsated. Nobody could possibly accuse them of being dispassionate and any presentation of understanding must be accepted as having

---

6. Schaeffer, *Escape from Reason*, 21.

been influenced by the worldview that spawned it. It is just that sometimes I think we have a tendency to mold the facts beyond recognizably tolerable boundaries. We must guard against failing to distinguish between truth and reality as we perceive it to be. Moreover, there is a world of difference between accepting Christ as God's provision for our salvific atonement and embracing Christianity as a superior brand of sociological utilitarianism; it demands a far more radical response.

Truth and love in tandem

I am of the opinion that this is what Schaeffer was getting at by coining the phrase "true truth," at least in part. In greater measure, however, it cannot escape the attention of anyone who either knew him or knows of his work that such truth was never preached or practised in isolation from or independent of love. Even his critics were met with nothing more threatening than a dismissive shrug of the shoulders. This emptiness of truth devoid of love was a major concern for the apostle Paul, most notably in his dealings with the church at Ephesus. Having already extolled the supremacy of love above every other gift, disposition, or virtue to the believers at Corinth (1 Cor 13), Paul suggests that love itself, if it is to be identified as true love, must be subject to truth (Eph 4:15).

This presupposes the idea that it is possible to speak the truth in the absence of love. It is also not inconceivable to experience a kind of love that is false. Truth and love are divine qualities and, therefore, exist in God—and only in him—as absolutes. When we say of his acts or words that they are loving or truthful, they are so because they are but natural expressions of his supernatural essence. He can be no other. It would be both unethical and hypocritical to expect the same of fallen finite beings, even redeemed fallen finite beings. And yet, as much as it is still possible for us to replicate the image of God in created man, Paul insists that we do so.

But that element of redemption cannot so easily be swept under the carpet. Christian discipleship demands that we follow the example of Jesus as closely as the boundaries of finite beinghood will allow. This Jesus is God, but he is also human flesh, of whom that beloved disciple, John, wrote "came from the Father, full of grace and truth" (John 1:14). Of course, he was full of truth because he is truth (John 14:6), just as God exudes love because he is love (1 John 4:8). Because the word "Christian" means "Christ in us and us in him," we now have access to all that was made available to us by virtue of his atoning sacrifice, including an increased and growing capacity for love and truth.

Deceit is never loving

Why then, you may well ask, do some believers find it so easy to embellish the facts, bear false testimony, be so economical with the truth as to intentionally create a wrong impression, or just blatantly lie? And I am not restricting that observation to the occasional pewfiller; some of the worst culprits I have encountered have been those with a measure of leadership responsibility in the local church.

Without attempting to excuse such falsehood, I do think one of the reasons is social acceptance. What has become the norm in society has infiltrated the church by virtue of nothing more sinister than the fact that the latter is part of the former. We are constantly inundated with marketing claims of advertising analysts that not only do not bear scrutiny, but are so ridiculous that they could not possibly hope to do so. Constant striving in the workplace to meet targets that are ultimately unachievable has generated a culture that is deliberately manipulated from finding satisfaction, lest it impede the employee's motivation to reach yet further goals.

At the other end of the scale, but similarly deceitful, is the practice that has moved away from rubbishing the efforts of children to congratulating them for the most meaningless of contributions. The result of all this is that by the time they reach mid-to-late teens, there is an expectation that they are now ready to conquer the world in whatever field they choose, regardless of genuine skill or talent other than that discerned by wholly unqualified aunts and uncles from an early age.

Is it any wonder, then, that when the church reaches out to such a generation, it brings with it a warped sense of reality? The difficulty facing those already in the church is not in daring to challenge the wrongful perception of truth, but in finding a way to do so that will achieve its desired objective. Those unused to being told they are wrong seldom embrace correction sternly administered. They will often remove themselves from the threatening environment, lest it endanger the perception of their omnicompetence. This usually means they will either opt out altogether or set up their own thing where they rule the roost. Hence, the emergence of a plethora of new denominations where virtually anything goes, because there are no governing guidelines. Scripture is often either ignored or rewritten to accommodate politically correct sensitivities, liturgy is relaxed to mimic the after-work party, authority is dismissed as restricting the flow, and any hint of teaching—such as it is—more resembles the advice you might glean from a self-help seminar for would-be hedonists. Some of us never seem to learn that empty earthenware jars do not become filled by relocation, joining with others similarly devoid of content, or the self-application of a decorative glaze (John 2:1–11; 2 Cor 4:7–9).

True freedom

When Jesus said, "[T]he truth will set you free" (John 8:32b), this was preceded by the assumption that his addressees would "know the truth" (John 8:32a), itself governed by them "holding to [his] teaching" as indicative that they were "really his disciples" (John 8:31). What may we say of such freedom? That it is aligned to rebellion, disobedience, and self-gratification? Is the root of all these things not sin? And is it not sin's dominance from which we have been set free? We are now free to honor, obey, and serve God; that is the truth of the matter.

Apathy, angst, and submission have one thing in common: none of them affect the truth of truth, only its effect upon each response (I suppose that makes two things in common). "God is the Creator of the universe" is both a Christian proposition and a theological statement. A proposition may be true or false, an object may be real or imaginary, and the mind of the individual may be knowing or ignorant.[7] My mind owns God to be real and this proposition to be true. My brother-in-law would disagree. If I am correct, the value of my brother-in-law's opinion on the propositional truth of God's role as Creator of the universe is zero.

The revelation presented to Daniel, though it concerned future events, was true; just as true as those events that were at the time consigned to Daniel's past. Such truth is true, regardless of either our acknowledgment or our understanding of it.

I, Daniel

> On the twenty-fourth day of the first month, as I was standing on the bank of the great river, the Tigris, I looked up and there before me was a man dressed in linen, with a belt of the finest gold round his waist. His body was like chrysolite, his face like lightning, his eyes like flaming torches, his arms and legs like the gleam of burnished bronze, and his voice like the sound of a multitude. I, Daniel, was the only one who saw the vision; the men with me did not see it, but such terror overwhelmed them that they fled and hid themselves. So I was left alone, gazing at

---

7. See Trueblood, *General Philosophy*, 47.

> this great vision; I had no strength left, my face turned deathly pale and I was helpless. Then I heard him speaking, and as I listened to him, I fell into a deep sleep, my face to the ground. (Dan 10:4–9)

By the time readers of Daniel arrive at chapter 10, they already know that he specializes in descriptive terminology. We also have a shrewd idea that some of the things he "saw" in his visions were really beyond the limits of his vocabulary, and so—gifted as he was—he had to resort to simile. Though not identical, this section is particularly reminiscent of John's Patmos experience (Rev 1:12–16). Commentators are reluctant to find consensus regarding the identity of Daniel's linen-clad man. Even those who argue that he was an angelic messenger cannot agree on which, some insisting it was Gabriel, while others posit Michael. Some even propose that Michael was the preincarnate identity of Christ.

It is my opinion that there is an identity change at verse 10, the hand that touches Daniel and thereafter addresses him not belonging to the person described in these earlier verses. I concur here with Edward Young:

> However, the description seems to indicate that the Person here presented is none other than the Lord Himself. The revelation therefore is a theophany, a preincarnate appearance of the eternal Son.[8]

Young cites the likeness between this passage and that of John in Revelation as evidence for his position, but I think there are stronger clues in the description he mentions. The man's clothing alone speaks of two things: royalty and purity. The white linen is often associated in Scripture with angelic beings (Ezek 9:2; Rev 15:6) and the priesthood (Lev 6:10; 16:4). I was tempted to add virginal females, but could find no unambiguous biblical evidence to warrant such a premise. The regal aspect of clothing adorned by the man in Daniel's vision leans toward a royal priest, but the idea that it could have been an angel is not entirely without support.

Asleep on the job?

What is indisputable, however, is the effect the vision had on Daniel. It might be an idea to read passages like this before we glibly pray or sing about wanting to see Jesus or yearning for more of God's presence. Such experiences are precious and to be welcomed, but their design consists of immeasurably more than scratching an itch in their direction. Equally, if

---

8. Young, *Daniel*, 225.

the extent of your exposure to divine visions consists of little more than the pastor's wife closing her eyes and seeing a bowl of fruit, whereby the grapes are spoken of in *faux* seventeenth-century English as God's sign that: "Lo, though thou art troublest with the hemorrhoids, knoweth for a surety that he hath it in hand," then the authenticity levels have been raised several notches here. We are not at liberty to believe the convenient to be true with absolutely no other qualifying factors.

I wonder how many readers are able to identify with the experience of having become so overwhelmed with exhaustion during your quiet times alone with God, that the foremost item on your agenda was not to tell everyone about how it made you feel, but immediately to seek another quiet time alone, this time without God, just so that you might recover. I'm guessing not many. This is not a criticism. I can number such experiences on one hand, and I wouldn't need my thumb or index finger to do so. Even my pinky was used only to register a friend telling me it had happened to her.

In fact, almost everything about Daniel's experience, as recorded here in chapter 10, runs counter to twenty-first century Christian expectations and practice. Not least amongst these was the fact that Daniel fell asleep while listening to the "man" speak. We must remember, of course, that the earlier message (Dan 10:1) had so troubled him that he "mourned for three weeks," enjoying only a meager diet (Dan 10:2–3). There may also be some significance in the fact that all this took place during the first month of the year (Dan 10:4), during which both Passover and the Feast of Unleavened Bread were celebrated. Although the climax of each occasion included joyful festivities, they were also precipitated by periods of sober fasting.

Even allowing for this, however, Daniel didn't just nod off or wait until the object of his vision had finished speaking before catching forty winks: "as [he] listened to him, [Daniel] fell into a deep sleep" (Dan 10:9). Young and Darby translate this as "trance" and "stupor," respectively. Both appear to be closer to the original than most other attempts. This puts a completely different complexion on our tendency to assume that Daniel's falling asleep interrupted the message he was being given at the time. Although far from unequivocal, we must at least entertain the possibility that his sleep was divinely induced so that his spirit might be more receptive to understanding what would otherwise have been beyond the capacity of his natural intellect. The effect this would have on the foregoing clause would thereby be minimal, but not without import: no longer "as I was listening," but "as I continued to listen."

As old as Adam

Although not commonplace in Scripture, neither is this act of being put into an involuntary state of sleep a unique one. If we were to adopt the law of first mention, we would not have to turn many pages from the beginning of our Bibles:

> So the man gave names to all the livestock, the birds of the air and all the beasts of the field. But for Adam no suitable helper was found. So the Lord caused the man to fall into a deep sleep; and while he was sleeping, he took one of the man's ribs and closed up the place with flesh. Then the Lord made a woman from the rib he had taken out of the man, and he brought her to the man. (Gen 2:20-22)

Most commentators remain silent on the "why" of Adam's sleep, preferring to focus exclusively on the "wherefore." The majority of the bloggers I have come across should have followed the commentators' lead, choosing instead to fill their sites with what they do best: voicing opinions of which the fine line between subtlety and spuriousness is often breached. That is not to say that nothing may be deduced from this context. As the first of only seven occasions where the word *tardema* is used, something of significance must be discernible. According to Bill Williams: "Yahweh causes a deep sleep to fall on people to allow him to do his work without interference . . . or reveal himself in a special way."[9] Certainly, Williams' definition can be seen to apply to each of its uses in the Old Testament, though I'm not sure about the validity of suggesting that God's work can be subject to such interference that might hinder its progress. That God often chooses to "do his work" without deeming it necessary to bring about such a deep sleep serves only to confound the theory further. However, the idea that it allows for special revelation, either to or through the individual subject to such stupor, is devoid of similar objections.

If there is anything of more meaningful significance concerning Adam's experience, I think it is more typological than lexicographical. Several times in the New Testament, death is referred to as sleep (e.g., Matt 9:24; John 11:11-14; 1 Thess 4:15-17). This figurative use may have been entirely because of the resemblance between a recently deceased cadaver and a sleeping person. Perhaps an even deeper symbolism was attached, as endorsed by Martin Luther:

---

9. In VanGemeren, *Dictionary of Old Testament Theology*, 3.1057.

> It is probable, in my opinion, that, with few exceptions indeed, the dead sleep in utter insensibility till the day of judgment . . . On what authority can it be said that the souls of the dead may not sleep . . . in the same way that the living pass in profound slumber the interval between their downlying at night and their uprising in the morning?[10]

It is difficult to imagine the typology being universally applicable across all Old Testament examples of God placing individuals into a deep sleep, but I do think the case of Adam as a type of Christ makes it more likely that Jesus' death is being alluded to there. This really doesn't help us in our understanding of the incident with Daniel, except insofar that we are able to rule out the Adamic analogy.

God's presence is exhausting

So, is there anything more meaningful that might be gleaned from Daniel being put "into a deep sleep"? Most commentators retain the figurative idea, but do so in the sense of Daniel being stunned with astonishment. Other Old Testament examples of similar occurrences aid us only to a point, that of Abram perhaps being the most helpful (see Gen 15:17–18). I believe it is to the pages of the New Testament to which we must turn for further enlightenment.

There are, I believe, similarities between Daniel's experience, here and elsewhere (see also Dan 8:18), and that described of the "man in Christ" known to the apostle Paul (2 Cor 12:1–4). On the basis of what follows (i.e., 2 Cor 12:5–10), it is generally regarded that Paul is speaking of himself, but establishing his identity is irrelevant here. The trancelike, or ecstatic, experience of being "caught up to the third heaven" (2 Cor 12:2) seems too similar to that of Daniel to be coincidental, but neither is it conclusive.

To my mind, the most comprehensive likeness is that alluded to earlier. Let us revisit it together, this time in more detail. John was in the Spirit on the Lord's day, when he heard a loud voice behind him (Rev 1:10). Turning, he saw one "like a son of man," in a long robe with a golden sash. With head and hair as white as snow, eyes blazing like fire, feet glowing like bronze in a furnace, a double-edged sword coming out of his mouth, and face like the radiance of the sun (2 Cor 12:12–16), John's reaction is unsurprising: "When I saw him, I fell at his feet as though dead. Then he placed his right hand on me and said: 'Do not be afraid'" (Rev 1:17a). Sound familiar? When I mentioned earlier that Daniel's experience was reminiscent of that of John

---

10. In Michelet, *Martin Luther*, 133.

on Patmos, perhaps the phrase I should have used is almost carbon copy. This likeness is not only restricted to what each man saw and recorded, nor even the effect it had upon them both, but their circumstances were also similar. Where it might be said that they differed is that the object of Daniel's vision was personally unknown to him. And yet, as Trench points out: "The beloved disciple, who had handled the Word of life, lain in his Lord's bosom in the days of his flesh, can as little as any endure the revelation of his majesty."[11] In both cases, the Hebrew and Greek words employed for their respective falling ("into a deep sleep" and "as though dead") do not rule out the possibility of them being voluntary acts. However, it is unlikely for Daniel and only marginally less so for John. Had the latter's experience been "as though dying" (i.e., a process akin to making oneself prostrate), then perhaps such an argument would acquire a greater degree of plausibility.

That both men were told not to be afraid (Dan 10:12; Rev 1:17) could have been pre-emptive, but more probably suggests the correction of an already obvious demeanor. What is actually recorded of Daniel and cannot be dismissed of John, despite its absence, is the state of utter exhaustion wrought by being envisioned thus. Their advanced years may have contributed to this. However, personal experience testifies to the draining effect of meeting with God in this way.

In the early part of 1981, I had a vision. Although it was not a vision of God, I believe it to have been one given by him. I had never experienced such a thing prior to this, nor have I since. I was in a Friday evening prayer meeting in a church in South Wales, the pastor of which was one of my College tutors. The particulars are not material here, other than to say it was like a vivid unfolding of events, every detail of which I remember to this day.

I wasn't primed for such an occasion; I don't remember feeling particularly spiritual or attuned to meeting God in that way. I'm not even sure that type of church welcomed the admission of such episodes beyond the pages of Scripture. I do remember my position as the images unfolded in my mind: I was kneeling facing the chair upon which I had been sitting. As I began to regain awareness of my surroundings, two things struck me: I was prostrate on the carpeted hall and I was absolutely and inexplicably enfeebled. To those who claim to be regular recipients of divine visions, I am left only to presume that the experience becomes less debilitating with practice or that I was a particularly delicate twenty-one-year-old. I suppose there could be one other possible explanation.

---

11. Trench, *Synonyms*, 45.

Awestruck, Yet Obedient

> A hand touched me and set me trembling on my hands and knees. He said, "Daniel, you who are highly esteemed, consider carefully the words I am about to speak to you, and stand up, for I have now been sent to you." And when he said this to me, I stood up trembling. (Dan 10:10–11)

As mentioned earlier, I think there is a change of identity here in Daniel's vision. It is no more than an opinion, and I admit that the evidence either way is inconclusive. The lessons we may learn from these verses, however, are both unhindered and unimpinged by knowing the precise identity of the addressor. What ensues develops smoothly from what has gone before; there is no sudden change of direction.

The sense of what follows after these verses would not have been affected had Daniel been addressed thus: "Daniel, consider carefully . . . " But to be reminded of the esteem with which he is held is more than mere comforting words. Other versions translate: "man greatly beloved" (e.g., KJV, ESV, ASV), while others still speak of him being "treasured by God" (HCSB) and "very precious to God" (NLT). This is not the only time Daniel has been thus identified (see also Dan 9:23), each occasion precipitating significant revelation. And yet for Daniel, those words would have been a revelation in themselves.

Knowing and known

When it comes to corporate worship, it seems I share a weakness with countless others, some perhaps without even realizing it: I'm a sucker for the slow melody in a minor key. I must also confess that my penchant is not restricted to worship material or even songs with an overtly Christian message. A gentle ballad with a crescendo climax can touch my emotions almost regardless of its lyrical content. Within a Christian context, however, one of my favorites is *Knowing You, Jesus* by Graham Kendrick. The refrain adds, "there is no greater thing." Very touching, very moving, incredibly comforting, and guaranteed to have the whole congregation at the disposal of the preacher for the next hour or so. But is it also very true? Subjectively, it probably is; objectively, I'm not so sure.

Please don't misunderstand me. Being allowed to experience that level of intimacy with the Son of God is as unfathomable as it is insatiable. Knowing Jesus is an almost insurmountable thing. But I believe there is something that exceeds it. Jesus implied as much himself:

> Not everyone who says to me, "Lord, Lord," will enter the kingdom of heaven, but only he who does the will of my Father who is in heaven. Many will say to me on that day, "Lord, Lord, did we not prophesy in your name, and in your name drive out demons and perform many miracles?" Then I will tell them plainly, "I never knew you. Away from me, you evildoers!" (Matt 7:21–23)

How astonishing! And on so many levels. Arguably the most striking feature of this is the implication that prophesying, driving out demons, and performing miracles are insufficient in themselves to constitute doing the will of the Father. And yet, I know quite a few in my albeit limited social circle who would point to such things as evidence of their spiritual relationship: "I must be right because I pray for the sick, invite my neighbors to special church events, and go around the church after the benediction has been pronounced laden with coffee cups, cream buns, and gospel tracts at the ready."

If we only had Jesus' opening sentence without this back-up, we could confidently assert it to be an example of disharmony between life and lip: saying, but not doing. But he goes on to dismiss those who not only do, nor even merely do apparently laudable deeds, but they do them in his name. How can this be? A couple of possibilities present themselves. It may be that the cited deeds were sham performances and their perpetrators were also wrongly appealing for Christian authenticity. Another plausible explanation might be that "in the name of Jesus" was being used as some sort of mystical formula by those with no rightful claim to its authority. That debate belongs to a different time and probably those more sufficiently qualified than I to appraise the arguments of contending scholars.

It is what Jesus pronounced upon such people that concerns us here: "I never knew you." Obviously, Jesus is not denying any mental awareness of these "evildoers." He had just demonstrated his knowledge of their acts. But the knowledge of which he speaks here is intimacy of relationship. Hendriksen paraphrases thus: "Not for a single moment have I acknowledged you as my own, or known you to be my friends."[12] Is there something greater than knowing Jesus? Oh, yes! It is that he knows us.

God is truly awesome

Daniel was known by God. Well before the incident we have in front of us here, Daniel will have known that he was known by God. Despite his previous experiences—or, perhaps in some measure, because of them—the

---

12. Hendriksen, *Matthew*, 377.

current circumstances caused him to tremble. I cannot say for certain on the basis of the evidence we have, but I can imagine myself in Daniel's position: God knows me; I know he knows me; but if I had a vision of someone reaffirming that fact, whatever my condition before, that information alone would also cause me to tremble.

I was tempted to add at the end of the previous paragraph something along the lines of, "but not with fear." But it would be fear of a certain kind. Although most dictionary definitions focus on negative associations, such as "an unpleasant emotion caused by exposure to danger," "anxiety for the safety of," "the expectation or likelihood of danger," or "uneasy apprehension," a plausible alternative would be "to show reverence towards." A less ambiguous option might be "awe."

How casually that word is often used! An outstanding sports performance is described as "awesome." A memorable concert, film, or stage production earns the accolade "awesome." Some time ago, a friend of mine labeled her experience of the view of the UK capital from the London Eye as "awesome." As spectacular as each of these may have been, none of them compare with the sense of absolute wonderment of God's presence. Daniel truly was awestruck.

On such occasions, even those where we misuse the word, there is a natural inclination to want to capture the moment. In my lifetime, technology has developed from the cine camera, through the insta-matic, via the videocam, and on to the pocket-sized cell phone. Possibly the most overwhelming spectacle of the New Testament was the Transfiguration of Jesus (Luke 9:28–36). There are arguments to be heard for other candidates, but I would contend that this is the one that was recognized as such by its albeit limited audience without the need for hindsight. And how did that band of brothers respond? With such short-sighted relish that they wanted to build a shrine (Luke 9:33). How did Daniel respond to his awesome experience? He was told to stand up, so he stood up (Dan 10:11). Trembling, yes; but he did obey.

Obedience unobstructed by instincts

There is a beautiful episode in the Old Testament concerning the return of the ark of God to Israel. Philistine hordes had seized the ark in the same battle that saw the death of Eli's two sons, Hophni and Phinehas (1 Sam 4:1–11). So representative of the divine bond between Yahweh and his people was the ark, that when the already pregnant widow of Phinehas gave birth, she prophetically named her son "Ichabod, saying, 'The glory has departed from Israel'" (1 Sam 4:19–21a). The Philistines had taken the ark, believing it to be the key to Israel's might in battle. They were correct, but hadn't thought the capture fully through. In the hands of God's people, the ark had been a symbol of their covenant relationship; in Philistine possession, it wrought only devastation and destruction. Ashdod, Gath, and Ekron all suffered for illegitimately housing God's ark.

Seven months later, the Philistines decided to return the ark to Israel. Following the advice of those familiar with cultic matters, they opted to send it back to Beth Shemesh on a cart pulled by two milking cows that were unused to being yoked (1 Sam 6:7). Their calves were removed to a pen and the cows were sent on their way. As they journeyed, Scripture describes the scene thus: "Then the cows went straight up towards Beth Shemesh, keeping on the road and lowing all the way; they did not turn to the right or to the left" (1 Sam 6:12). The cows' natural inclination would have been to follow their motherly instincts toward the sound of their hungry bleating calves. But they continued on their appointed contrary trek, lowing as they went. The Hebrew word used here is *ga'ah*, the root of which indicates an intense aversion, often expressed amid punitive, adverse, or unfamiliar action. I am sure that God much prefers co-operative collaboration to reluctant coercion. I am also confident that he remains relatively untroubled by us adopting a similar stance of lowing, so long as we, too, low as we go.

Obedience is not a natural tendency. In fact, rebellion is never more vibrant than when in response to a more recent prohibition. If any readers are in doubt, just observe your local park keeper put up the temporary "Keep off the grass" signs, after putting the mower away. Passersby will not be able to resist placing at least a toe beyond the footpath's edge. Parents of small children need no convincing about this natural proclivity to defy. "Switch that off," "Hurry up," "Go to bed," "Come now; your dinner is on the table," and "Tidy your room" are all met with the same level (i.e., lack) of enthusiasm, with or without a mild-mannered "Please!" being attached to them.

Action required

It is not always easy to detect obedience or to notice rebellion that is subtly disguised. An oft-witnessed reply to each of the above commands might well be a cheery, "Yes, I will," followed by an equally joyful period of unresponsiveness. It is not a new phenomenon. Jesus told a parable of a man who had two sons. The man also had a vineyard that needed tending. He asked each of his sons in turn to help. The first son initially refused, but later changed his mind. We are not told why. It could have been conviction, convenience, or a change of circumstances. The original text seems to indicate a measure of remorse for his earlier snub, though the intricacies of linguistic meaning outside of such a context are not so easy to apply to parables. It matters not; he said he would not help, but he did so.

The other son immediately answered in the affirmative, but his words proved empty. Whether there was ever any genuine intention in his earlier response is not clear. There is no such ambiguity concerning the end product, however: he did not fulfil his promise. Jesus then asked his audience which of the two boys had done as their father requested (Matt 21:28–32). The answer is so obvious as to warrant no further comment here, though the religious leaders were more willing to answer it than Jesus' earlier question about the authority of John the Baptist (Matt 21:23–27a). Suffice to repeat, I am certain that God would prefer willing obedience on our part; I am equally sure that he will accept reluctant obedience over unfulfilled promises.

The idea of submission cannot be separated from that of obedience: obedience is essentially submission to the will of another. It may or may not include persuasion by way of reasonable argument: "Please do this, because . . . " Autonomy or self-government is obedience only to one's own inclinations; it is submission to selfish desires. To submit to the will of another only when that will corresponds with our own or when we regard it solely as an opportunity to further our own cause is not obedience in the truest sense. So guys, if like me you exude a certain "Oh! What a good boy am I?" quality when responding favorably to your wife's request to prepare the vegetables, when deep down your "submission" is motivated only by the fact that you are contributing toward your own later enjoyment of the evening meal, then we really need to stop sticking out our thumb in the hope that it will be rewarded with a plum. It is the kind of obedience demonstrated by Jesus' addressees, from whom it derives its pejorative name: it is Pharisaical.

Pride versus humility

The association with disobedience of pride cannot be overlooked. A refusal to submit to another's request for action has at its root the notion that "I'm not going to do it your way, because my way is better." To put it another way, obedience is the fruit of humility. Just in case further doubt remains, consider the following:

> God opposes the proud but gives grace to the humble. (Jas 4:6)

> When pride comes, then comes disgrace, but with humility comes wisdom. (Prov 11:2)

Which of these qualities would you say best describes what we know of Daniel: proud or humble, disgraceful or wise? Here is a clue from the pen of Derek Kidner:

> This word for pride is from a root that suggests boiling up, and is used of the arrogance of those who must have everything their own way and will not be "kicked around": e.g., Pharaoh (Neh 9:10), Israel (Neh 9:16, 29), the social rebel (Deut 17:12–13), the bogus prophet (Deut 18:20), the murderer (Exod 21:14).[13]

By contrast, the Greek word translated "humility" in both the New Testament and the Septuagint version of the Old is *praotes*. The biblical use of this word is not entirely consistent with that of classical Greek scholars, though Trench makes the following erudite points:

> The Scriptural *praotes* is manifested not only in a man's outward behavior, nor merely in his relations with others, nor in his natural disposition. It is an inwrought grace of the soul that is exercised primarily toward God . . . It is a quality of spirit that accepts God's dealings with us as good, without disputing or resisting them.[14]

I will now repeat my earlier question: Which of these qualities would you say best describes what we know of Daniel—proud or humble?

Be Quiet and Listen

> While he was saying this to me, I bowed with my face to the ground and was speechless. (Dan 10:15)

While it must be acknowledged that part of the reason for Daniel's speechlessness was his continuing state of astonishment, the original word structure and what follows seem to suggest that Daniel was rendered incapable. Joyce Baldwin puts the case best:

> [Daniel] was literally deprived of the power of speech until he received a second supernatural touch, this time on his lips, and was given power of speech once more.[15]

---

13. Kidner, *Proverbs*, 86.
14. Trench, *Synonyms*, 166.
15. Baldwin, *Daniel*, 202.

However, there is also a more general lesson to be learned here: When God is speaking, all that is required of us is that we listen. Before we consider some practical pointers for hearing God's voice, I need to point out that despite my earlier Christian background being within a Pentecostal/charismatic setting, I have never had an experience quite like the one facing Daniel here. I have not knowingly heard an audible voice, nor have I ever made that claim. This is not to discredit those who make such assertions, some of whom are personally known to me and I have found to be otherwise entirely trustworthy. Some might even say that I was gilded by the joy of unvarnished experiences. Be that as it may, it would be unwise of me to speak too much of an experience with which I am personally unfamiliar.

But God still manages to speak to me. For the most part, he does so through his written word, the Bible. He speaks to me often through the lives and circumstances of others, especially—but not exclusively—Christian brothers and sisters. It is also important to note that when we look for godly lessons in others, their conduct may equally be an example of how not to live as it can be one to replicate. I spent three years serving a pastor in my twenties and that was pretty much the sum of my instruction from him. And yet, it was vital that I remained to learn that lesson; God had devised it so.

For the rest of this section, I want to draw the reader's attention to seven principles associated with listening to God:

A sheep's divine right

> My sheep hear my voice; I know them and they follow me.
> (John 10:27)

The context of Jesus saying this was in response to being approached at the Feast of Dedication by certain Jews, who asked him to confirm that he was the Christ (John 10:22-24). Of course, their motivation was not that they might thence leave all and become his disciples, but they wanted further ammunition with which to hold him accountable for blasphemy. Without directly answering their question, Jesus did suggest that the converse of the above statement is equally true: "[Y]ou do not believe because you are not my sheep" (John 10:26).

Sometimes, when my wife asks me to help with a chore around the house or gives me advance notice of a planned day out, I either forget momentarily or have absolutely no recollection of the alleged conversation. This can be because I have other things on my mind at the time, or I am in the middle of doing something else that requires complete concentration. When later reminded that the potatoes still need pealing or being informed, "I told you weeks ago," my stock reply is: "I didn't hear you." Even as I'm saying it, I know what is coming next: "You only hear what you want to hear!" As sheep, we have the right to hear the Shepherd's voice; do we also have the desire?

As Christians, we have the right to expect to hear God directing us, congratulating us, chastising us, speaking words of comfort to us, giving us insight into otherwise problematic decisions that we may have to make, enabling us to become aware of potential difficulties before they arise, or helping us to know how best we may help others. Such communication is an expression of fellowship based upon relationship.

In the same—but obviously restricted—way, my wife hears my voice. Others may hear it too, but not with the same level of intimacy or, dare I say it, accountability. If Barbara asks for advice on how I think she should proceed with a situation, she is obliged only to listen. What she then does with that counsel is nobody's responsibility but her own. She is free to follow my instructions, hold them in abeyance for later application, or utterly disregard them. Each position has its own consequences. If she takes the latter course, one outcome might be to hear my voice again, this time saying: "I told you so!" God has had cause to say that to me on more than one occasion.

Beware of other voices

Sheep have the distinct advantage over goats: they hear the Shepherd's voice. The disadvantage they share is that both are capable of hearing other voices, too. There appears to be a safeguard to this as far as believers are concerned. Earlier in the same chapter, Jesus had first mentioned to his audience that: "his sheep [will] follow him because they know his voice" (John 10:4). He then goes on to offer further reassurance: "But they will never follow a stranger; in fact they will run away from him because they do not recognize a stranger's voice" (John 10:5). (We are then told, somewhat ironically, that his audience "did not understand what he was telling them.") So far, so good! But what if the other voice belongs to someone who is not entirely unknown to us?

Many of the New Testament epistles were written as an apostolic response to problems encountered by their early church recipients. Some were individual errors that had not been nipped in the bud, whereas others involved a significant proportion of the local church. Divisions, party spirit, legalistic tendencies, inappropriate relationships, and impropriety in worship did not just manifest themselves overnight. I have witnessed some of these first hand. Though I have never been so close to the hub of the action to know how they began, I can say how they developed: by unsuspecting and inexperienced believers placing too much trust in the voices of those from whom more maturity was expected. We shouldn't automatically assume that the voice of those over us in the Lord is necessarily an echo of the Shepherd's voice.

A preacher friend of mine recently said from the pulpit: "There are essentially three voices we may hear as Christians: God's voice, the devil's voice, and the voice of our own selfish desires." I can find no legitimate reason to disagree with him, but I would also add that the loudest voice, the most apparently rational, or the one designed to bring the most immediate comfort is not necessarily the one we should follow. Indeed, I would have to confess that on every occasion where the unfolding of events has proved that I followed my own inclinations, at least one of these features could have been attributed to its persuasiveness. All I can say is thank God that the achieving of his purpose for my life was not always dependent upon me always having made the correct decision.

Clearing the tracks for discernment

Is there a sure-fire way of knowing every single time which voice to heed? Let me put it another way: Is it possible to determine God's will, "his good, pleasing and perfect will" (Rom 12:2)? Yes, there is, and we have already covered it in a slightly different context. That "the renewing of [our] mind[s]" features here also serves only to emphasize its importance. What is the connection here? True discernment requires avoidance of distractions. In other words, we need to clear away the trash.

One of the distinct disadvantages of the technological age is the potential for even more garbage to clutter our minds, due in no small part to the increase in media platforms. This can be perceived as advantageous. After all, no previous generation has been as socially aware, as culturally enlightened, or as prepared to adjust to the ever-changing political uncertainties. But these benefits bring with them also certain hitherto unknown pressures, the mental burden of which is incalculable.

"Keeping up with the Joneses" has always been used in a disparaging way to refer to third parties who perceived a need to be seen on at least equal terms with their next-door neighbor. As the world shrinks metaphorically through travel and employment opportunities, those Joneses are no longer restricted to the family on the other side of the partition wall. And so, many find themselves gripped by a credit system that asks, "Why wait?" without even having the decency to conclude: " . . . to become a prisoner to debt?" Variable interest rates, short-term contracts, and unforeseeable price increases are the enemy of financial planning for everyone except those with vested interests in the economy.

Of course, we may all be unwitting victims. Having found ourselves so, we must seek a satisfactory resolution. But if such possibilities exist, and the consequences of falling foul to them include a debilitating effect on our capacity to focus on more spiritually enhancing matters, like hearing God's voice, is it really worth the risk to get involved more than is absolutely necessary?

Presumption the enemy of faith

> Consequently, faith comes from hearing the message, and the message is heard through the word of Christ. (Rom 10:17)

The context of this verse makes it clear that Paul is obviously referring to saving faith. The original setting of the previous verse serves only to confirm this. The principle underscoring it, however, is equally applicable to living faith. To believe God's promises—any promises—must be preceded by the individual (or corporate body) having first heard from God on the matter. Having done so, the arrival of faith, and its object, is a foregone conclusion. There is no sense here that "faith might come" or that there may be other conditions to meet, except perhaps for patience in awaiting God's appointed time.

Not only does faith come as a consequence of having heard the message—that message being heard through the word of Christ—but the same is true also of faith's development, growth, coming to maturity, and increasing in both measure and potency. The inverse is equally true. Faith does not come, cannot be conjured, will not arrive at some long-awaited future date, just so long as we persevere, cast aside all doubt, or believe sufficiently. No matter how many seminars we sign up for where the theme seems to be related, such as *Believing God in a Cynical Church* or *Faith to Fortify the Spiritually Naïve*, if God has not spoken we have not heard from him. This being the case, call it what we will, it does not conform to the biblical presentation of faith. Rather, it is baseless presumption and, therefore, an enemy of true faith.

The difficulty with which Paul was faced by the Galatian churches was not very different to that at Rome: "For in Christ Jesus neither circumcision nor uncircumcision has any value. The only thing that counts is faith expressing itself through love" (Gal 5:6). I had to re-read this. If anyone had asked me to quote it without looking it up, I would have missed the part about uncircumcision. But Paul is saying that not only are ritual and ceremony in isolation unable to commend us to God, but resistance to them based on anything other than faith is equally without merit. This is not to say that rituals are inherently wrong, so long as they do not provide the basis for our confidence in God. Where faith is present, not only must it be allowed to express itself if it is to achieve its goal, but it must do so "through love." To presume otherwise is at enmity with genuine faith.

Be still and know that he is God

> Be still and know that I am God; I will be exalted among the nations, I will be exalted in the earth. (Ps 46:10)

I realize I run the risk of citing this verse out of context, so let us take a look at that first. Although recorded by the Psalmist, wherein the earlier encouragement was to remind God's people of their refuge and strength (Ps 46:1), the immediate context of verse 10 suggests Yahweh is there addressing their enemies. In effect, we might paraphrase: "You are planning to do my people harm; desist or you will have me to answer to. This is a battle you would be better advised not to engage."

This does not prevent us from applying the verse in a more positive manner to believers. Its meaning can still instruct us. At its most basic, it means: "Stop what you are doing and acknowledge me." Many of us, even with the best intentions, often only consult God in the decisions we face when we have already taken several steps down a chosen road, only to find it leads to disaster: "Help, Lord; please bail me out—again!" Amazingly, yet graciously, he often does. But should we really be using God as a back-up plan? And would we have found ourselves in such a mess if we had rather learned to be still at the outset, in the full knowledge that he is God?

Some situations are more conducive to stillness than others. The more intense the pressure, the higher the stakes; the closer a designated deadline looms, the higher panic levels rise. Conversely, sitting in the cool summer breeze with your nearest and dearest, sipping your favorite tipple after a wonderful meal, having enjoyed an exhilarating exposition on the love of God earlier in the day, and no immediate work schedule to invade your thoughts, brings about its own unique brand of stillness. Even to imagine it is not an altogether unpleasant assault on the senses. However, the Psalmist doesn't invite us to "Be still, because your present situation lends itself to a restful disposition," but to be still in every circumstance of life because God is in control. Perhaps unsurprisingly, the more we come to know, appreciate, and understand God and his ways, the less we experience resistance to stillness. Many moons have waned since I vowed that a troubled mind and my free evenings should never again coincide.

God's voice is consistent with his character

The next two points are closely connected, but there is a subtle distinction that renders them worthy of separate consideration. That College friend I mentioned earlier was a couple of years older than me; to save any potential embarrassment, let us call him Dave. Although we shared a similar denominational background, Dave had been a Christian considerably longer than I had. I suppose I initially looked up to him as an older brother figure. His approach to divine guidance consisted as much of omission as it did communication. Dave believed he was permitted to do anything he liked unless specifically forbidden.

Bizarrely, the nature of such prohibition was also subject to personal interpretation, which was often conditioned by convenience. For example, he would occasionally claim to have received a vision from God, with himself playing the lead role enacting precisely that for which he assured others he had asked guidance. I suspect he was probably fantasizing the scene in his own imagination and then projecting the image displayed there as if from God, as some sort of pseudo-blessing.

No matter how exhaustive when compared to others, our understanding of God is always confined to finite parameters. Within those restrictions, however, Scripture does provide clues concerning his nature. Defense mechanisms that contravene what we know of him can only ever be doomed to failure. "A voice in my head, which I believe to have been God, told me to kill prostitutes" is nonsense and should always be regarded as such. Blaming him for our infidelity, marital or otherwise, is similar drivel. Moreover, asking others to pray on our behalf in the hope that their ill-advised conclusions will match our own legitimizes neither our ignorance nor theirs. Any notion of democracy being an avenue that leads to divine guidance is limited to the three persons of the Trinity; it does not include the church flower arranger, the chief chorister, or the organist's current beau. Nor is God in need of a second opinion.

God doesn't speak contrary to his revealed word

> Let the word of Christ dwell in you richly as you teach and admonish one another with all wisdom . . . (Col 3:16a)

Although the NIV (or, at least, my edition of it) is correct to show that "with all wisdom" modifies "teach and admonish," both are dependent on the preceding clause: "Let the word of Christ dwell in you richly." Without that qualification, any teaching and admonition that takes place is devoid of true wisdom.

What is that "word of Christ"? Some might argue that it is restricted to the teaching and example of Jesus as found in the Gospel accounts, while others might also include their apostolic interpretation elsewhere in the New Testament. First of all, we should understand that at the time of Paul writing to the Colossians, this "word of Christ" was not as accessible as we now find it. Secondly, even if we were momentarily to ignore the finer intricacies of detail surrounding the doctrine of the Trinity, Jesus identified himself with the Father, his will with that of the Father, and his words with those of the Father. Is it, therefore, unreasonable to perceive the "word of Christ" as synonymous with "the word of God"?

Even were this not the case, there is nothing that may be attributed to what we know of Jesus from the pages of the New Testament, either in word or in deed, that is inconsistent with what is revealed of God throughout Scripture. When God speaks, he does so with absolute clarity and consistency. It behooves us, therefore, to fill our minds with his revelation, through which we might filter all else that would present itself as God's voice. If it genuinely is, not only must it be subject to that test, but it will remain unoffended by being so. Thus, "the word of Christ" employed here may be regarded as complementary to Paul's earlier use of the phrase, "the word of truth" (Col 1:5).

Empowered by Peace

> Again the one who looked like a man touched me and gave me strength. "Do not be afraid, O man highly esteemed," he said. "Peace! Be strong now; be strong." When he spoke to me, I was strengthened and said, "Speak, my lord, since you have given me strength." (Dan 10:18–19)

It should perhaps not come as such a surprise that one of the consequences of having peace divinely bestowed upon us is immediate strengthening. Yet, how often do we seek empowerment by other means? Maybe this is partly because we are so used to dealing with symptoms rather than root causes, and do so little realizing that the inverse is equally true: dispeace can only ever produce feebleness, leading to inadequate preparation, poor levels of awareness, and insufficient understanding of the issues with which we have to deal.

How Daniel was able to recognize the change within himself can only ever be, at least in part, speculative. I don't think it is too much of a stretch to draw the inference that he felt strengthened, but what form might this have taken? The problems Daniel faced previously had not been removed; they still awaited their unfolding in time. The blessing of peace does reduce anxiety levels. For Daniel, it may have been enough to be reminded that his confidence was not in the favorable development of historical proceedings, but in the One who ordered such events. For us, it is best encapsulated in the adage: we don't know what the future holds, but we do know who holds the future.

More than a well-wisher's salutation

When Jesus informed his disciples of his pending death, he did two remarkable things: he promised the coming of the Holy Spirit and he pronounced his peace upon them (see John 14:16–27). I am not entirely convinced that the two can easily be separated; they are mutually identifiable. We will consider this in due course. For now, let us content ourselves with taking a look at Jesus' words at the end of the citation: "Peace I leave you; my peace I give to you. I do not give to you as the world gives. Do not let your hearts be troubled and do not be afraid" (John 14:27). This was no first-century Buzz Lightyearism. The first part was a common Hebrew greeting. Its familiarity had perhaps robbed it of some meaning. As if to counter that possibility, Jesus reaffirms his intention, effectively saying: "I'm not just leaving my wishes for you to enjoy a peaceful existence, in some passive cavalier fashion, but I actively bestow upon you my peace. My giving of it is not the same as when others pronounce a hoped-for blessing. Therefore, whatever circumstances you find yourselves in, however apparently difficult the situation or potentially traumatic the outcome, the peace I give you now will strengthen you, so don't yield to your natural tendency to fear."

In the context of inferring this to be Jesus' last will and testament, it is easy to imagine the peace of which he speaks here to be entirely related to the atonement, that is, peace with God. But context must take cognizance of its entire surroundings, what precedes as well as what follows. By adopting such a panoramic view, we are able to identify a subjective quality to Jesus' parting gift. That he almost immediately annexes this peace to joy and faith (John 14:28-29) attaches also emotional and rational responses.

Is this not too personal, too parochial, too selfish for a people with a global mission? When Jesus speaks of peace, joy, and faith, isn't he rather doing so in relation to the hostility they will face? And when we embrace those principles in our own day, should we not apply them rather to the persecution we might face, or the crises of the age, the political unrest, social injustice, economic frailty, the dangers associated with climate change, poverty and hunger due to governmental irresponsibility, and community disarray caused by ill-advised lowest-common-denominator cohesion? Take any one of these; take them all as a package, if you like; add some more that I haven't included, more grotesque and gratuitous than the rest, such as white collar corruption at the expense of blue collar exploitation, and consider this: Do they not exist primarily because their perpetrators are singularly lacking in the peace of Christ? And is not that peace attained essentially and exclusively by faith in Christ? And does not such true faith express itself involuntarily joyfully?

All of the above have one thing in common: innocent victims. Those caught up in the schemes of others and trapped by egotistical marches toward self-achievement, individualistic expressions of what they perceive in law to be their rights at the expense of the common good, and garnering support for the celebration of mediocrity while the truly gifted are sacrificed on the altar of unpopularity, infrequently find their conditions altered by the peace of Jesus coming into their lives. The early disciples didn't and Daniel didn't, because it doesn't promise to deal with external issues. Nobody experienced the peace of Christ more than Christ himself, but he still had to endure the cross. He did so from a position of strength.

Jesus' heart was not troubled; neither was he afraid. Knowing what lay ahead and his command over the situation, he directed his concern toward the well-being of his disciples. He saw a need—or, at least, the potential for one to develop—and he knew there could only be one solution, and he had it in his gift—his peace.

Peace without concession

Although there is something different about this kind of peace when compared to that on offer elsewhere, they also share certain qualities. Outside of this context, I wonder what other words the reader would instinctively associate with peace: amicability, becalmed, contentedness, fearlessness, quietness, serenity, unflustered, absence of unrest, taking things in one's stride.

The world and its agents attempt to provide all of these things by seeking to change our environment, and so the things that would cause their opposite are removed from our sphere of influence. This is not always possible due to conflict of interests: one man's eclecticism is another's eccentricity. In such cases, an attitude of give and take is encouraged; we are invited to compromise so that a measure of peace may be maintained.

Now, take the above list of words and phrases and try to imagine their opposites: disagreeable, anxious, malcontent, fearful, disquieted, agitated, unnerved, restless, disturbed. The kind of peace Jesus is able to provide is not attained by changing our surroundings, but is ours for the asking amid situations that might otherwise cause us to be described by any or all on this second list. Again, the change is not external but internal.

Many of us welcome or covet peace for its own sake. It is a mindset with which I am familiar. Periods of intense pressure to meet targets by a specified deadline, whether at work, at school, or in the home can all cause us to yearn for the day when the burden of responsibility diminishes or ceases. Towards the back end of last year, my wife and I completed the decorating of our hallway, stairs, and landing area. We had engaged the services of a plumber to remove and re-site one radiator, and a decorator to re-paper the walls. I am no expert in home improvements but am willing to have a go at most things, so I had decided to tackle all the preparation work, such as filling and sanding holes and cracks in the plaster, priming and undercoating the woodwork, and emulsioning the ceilings. My attempts at anything more elaborate are best viewed with a somewhat jaundiced eye.

I always try to err on the side of caution, so we had given ourselves what we imagined to be ample time to finish our tasks before the professionals were due. I normally complete summer marking duties for an examination board by around the middle of July, so we had four months to casually sand and paint. As a new specification, my marking period was extended by about a fortnight, but that presented no real problem. I was then given a contract to remark those papers that had been queried by the parent schools. As a result, Barbara and I found that we were still washing bare floors less than an hour before the carpet fitters arrived. Our relation to peace was not what it had been three months earlier.

Beyond comprehension, but not without purpose

Paul instructed the believers at Philippi that "the peace of God . . . transcends all understanding" (Phil 4:7). As it appears in full and in context, the second part is more of a parenthetical aside: "And the peace of God, which transcends all understanding, will guard your hearts and your minds in Christ." It is almost as if the apostle is diverting his readers' attention from any attempt to rationalize the peace of God, focusing only on the conditions by which it may be attracted and the consequences of having done so. The conditions appear in verses 4 to 6:

> Rejoice in the Lord always. I will say it again: Rejoice! Let your gentleness be evident to all. The Lord is near. Do not be anxious about anything, but in everything, by prayer and petition, present your requests to God ... (Phil 4:4-6)

Notice both the imperative nature and the adverbial all-inclusiveness of each sentence. If any reader is currently struggling to think of anything for which to rejoice in God, then allow me to come to your aid: rejoice that none of us had any part in the writing of Scripture. Had this letter been penned by some of those I have met over the years, it would probably have included:

> Rejoice in the Lord sometimes. I repeat: Sometimes! Let your gentleness be evident only to those who deserve it or who you think may do you some good in the future. Your celebrity status could depend on it. Don't be anxious about most things, but if you are, as a last resort, it might be an idea to pray about it. You never know; anything's worth a try. But only if all other financial, social, medical, and governmental resources have been fully exhausted.

The peace of which Paul speaks here is not presented as something for which we have any obligation to pursue, but rather is indicative of the required conditions by which it may be attained having already been met. Whether the nearness of the Lord is also suggestive of what precedes it, or is issued as a warning that nothing is unseen, or an encouragement to persevere in the light of Christ's imminent return, is unclear. Scholars better qualified than I cannot agree.

What is utterly lacking in ambiguity is the fact that none of Paul's letters find the mention of peace absent. It may appear only as part of the introductory salutations, or in the closing greetings, or as a main topic of instruction within the corpus of the epistle, as here. What we are also able to discern is that whenever Paul mentions peace, he does so either alongside grace or in the vicinity of having exhorted or encouraged gracious conduct on the part of his addressees. Moreover, the relationship between the two is invariably seen as gracious actions or acts motivated by the bestowal of grace producing a peaceful disposition. I was tempted to add "even when those acts or actions are undeserved," but that is precisely what constitutes their graciousness: "spontaneous, unmerited favor in action."[16]

The implication behind Paul's use of the concepts of grace and peace is that true peace cannot be our experience unless we have first known true grace. But the testimony of Scripture, including its presentation of the experience of Daniel, is that the receipt of God's peace has such an effect on us that it refreshes, strengthens, reinvigorates, and empowers us. I guess that many of us would have settled at peace. There have been times when I certainly would have done so. Those who would not might now be satisfied to find that such peace produces the above-mentioned rejuvenation. But it does not end there, either. What we learn from Daniel's experience is that not only does God's peace precipitate strengthening, but it also has the capacity to fortify the over-forties and the over-fifties, satisfy the over-sixties and the over-seventies, and edify even the eighty-somethings, thereby fostering perseverance.

Whatever our age, this is why the peace of God strengthens us: that we might continue the tasks he has set us, having been "strengthened with all power according to his glorious might so that [we] may have great endurance and patience" (Col 1:11). Endurance and patience for what exactly?

- That we might continue to demonstrate our love for Jesus by keeping his commands (John 14:15)
- That our petitions may be unhindered (John 15:7; 1 Pet 3:7)
- That we may "never tire of doing what is right" (2 Thess 3:13; see also Gal 6:9)
- That we might not abandon the faith (1 Tim 4:1)
- That our hope might be fully realized (Heb 6:11)
- That we may receive the promised crown of life (Jas 1:12; Rev 2:10)
- That we will not have to endure end-time affliction (Rev 3:10)

Victory validates the strategy of the overcomers, as eternity will amply demonstrate. Only the peace that Jesus gives can produce these benefits. In an age where the worth of a gift is often determined by its size, how much was spent in attaining it, or its collectability based on rarity value, it is perhaps not easy to appreciate the gift of a quiet disposition. That is, unless you have experienced turmoil, known hostility, or suffered extreme tragedy. The peace on offer is not merely a measure of peace, like some medicinal dose to get you through your present trial; it is not even the recovery or

---

16. Hendriksen, *Philippians, Colossians & Philemon*, 49.

rediscovery of our peace, having previously squandered it in the heat of battle. "My peace I give you," said Jesus. It is *his* peace.

Summary

The book of Daniel continues to inspire and flummox, and I have yet to discover anyone who claims to sit exclusively in one camp or the other. Having looked at his output in more detail than previously, I can say that I am now only slightly less baffled than before, though incredibly stimulated to delve deeper into its secrets, so long as they prove true. May that be the filter through which we all pass the revelation of God's word, both directly to us and through the interpretive skills of others.

God's word is not lightweight trivia, and it is to our discredit to treat it as such. Neither is it within our gifts to edit its contents for the sake of personal comfortability or political correctness. The books of the Old Testament are not inconsequential or outdated. As we approach difficult passages, like those Daniel presents in abundance, we do well to ask ourselves what kind of Christianity we pursue: one that is predictable and pedestrian, or one that is powerful and engaging. Perhaps it is time to adopt a Daniel-like approach to recognizing and receiving God's truth, whereby we might better be equipped to silence its critics, rather than the other way around.

If we are to learn just one lesson from the example of Daniel as demonstrated in the book that bears his name, and especially so in these verses we have considered, it is this: God is entirely unsurprised by the unfolding of world events. History truly is his story.

Conclusion

My one-time mentor once told me that there are essentially three questions confronting the theologian:

i. Is there a God?

ii. Has he spoken?

iii. What has he said?

Together, the prophets of the Old Testament comprise around a quarter of the Bible's total output and are critical to our understanding of its message, both doctrinally and historically. One of the issues I raised when dealing with the Minor Prophets was the tendency amongst some Christians to overlook, underestimate, or devalue certain portions of Scripture. The question may well have been asked: Do Christians afford the Minor Prophets the attention they deserve? Perhaps the Major Prophets do not quite fall into that category, but our understanding of them is sometimes fraught with precisely the opposite problem: they are so familiar to us that our reading of them often takes us down such well-trodden paths that we are reluctant to ask questions of the text.

Although the immediate function of the Old Testament prophet was to challenge God's people in relation to their covenantal responsibilities, often in the context of their abrogation, always in the background was at least a hint of a coming Messiah who would usher in a kingdom of righteousness and establish a new covenant relationship between God and his people. Thus, we deprive ourselves of vital tools of understanding if we fail to read the Old Testament in the light of the New and *vice versa*. Nowhere is this more true than concerning the books of the prophets.

Readers who have arrived at this point may well have done so having avoided the sections labeled "Historical" and "Personal Background" and "Overview" for each prophet. You are perfectly entitled to have done so and,

I trust, you will have been amply rewarded by the meatier teaching sections. However, I would encourage you to go back and read each chapter in its entirety, as those oh-so-skippable portions provide the contextual setting by which your understanding of the rest might be enhanced. Who, for example, would fully comprehend the incredulity experienced by Isaiah's listeners without some understanding also of Assyria's role in eighth-century BC world events? At the same time, who better to employ as an instrument of God's judgment than a near-neighbor with more than one eye looking toward territorial expansion?

Similar questions might be asked of the issues we considered under Jeremiah. Israel's persistent refusal to heed the sugarless messages of God's true prophets must be seen in the context of their commensurate appetite for the comforting words of those who spoke lies in God's name. They much preferred to hear, "There, there!" than, "You have forsaken your God!" And remember, this was a good two-and-a-half-thousand years before the advent of political correctness. The prophets of old were more interested in changing hearts than tickling ears, though they should not be judged by either their popularity or their success rate unless, of course, that success is understood exclusively in terms of obedience to God's calling. Whatever the background, this was their default filter.

Because of the way I approached the book of Lamentations, it might be argued that the background wasn't quite so important here as elsewhere. You will remember that I preferred to respect the author's anonymity. I trust I will not be misunderstood or misrepresented in this. It is not that I find the positing of Jeremiah to be implausible; rather, that I consider the evidence in support of such a claim to be underwhelming. But that should not detract from us seeing the message contained therein in some sort of contextual setting. If it was Jeremiah—and I concede the possibility as much as any alternative—then his background provides a reasonable one by which to read Lamentations. Even if it was not, there are sufficient clues internally to ensure that our quest for context is not entirely devoid of hope. For example, it had to have been written by someone who was personally familiar not only with the divine judgment on Israel in 586 BC, but also with the crushing sense of loss experienced by those upon whom that judgement came.

I remember reading Daniel for the very first time and being completely bemused by its contents. I must confess to being only marginally less so nowadays. Any differences have been aided by a more learned grasp of the historical and political landscape of the period covered by its contents. To an admittedly lesser degree, the same could be said of the book of Ezekiel. His vision of the valley of dry bones not only begins to make more sense when we understand something of its original context, but it also enables us to apply it to our situation without extending beyond the boundaries of God's design. Similarly, the apparent minefield of Daniel's musings loses a little of its bewilderment, if nothing of its requirement for navigational skills, when we view it through the lens of his specific circumstances. I trust I have shown this to be the case.

Of course, there is one aspect of context that we share with all generations: the sinful human condition. Take any Old Testament passage bar its first three chapters and you will find some measure of identification. There is also one major difference: though every generation finds rebellion toward its Maker the easier option, with no intrinsic way of bridging the gap that exists between them and, therefore, in need of a Savior, we have the benefit of that requirement having been made for us. Thus, when Isaiah speaks to Israel of woe and judgment, God's woe for those who are willing to embrace his provision passes to that provision, thereby allowing him to judge us as righteous in his sight. Like Jeremiah's audience, the choice of where to draw water on this side of Calvary remains the spring of living waters or unreliable cisterns, but the spring is now more readily accessible for all and the life it gives is eternally replenishable.

We may not know for certain who wrote the book of Lamentations, but we can say quite unequivocally that its divine author is ascribed with the same degree of faithfulness today as then; there truly is no shadow of turning with him. The issues facing post-exilic Judah were matters of spiritual death and life; they are no less so for the post-twentieth-century church. The choice is ours, but the offer is made by the Giver of life and is available only on the basis of his Son's sacrificial death. Loyalty will be rewarded, but recipients of that reward must first have accessed the membership scheme by the only prescribed means: Christ Jesus.

Bibliography

Albright, William F. *The Archaeology of Palestine*. Harmondsworth, UK: Pelican, 1956.
Archer, Gleason L. *Old Testament Survey: Introduction*. Chicago: Moody, 1974.
Augustine. "Questions on the Heptateuch." In *Writings on the Old Testament*, edited by Boniface Ramsey, 3–478. Hyde Park, NY: Augustinian Heritage Institute, 2016.
Baldwin, Joyce G. *Daniel*. Vol. 23, *Tyndale Old Testament Commentaries*. Leicester, UK: InterVarsity Academic, 2009.
Berkhof, Louis. *Systematic Theology*. Edinburgh: Banner of Truth, 1988.
Bonhoeffer, Dietrich. *The Cost of Discipleship*. London: SCM, 1975.
Bright, John. *A History of Israel*. London: SCM, 2000.
Bruce, F.F. *1 & 2 Corinthians*. London: Marshall, Morgan & Scott, 1981.
Byrne, Brendan. *Life Abounding: A Reading of John's Gospel*. Collegeville, PA: Liturgical, 2014.
Calvin, John. *Genesis*. The Geneva Series of Commentaries. Edinburgh: Banner of Truth, 1992.
Douglas, J.D., ed. *New Bible Dictionary*. 2nd ed. Leicester, UK: InterVarsity, 1992.
Elliot, Elisabeth. *Through Gates of Splendor*. London: Hodder & Stoughton, 1966.
Girdlestone, Robert B. *Synonyms of the Old Testament*. Peabody, MA: Hendrickson, 2000.
Gottwald, Norman, K. *Studies in the Book of Lamentations*. London: SCM, 1962.
Grudem, Wayne A. *Systematic Theology: An Introduction to Biblical Doctrine*. Leicester, UK: InterVarsity, 1994.
Guthrie, Donald, and J. Alec Motyer, eds. *New Bible Commentary*. 3rd ed. Leicester, UK: InterVarsity, 1992.
Harrison, Roland K. *Jeremiah and Lamentations*. Vol. 21, *Tyndale Old Testament Commentaries*. Leicester: InterVarsity Academic, 1973.
Hemingway, Ernest. *Selected Letters 1917–1961*. Edited by Carlos Baker. New York: Scribner, 2003.
Hendriksen, William. *New Testament Commentary: 1 & 2 Thessalonians, 1 & 2 Timothy & Titus*. Edinburgh: Banner of Truth, 1991.
———. *New Testament Commentary: John*. Edinburgh: Banner of Truth, 1998.
———. *New Testament Commentary: Luke*. Edinburgh: Banner of Truth, 1997.
———. *New Testament Commentary: Mark*. Edinburgh: Banner of Truth, 1987.
———. *New Testament Commentary: Matthew*. Edinburgh: Banner of Truth, 1989.
———. *New Testament Commentary: Philippians, Colossians & Philemon*. Edinburgh: Banner of Truth, 1988.

Jensen, Irving L. *Jeremiah and Lamentations*. Chicago: Moody, 1974.
———. *Survey of the Old Testament*. Chicago: Moody, 1978.
Johnson, Paul. *A History of the Jews*. London: Weidenfeld & Nicolson, 1987.
Kernaghan, Ronald J. *Mark*. Vol. 2, *New Testament Commentary Series*. Leicester, UK: InterVarsity, 2007.
Kidner, Derek. *Genesis*. Vol. 1, *Tyndale Old Testament Commentaries*. Leicester, UK: InterVarsity Academic, 1967.
———. *Proverbs*. Vol. 17, *Tyndale Old Testament Commentaries*. Leicester, UK: InterVarsity Academic, 1964.
Lloyd-Jones, D. Martyn. *Romans: An Exposition of Chapters 3:20—4:25*. Edinburgh: Banner of Truth, 2003.
McGrath, Alister E. *The Future of Christianity*. Oxford: Blackwell, 2002.
Michelet, Jules. *The Life of Martin Luther: Gathered from His Own Writings*. Translated by William Hazlitt. London: G. Bell, 1862.
Moo, Douglas J. *The Letter to the Romans*. New International Commentary on the New Testament. Grand Rapids: Eerdmans, 1996.
Motyer, J. Alec. *Isaiah*. Vol. 20, *Tyndale Old Testament Commentaries*. Leicester, UK: InterVarsity Academic, 1999.
Pfeiffer, Charles F., and Everett F. Harrison, eds. *The Wycliffe Bible Commentary*. London: Oliphants, 1968.
Phillips, John. *Exploring the Scriptures*. Chicago: Moody, 1970.
Schaeffer, Francis A. *Death in the City*. Wheaton, IL: Crossway, 2002.
———. *Escape from Reason*. London: InterVarsity, 1972.
Seboek, Thomas A., ed. *Current Trends in Linguistics*. Vol. 6, *Linguistics in South West Asia and North Africa*. The Hague, Paris: Mouton, 1970.
Stedman, Ray C. *Hebrews*. Vol. 15, *New Testament Commentary Series*. Leicester, UK: InterVarsity, 1992.
Taylor, John B. *Ezekiel*. Vol. 22, *Tyndale Old Testament Commentaries*. Leicester, UK: InterVarsity Academic, 1969.
Tozer, A.W. *The Pursuit of God*. Chicago: Moody, 1996.
Trench, Richard C. *Commentary on the Epistle to the Seven Churches in Asia*. Eugene, OR: Wipf & Stock, 1997.
———. *Synonyms of the New Testament*. Peabody, MA: Hendrickson, 2000.
Trueblood, David E. *General Philosophy*. Grand Rapids: Baker, 1976.
VanGemeren, Willem A., ed. *New International Dictionary of Old Testament Theology & Exegesis*. 5 vols. Carlisle, UK: Paternoster, 1997.
Vine, William E. *Expository Dictionary of New Testament Words*. Iowa Falls, IA: Riverside, 1975.
Whitcomb, John C. *Darius the Mede: A Study in Historical Identification*. Phillipsburg: Presbyterian & Reformed, 1963.
Wiseman, Donald J., et al. *Notes on Some Problems in the Book of Daniel*. London: Tyndale, 1965.
Woodall, Chris. *Covenant: The Basis of God's Self-Disclosure*. Eugene, OR: Wipf & Stock, 2011.
———. *Kingdom: The Expression of God's Rule*. Eugene, OR: Wipf & Stock, 2012.
Young, Edward J. *Daniel*. Geneva Series of Commentaries. Edinburgh: Banner of Truth, 1997.

www.ingramcontent.com/pod-product-compliance
Lightning Source LLC
Chambersburg PA
CBHW060607230426
43670CB00011B/2016